VICE COP

"Most escort agencies have two categories of whores: the ones billed as 'Models' and the ones billed as 'Actresses.' 'Models' cost about three hundred to four hundred dollars an hour. 'Actresses' run about four to five hundred. The actresses are supposed to be the much better-looking girls, the elite. I believe they're the same girls."

ARSON COP

"You can look for external marks on a body that's been in a fire to determine homicide. But sometimes external marks are not indicative of a homicide. When a body burns . . . you sometimes get heat fissures. In a body, skin and tissues actually split open. Oftentimes, they look like knife wounds."

HOSTAGE COP

"Surrender is especially dangerous for police. They'll step back into that Kill Zone. The bad guy could still have a gun. And he's going through probably more psychologically traumatic times than ever. And *that's* the time the police start to let their guard down and move into the Kill Zone."

PURE COP

"People lie to us eight hours a day. Everybody lies to us: offenders, victims, witnesses. They all lie to the police. It gets so bad, you go to a party, somebody comes up to talk to you. You're thinking, 'Why is this guy saying this to me?' "

"We shot through the doorway in the direction of the gun-fire. The man inside knew what he was doing. He would fire . . . and stop and reload a different magazine . . . It was a .25 automatic."

•

"I'm telling him, 'Drop the gun. Drop the gun . . . Don't shoot.' I got my gun pointed at him. Instead of dropping the gun, he fires it at me."

•

"She keeps yelling, 'Kill him!' So I punch her in the face; I connected real good. She's out cold on the floor. 'Okay, okay,' the pimp goes. 'You're the police.' "

•

"The next thing I see is this guy coming up the stairs with the knife. He's got his arm extended and the knife's pointed right at me."

PURE COP

Cop Talk from the Street to the Specialized Units—Bomb Squad, Arson, Hostage Negotiation, Prostitution, Major Accidents, Crime Scene

CONNIE FLETCHER

ST. MARTIN'S PAPERBACKS

This book is dedicated to Trygve, Bridget, and Nick, the loves and lights of my life

Published by arrangement with Random House

PURE COP

Copyright © 1991 by Connie Fletcher.

Cover photograph by Charlie Westerman.

Library of Congress Catalog Card Number: 91-17049

ISBN: 0-312-92858-0

Printed in the United States of America

Villard Books hardcover edition / January 1992
St. Martin's Paperbacks edition / November 1992

10 9 8 7 6 5 4 3 2 1

PREFACE

Pure Cop is a trip into *terra incognita*. It ventures into the largely unexplored criminal landscape known only to law enforcement's highly specialized units, including Bomb and Arson, Hostage/Barricaded/Terrorist, Major Accident Investigation, and Crime Scene Investigation, units that have traditionally prevented journalists from getting any more than the briefest glimpses into their work. This book also explores the Vice Control Section, Prostitution Unit, whose undercover operations are the stuff of TV and film fantasies but rarely of full and accurate reportage. All police investigations center on or radiate from the street, and that is where *Pure Cop* ends.

Pure Cop presents a world of experts, of technicians and reconstructionists as well as beat cops, undercover cops, investigators and detectives. Here are cops trained in how to recognize bomb-makers' "signatures" as well as how to walk up to a bomb and render it safe. Here are cops expert in detecting the cause of fires; cops who shovel out evidence in perilous structures after the firefighters have gone; cops who apply the laws of physics to accident scenes in order to pinpoint guilt; cops who use the scientific principle of "transfer of material" to match the burglar, rapist, or murderer with the crime scene; cops who blend psychology and military tactics to get hostage-takers to surrender before they kill, or kill again.

This is an oral history. All these cops speak, in their own voices, anonymously and without authorial intrusion, about the intricacies of their work. Cops in specialized units (except for retired officers who write memoirs) are notoriously tight-lipped when it comes to the press. You can sense the "Police Line: Do Not Cross" policy of the specialized units in the terse newspaper accounts of the specialized units' work: Most hostage dramas are reduced to a few paragraphs or a photo caption. Bomb incidents are discussed and dismissed in a few prescribed phrases, and crime scene investigations are treated in the most cursory way. Some of the most intriguing conflicts of our time are given short shrift for the simple reason that the members of the specialized units don't want to talk to the press. "You know what we do as soon as an incident is over?" said one hostage negotiator. "We run like hell. We sneak off real fast. We don't want to talk to any reporters." A bomb squad technician said, "You don't want to talk to the press. You just tell them the bomb was successfully rendered safe. That's it."

The men and women in the Chicago Police Department's citywide specialized units talked to me on the strength of referrals from other cops I interviewed during the course of researching my previous book, *What Cops Know*. I was propelled into this strange land on a string of "She's okay" 's, which is cop for "as trustworthy as any scumbag journalist can be." Here was a typical scenario: I'd be talking to or walking with Cop A when Cop B would be sighted. "I'll introduce you to Cop B," he'd say. "He's a great guy." Cop A would introduce me, "This is Connie Fletcher. She's a writer." Cop B would shrink away from me with a sort of horror mixed with contempt. "But she's okay," Cop A would add quickly. Cop B would respond, "She's okay? Okay. If you say she's okay, she's okay." Or I'd call people up: "So-and-so says I'm okay. You can call her up and she'll tell you I'm okay." "Okay. I'm gonna check you out to see if you're okay." Or: "If you talked to So-and-so, then I know you're okay." The other cop encomium I received was "half-way decent"—"You know, you're half-way decent." Okay.

Pure Cop is a continuation, and completion, of *What Cops Know*. In *What Cops Know*, cops (mostly centered in Chicago's Area Six) who had long worked the street, homicide, robbery, narcotics, sex crimes, burglary, big-time theft operations, and organized crime talked anonymously about what the rest of us either don't have the opportunity (or the tragedy) to witness, or what we choose to ignore. In *Pure Cop*, cops from all over the city talk about crimes and scenes and specializations previously cordoned off from the public.

The shaping idea behind both *Pure Cop* and *What Cops Know* is the same: that cops, by virtue of their experience and expertise, know things that are hidden from the rest of us and that this knowledge, in turn, can be a redemptive and/or shattering force in their own lives.

Neither *What Cops Know* nor *Pure Cop* is a primer for would-be criminals. While there's a great deal of information on the way criminals operate today, none of it is how-to or step-by-step. On several occasions, cops would stop themselves after they'd told me something and say, "Don't put that in. That would help the bad guy." There is, however, much information in both books that can help people avoid becoming victims in the first place or stay alive if they're placed in a high-risk situation, such as being taken hostage.

Both books focus on cop experience and expertise. While negative aspects of police work and tales of lazy, incompetent, brutal, or corrupt cops can be found in both works, the overwhelming emphasis is on expertise rather than exposé.

In both *What Cops Know* and *Pure Cop*, cops themselves take center stage, relating cases, war stories, anecdotes, gallows humor, findings, musings, all in their own words. This is designed to let the reader share the remarkable experience I had in interviewing cops over four years. Cops are consummate storytellers. They turn street grit into powerful poetry. In each book, I've tried to make each chapter flow as both a logical and an emotional argument and to capture the cops' individual voices. My hope is that readers of both books will feel that they've pulled up a chair or a barstool and are eavesdropping on some of the best stories they've ever heard—the experience of listening to a bunch of cops holding forth. What follows is pure cop.

ACKNOWLEDGMENTS

It's hard to get to cops in specialized units. If you do get to them, it's hard to get them to talk beyond the most condensed and careful summaries of incidents resolved.

I was lucky enough to be able to contact officers with a great deal of expertise in the Chicago Police Department's specialized units and to have these people talk openly and freely about their work. An accident of birth gave me this access. My sister, Julie Schalk, a supervising CPD sergeant, has been a Chicago cop since 1981. She is greatly liked and respected by the officers who know her, and those officers were willing to give me, even with the highly dubious blotch of being a journalist, the benefit of the doubt.

Captain Tom Cronin is one officer who took a chance on me and helped me tremendously, both with *What Cops Know* and *Pure Cop*. Cronin, one of only twenty-seven police officers in the world trained by the FBI in criminal assessment and profiling, referred me to cops renowned in police circles for their expertise but, especially in the specialized units, virtually inaccessible to the press. Cronin also gave me the benefit of his considerable insights and psychological perspectives into violent crimes, crime scene investigation, and the street.

Lieutenant Ted Head of the Seventeenth District has also been a stand-out mentor, encouraging me from the very outset, proffering leads, referrals, and great advice. Several other officers went above and beyond the call of duty in helping me: Jack Hinchy, John Volland, Ted O'Connor, Phil Cline, Bill Pederson, Kim Anderson, Linda Reiter, Tony Bertuca, Joe Laskero, Ted Faulkner, and Mort Franklin.

All the cops I interviewed were unstinting in their generosity to me. When I read passages now, without trying to remember,

I can hear the cop's voice telling the story, see the waitress standing by with coffee or waiting for the order, remember the tape recorder being passed from cop to cop or standing in the middle of plates—but mostly I remember my sense of wonder that cops, who I always expected to sit with arms and lips tightly folded, were talking so unrestrainedly. I owe every one of the officers in *Pure Cop* and *What Cops Know* an enormous debt of gratitude.

None of this would have been possible without Tina Vicini, spokesperson for the Chicago Police Department, who gave me permission to contact and interview Chicago cops off-duty. And the project would have been much rougher were it not for my friends and colleagues at Loyola. Chief among these for his unfailingly trenchant advice and unflagging support is Ed Rooney.

My thanks to attorney Steven Molo of Winston & Strawn for his expert legal advice and superb subpoena quashing.

My gratitude to Will Beaton, who has served as chief special investigator responsible for all special investigations for the chief medical examiner since 1987, for sharing his considerable insights into crime scene investigation with me.

My deep gratitude to Diane Reverand, my editor at Villard, my production editor Beth Pearson, and my agent, Nat Sobel.

My best love and thanks to Trig, Bridget, and Nick. Trig makes everything possible. Bridget has helped most of all, every step of the way, in researching and writing *What Cops Know* and *Pure Cop,* and Nick makes it all fun.

My love and thanks to everyone in my family, living and dead, especially everyone who ever gathered in Mum Mum's and Nonnie and Nonie's kitchens, where I learned to love to listen to great storytellers.

CONTENTS

BOMB SQUAD

No one bomb is any deadlier than any other bomb. The only thing is, high explosive and low explosive, the only difference is the number of milliseconds it's gonna take you to die if you're on top of it. That's all. Funeral arrangements will be different—whether to use a big bag or a little bag, is it gonna be open casket or closed casket?
CPD bomb technician

Whenever I go up on a bomb, I always think of what an instructor told us in bomb school. He said: "One day you're the windshield and one day you're the bug."
CPD bomb technician

Bomb Squad officers are on an everlasting blind date with any bomb—found, reported, or suspected, before or after it goes off. If the bomb *has* exploded, the bomb techs, more formally known as "explosives technicians," conduct a post-blast investigation, hoping to gain insight into the M.O. of the bomb-maker by piecing together bits of bomb, alert to the possibility that another, undiscovered bomb may be about to go off as they work. Or, if they get an unexploded device, bomb techs "render it safe," a pallid understatement for the practice of walking up to a bomb that may go off at any nanosecond, figuring out what to do about it—and then doing it.

"There's one thing we kind of work by: It *is* a bomb until it is *not* a bomb," says one CPD bomb tech. "You've got a real bomb till you know that it isn't.

"If you don't operate that way, you don't belong in the business. I don't care what the package is, what it looks like, what it's supposed to look like—if you don't operate that everything is a bomb until you prove otherwise, then you shouldn't be here doing the job, because you're doing a disservice to yourself, your family, everybody else, plus your partners.

"You cannot become complacent. The pucker power is always there. Every device you go up on is a bomb. Whether you're taking apart a real nuclear device or some kid's hoax, with flares and an old alarm clock, you better feel the same way."

The Bomb Squad is part of Bomb and Arson, one unit with, for the most part, two very different functions going on within it. The link is "arson"—arson is considered, legally, to have two components: "arson by explosives" and "arson by fire."

Currently, the strength of Bomb and Arson stands at thirteen explosives technicians and thirty-six arson detectives, three of whom work jointly with ATF (the Bureau of Alcohol, Tobacco, and Firearms) on the Arson Task Force. Both bomb techs and arson investigators are highly trained: bomb techs are trained by the FBI at Redstone Arsenal in Huntsville, Alabama; arson investigators receive technical training from the University of Illinois and the state fire marshal.

Bomb and arson investigations sometimes overlap, with the arson detectives seeking the maker and motive behind the explosive device the Bomb Squad discovers, as in the drama of the freelance armorer on the West Side who spent the mid-to-late eighties selling hand grenades to street gangs and drug dealers— the grenades had been altered so there was no delay between pulling the pin and the grenade exploding; they went off in the bomber's throwing hand. The armorer has been caught and indicted, but Bomb and Arson detectives are still picking up the pieces from the armorer's masterworks, or from copycat grenades: "We keep going out and picking up fingers and parts of hands on the West Side," explains one arson investigator.

CPD bomb techs and arson-for-profit investigators also worked together and with ATF in cracking the largest arson-for-profit ring ever uncovered in the U.S. This ring, headquartered in Chicago, spread arson and extortion as far as Greece, and was based upon a single bomb-maker's expertise.

CPD bomb techs average about twenty-four bomb-ings a year. Their investigations encompass everything from simple revenge bombings to business, Outfit, street gang, drug trade, and terrorist bombings. "Illinois always ranks one, two, or three in bomb-ings," says Captain Joseph Grubisic, head of Bomb and Arson and an explosives technician himself. "Florida's really coming up now, though, because of all the dope activity."

A bomb tech is only as good as his guess as to what he's walking up on. Even the simplest-seeming device can be booby-trapped, or made either so cleverly or so amateurishly that the slightest movement sets it off. The guesses keep getting harder as bomb technology explodes.

What follows in this chapter and every other chapter in this book is a series of direct, unedited, unexpurgat-ed cop quotes. Quotation marks, except as they occur within the quotes themselves, have been omitted. The best way to read these chapters is straight through, listening to the voices jostle one another . . .

A bomb is only limited to the imagination of the builder. He can build a bomb that he can put in a tackle box, he can put a bomb in a coffee can, he can put a bomb in a thermos jug, he can have a bomb that *looks* like a thermos jug—it's however he wants to disguise it. They don't build them like they do on television with an alarm clock and three sticks of red dynamite wrapped in black tape—you don't find them like that.

A bomb is just an exploding device that's initiated by some-thing—it can be mechanical, chemical, or electrical. And that's why bombs can be so sophisticated now, because of electron-ics. Electronics has revolutionized bomb technology.

You know those tape recorders that work with slide pro-jectors—they narrate and then you hear a beep and the slide projector moves to the next slide? All that beep does is activate an electronic circuit to make something happen. It's just an electrical signal.

Take away the projector. Put a switch in there that will initiate a bomb.

You can do this with anything. A doorbell. Anything. Something that initiates.

You have the recording devices that answer your telephone—set a system up like this, you call the number, the device comes on, it closes an electrical circuit, therefore setting the bomb off.

A beeper creates an electrical circuit, doesn't it? If I were to wire a battery onto a beeper onto a bomb and put this under the couch in your apartment—and I sit and I watch you go into your apartment—okay, she's sitting down now. Now all I do is dial the number of the beeper, the beeper goes off—beep, *boom*. That's it. That's all it takes. It's ingenuity.

We had a guy killed in his Mercedes driving in from the suburbs to work. This was an Outfit hit.

Some guys put dynamite under the front seat of his Mercedes. Then they took an electric garage door opener, put it in a stolen car; they taped it in the ON position and then taped it to the sun visor of the car.

This guy took the same route to work every day; he drove the Tri-State in. He was on an on ramp on the Tri-State when he died. The car with the garage door opener was off in a parking lot within a hundred feet of the on ramp.

It was a radio-controlled device. So when he drove into the radio signal, it activated the device just like when you pull up to your garage, you push the button on your garage door opener—the radio signal goes out, activates the transmitter. So when he got in range of the electric garage door opener, the electronic signal—this car went to the moon with him in it. He was a mess. He was in about four-pound pieces. The biggest chunk they found of him was about six inches square.

*   *   *

The ultimate nightmare, probably, is a remote-controlled device that's activated by radio command or something along those lines. Because you don't have any control. I mean, we never have control in the first place, but the thing is, if the fellow's sitting three blocks down the street and sees you walking down the street as a bomb man, he can get you by pushing a button. That's the ultimate nightmare.

They have timing devices now that make . . . no noise. It's done electronically. Now they have LCDs—liquid crystal dials, the same as you have on your digital watch that let you read the numbers; they take just a minimal amount of electricity to make it function *and* they make no noise. That's one of the bombs I don't want to meet.

Bombers went down from a Big Ben alarm clock—they went down from that to a wristwatch and now they're going to microcircuits.

The big thing now is microcircuitry, the technology used in computers and stuff like that. They can make circuits any way they want to and miniaturize them, so all the coded instructions for the bomb, for how the bomb is controlled, the timer, whatever, can be miniaturized. They're very easy to conceal.

You can get down to making bombs that will fit into a letter—four, five, seven ounces of sheet explosives in there made to fit in a business-size envelope.

And all the new technology is just coming down the line. There's more and more of microcircuitry showing up, especially with the international terrorists.

Everything's becoming more and more sophisticated, more and more miniaturized, and it's becoming a horrendous headache.

They're talking about now—there's a conductive *glue*. A conductive glue—that's really going to be a problem because you can't X-ray it. Instead of running wires, which are susceptible to radiographs or X-ray or fluoroscoping, when you get into stuff like glues, you have nothing there to trace. It's a transparent thing and yet it still conducts electricity.

All these innovations are coming in and these terrorists are turning to them. We're in trouble.

The new bomb material now is Semtex—it's a plastique explosive. You can't detect it in luggage and things like that for the simple fact that the X-ray goes right through it. It doesn't show up. That's what's scary about it—for airlines, for anything. Even for a bomb technician; we go to X-ray it, it doesn't show up as an outline or anything.

If you're a bomb tech and you don't have a global perspective, if you don't keep up with all the latest technology, all the latest terrorist ploys, you're a damn fool.

O'Hare Airport's right here, eight to ten hours away from the home of some of the most active terrorists in the world. And it's a direct flight in here. A guy gets on a flight in Dublin, he's here in eleven hours. A guy leaves Frankfurt, he's here in ten and a half hours.

We work hand in glove with the FBI and their Antiterrorist people. The FBI Bomb Data Center is constantly sending out stuff. We talk to the bomb techs working Ireland all the time. And if you don't have some idea what you're looking for, if you don't know what the Lockerbie situation was and those kinds of devices, if you aren't aware of those kind of people and where they're coming from, then you're not a full-service organization. You gotta know what's going on or you're dead.

The IRA is in the forefront of bomb technology right now. They've got everything you can think of—timed devices, remote control devices, plastic explosives, military explosives, five-hundred-pound land mines, car bombs made out of fertilizer—they use everything, the whole full gamut of what's available out there.

And most of the antibomb technology the rest of the bomb world has comes from the British trying to defeat the IRA. That's where most of the equipment: the robots and the bomb suits and the research on rendering safe—it all stems from the problems in Ireland. The new robots that go up to explosives all come from England or Canada. Our CPD bomb suits come from England and Canada.

The Galt bomb suit is British. It has an extremely heavy helmet, an antiblast shield for the face, and a breast plate where the material is like what they use on bulletproof vests. And if the bomb goes off in your face, the bomb suit will keep all your body in one place. That's all. It's still going to kill you. If you're moving away from it, it may save your life. But if it goes off in your face, the bomb suit will help you have a better-looking corpse.

Now we use American Body Armor. It helps keep you in one piece. But if you're right over a device, you're probably going to be in one piece dead.

Terrorists are the best bombers. Oh, yes. They're more sophisticated than other bombers.

Most terrorist bombers—terrorists in foreign countries—are military trained. They've gone through some type of military training regarding bombs. Whereas bombings that happen here in the United States are amateuristic in comparison. So far.

Fifty percent of all bombings worldwide are terrorist bombings.

There was a guy who timed a bomb for 279 days. That's pretty tricky. Three of them in Chicago, three in New York, three in San Francisco. Nineteen seventy-one. He was a pretty smart guy. He put them in safety deposit boxes—one of them went off in San Francisco prematurely, maybe intentionally. He just wanted to show the establishment they're not immune from anything.

* * *

The FALN organization drove this city nuts for ten years and all their bombs were very crude. They were timed devices, utilizing a watch as one of the components and when the watch ran a certain amount of time, an electrical contact would be made and it would initiate the bomb. They put them in major corporation buildings and targets of opportunity all over the Loop for years and years and years. They'd stick small incendiary devices in the pockets of fur coats in downtown department stores. And all it was, was to cause panic.

FALN drove everybody crazy for years. New York. Two bomb techs were injured, horribly, due to an FALN device, and one policeman lost his leg. There were seven devices found in New York at one time; five had gone off. They found one behind a police station and a policeman, not a bomb tech, kicked it and it took his leg off. And the other one—two bomb techs were working over it as the time ran out. The time ran out. One guy died. The other guy is the director of an organization that counsels injured policemen and their families. He lost part of his hand, his sight. . . .

You know where some of the best explosives men in the country are? They're working in the movies.

When these guys go to work . . . they do things that are so well thought out, so well planned.

They bought a tavern on the North Side when they were doing *The Untouchables* and they blew that up. One time, one shot, and they bought the building and did a complete make-over for an eight-second effect. They had a scene where the little girl raises up a beer bucket and the building goes up. I was out there for four days while they blew up dummies of that little girl. They were trying to get the right type of explosives to accomplish this. We were viewing it. We said, "Hey, you're using too much." They said, "Yeah, we think so too." Then they reduced it down till they got it to where it worked fine; they were doing this right out into Clark

Street. It was a masterwork. The work going into that was incredible.

These guys are great, but they goof up a lot. They blow down hotel walls sometimes like they did here when they were making "Crime Story." They did an elevator scene where the Mafia guy was going to kill everybody on the elevator. But it got away from them. The explosion knocked out walls all the way up that elevator shaft, they happened to be kitchen walls of all the apartments going right up—they knocked out walls on the first floor too; a couple was sitting in a restaurant in a booth and the whole wall came in on them. The effects guys said it was too much dust built up in the shaft, but they snuck some gasoline in there, the gasoline vaporized, and then there was a delay and it built up its volume in there. They blew it; they made a mistake.

When they were making *Thief* here, they rented this guy's home. They built a front on the home and they were gonna blow the windows out. And the stunt people moved in much more gasoline and explosive than they anticipated. They ended up blowing the whole house down. They had to buy the guy a whole new home.

There's nothing beautiful about a real bomb. Bombs are mean, nasty, dirty things that go off with a tremendous amount of noise and a tremendous amount of percussion, fragmentation, and *dirt*. Usually dusty, smoky, black. You don't see this fireball they do in Hollywood—that's gasoline. Usually, you can count how big the ball is by how many five-gallon bags of gasoline they placed.

A bomb is very basic. It's a firing train. You've got an explosive, you've got a power source, and you have a way to initiate the bomb. In between the two you put any sophisticated or simple device that will make the thing initiate.

Most bomb-makers make bombs very simple, for a simple reason. The more sophisticated the bomb, the more chances the maker is going to blow himself up.

Two young men—brothers-in-law—had been making bombs for a grocery store owner, making and placing them, to eliminate the competition. One of them decided to do a little personal bombing one night.

This one guy had an argument with a neighbor over some allegedly stolen tools; he thought the neighbor broke into his garage and stole his tools. So he was gonna blow up his neighbor's car with the help of his brother-in-law.

This guy had a very unique system. He made a pipe bomb and put a timer on it, a Walgreen's travel alarm clock, set to go off at twelve-thirty in the morning.

So he and his brother-in-law went out and planted a pipe bomb under the guy's car. The bomb was set for 12:30. Sometime before twelve, they thought, "Wait a second! We've had a beef with this guy over tools. The police are gonna come to us right away if we don't establish an alibi." They went and retrieved the pipe bomb from under the car. They disconnected the battery. That was Friday night.

The next night they were going to go back and replant the bomb. The one brother-in-law sits in a tavern—that was gonna be his alibi: he was sitting there all night drinking. The second guy was gonna set the bomb, and then slide in the back door of the tavern and act as if he was there all night. That would establish *his* alibi.

He took the pipe bomb. It's 12:45 A.M. now. He forgot he had it set for 12:30 for the previous night. Now it's 12:45, close to 1.

As soon as he pulled the switch on the alarm clock to set the timer, as soon as he reconnected that battery, he probably got out *"Aw, sh—"*; never finished the last two letters of *"Aw, shit!"* —when it *shredded* him. I can see him looking at it with his hand on it— *"Aw, sh—"*

It actually, completely—well, it disemboweled him. It also blew his pants off. If you could have seen pictures—his brain, his guts out. His wife came down there and she was walking on him. She didn't even know. There were pieces on the floor, the walls, everywhere. Couldn't tell where he was. She had no idea what was going on. We found three more devices down there.

Most bombs are messages. They're sending somebody a message. Street gangs to other street gangs—"You're in our territory," or "You're in our business" with the Outfit or rival businesses. Now we get "You haven't paid the money you owe us" or "You cut it wrong"—that's with dope dealers. It can be anything. Bombs are to send people messages.

A domestic—a guy's playing around with my wife, I want to give him a message—we've had a lot of those. It's common. You put a bomb on his back porch, in his car, places where chances are he's not physically going to get hurt—it's property damage, not physical damage.

Business. Business competition. That's very common. If somebody says to you, "Hey, don't open this business," you'll say, "Get outta here. I'm opening the business. Don't tell me what to do." Three o'clock in the morning, you get a call, "You got a problem. A bomb went off in your business." You'd get the message.

So bombs are messages. You're not trying to blow the guy's building down or blow up his car, you're just trying to let him know, "Hey, next time it might be you instead of your car."

Terrorists use bombs to get the *media* to deliver their messages. Their bombs are to draw attention, to get media attention. If they can't publicize their beef or their organization, bombings will. Everybody's interested in bombings, so it's a great way of getting the news media's attention. It's PR, coming from the left-hand side, I guess.

Mobsters send a lot of messages with bombs. They always have and always will. Why do you think they call Outfit guys bomb throwers? They used to have a guy, Jimmy "the Bomber" Catuara, famous for his bombings. He's now "the late."

It's not just a message to the individual that blows up, but to everybody else in the organization.

* * *

Whenever you interview bombing victims, they never will tell you why they got the bomb, but in the back of their mind, they *know*.

In Europe, you always have different groups calling up claiming credit for bombs; they'll call up and say there's a bomb *going* to go off. But in the criminal world of Chicago, you aren't gonna get anybody claiming anything. Because the guy who's the victim knows who he's aggravated and he's gonna disavow any knowledge. And naturally the placer isn't gonna claim responsibility for anything.

We have numerous bomb threats, but we've never found a bomb. People call up and say there's a bomb in the building, but we've never found a bomb. A lot of bombs have gone off . . . but they never told us beforehand, though. Where in Europe, when they call up and say, "There's gonna be a bomb going off at two in the afternoon"—nine times out of ten, it goes off at two in the afternoon.

You can't say it's gangs, you can't say it's organized crime, you can't say it's politically motivated, because it's all of them.

At one time, it was FALN. Before that, the Weathermen. But now it can be anybody. It can be *anybody* messing with bombs.

People that make bombs generally are click-offs. They're nuts. They're very intelligent, but they're not logical thinkers.

Oftentimes, it's people with a paramilitary attitude towards life. They like guns. They like the military. *Soldier of Fortune* is one of their favorite magazines. We often find back issues of *Soldier of Fortune* laying around when we search bomb-makers' houses.

Many of these guys have the attitude that they want to destroy the person who's trained to defeat their efforts. Some of them will make complicated devices, with mercury switches, where all you have to do is pick it up and move it and it'll go off on you. They're trying to show their superior intelligence by making a device that you can't defeat and they can prove you can't defeat it by killing you. Their obvious aim is police officers who are going to render the devices safe. Not all; there are all kinds of different reasons to make a bomb.

Revenge and retaliation seems to be the biggest motive. For whatever reason somebody has a dislike for somebody else and decides to show it. Sometimes they're cars, they'll put a crude device in a car. It can be commercial; it can be domestic. But the common motive is revenge.

In 1984 and 1985, a businessman on the South Side of Chicago received some telephone threats, somebody BB-gunned his house—a number of other things happened. And then in 1985, somebody took a *large,* very extraordinarily large, pipe bomb, and put it under the businessman's front porch—lifted the house off its foundations while the family was sleeping inside. Nobody was injured, but it did major structural damage to the house.

At first he was suspect—why would somebody want to do this? He was suspect as knowing the reason for the crime. For a while we concentrated on him, thought maybe a gambling debt or something—he had nothing. He had a happy family life, he lived in a nice section of the city, had a very expensive house, was a businessman, was very successful, he just couldn't figure it out.

Then our focus turned to a neighbor that he had some bad words in the past with over cutting a tree down and then the neighbor became suspect.

It got to a point, we were stymied. We couldn't dig anything up. Then, on August 15, 1986, one year to the day, the one-year anniversary of the large bomb placed under his house, this businessman received a telephone call at his business office. The call was twenty seconds in duration. And the caller said: "Happy Anniversary, Steve. Boom."

We knew the caller was probably the guy who placed the bomb. We were able to trace the call to a house in the suburbs. That led us to a twenty-four-year-old man who admitted that he made the call for his dentist. He received free dental work from this guy and they were buddies. He went on to tell us that it was the dentist who did it and why he did it. He also told us the dentist had other bombs and a couple hundred other weapons, some of them machine guns, in his house.

Now here was the motive. The dentist and our businessman, in 1971, were costudents at Northern Illinois University. They had a fist fight in 1971 over a traffic accident.

Our victim didn't even remember him. But the dentist, for fourteen years he harbored this animosity for his fellow student to the point where he terrorized his family with the bombings and the BB-gunnings and everything. He got backtracked.

We raided the dentist's house. We recovered four fully operational assault weapons and one he was making; he was converting an AR-15 to an M-16 *as* we raided the house— he had the stuff on the table to make it a fully automatic machine gun.

This dentist was thirty-seven, single, living with Mom and Dad. He had so much money he didn't know what to do with it. He kept acquiring all these weapons. We found the receiver and the barrel of a .30-caliber German light machine gun in the trunk of his mint vintage 1968 Corvette that he had in his parents' driveway.

When we went into the basement, we found he had machine guns secreted behind the wall panel. There was a crawl space down there—when we entered that crawl space, by conservative estimate, we found fifty thousand rounds of spent ammunition down there. When Mom and Dad were out, this dentist would take his machine guns and practice.

A thirty-seven-year-old dentist with no criminal history. It was later proved that when he had an income tax problem one year, he decided to blow up the IRS office in Wheaton, which he did. He threw a pipe bomb at the IRS office because he was having a tax problem.

He went a year without making a bomb—I can't say without dropping them because he and a cohort were dropping them out in the forest preserves.

This is a man with a good education, an excellent income, had everything going for him, somehow just got—probably the hate in him. It lasted fourteen years. The hate consumed him to the point where he was doing all these stupid acts. His biggest mistake was the phone call on the anniversary of the bomb.

A dentist. Making $300,000 a year. Now he's pulling teeth in Lexington, Kentucky, in a federal prison.

There's homicide by bombs. Again, that's a message. You blow somebody up, it indicates a *lot* of anger. Or total frustration. One of the two.

We had an incident in Indiana, a love triangle. Two women and a vibrator. One of the girls fell in love with the vibrator and told her friend to leave. So the friend took the vibrator, cut the head off, filled it with black powder, put the head back on. The other woman, once she saw her vibrator, noticed the head was cut off and glued back on, thought something was wrong. Otherwise, she would have found out the hard way.

A young woman received a box of candy in the mail. It was from her ex-boyfriend. He had placed a shotgun shell in there. He also put a mousetrap inside the box. So the mousetrap would fly around, hit the shotgun shell and it would shoot off in the direction it was aimed in. She had the package, so to speak, backwards when she opened it, so the shotgun shell fired off, but it went the wrong way. Otherwise, it would have taken her face off.

The problem with a bomb, there's no guarantee that you're going to get your target—you can get anybody. You may make the bomb with the intention of blowing up Joe Schmoe, but you may get Joe Schmoe's kids or his wife or his mother. You're more certain you're getting your target if you kill somebody with a gun. But then you're missing the anonymity you get with a bomb.

We know one guy who should love his mother. This kid was sent a bomb through the mail. The package had the kid's name right, but the address was off. It went to a neighbor's, the neighbor brings the package over. The kid's mother was suspicious because of how the package was wrapped and because the name was off by one letter—everybody in the family had the first initial "J" and this had a different letter.

So the mother opens the package. Inside is a rattrap. She calls the police and the police open it. The rattrap had two shotgun shells in it. The bomber had soldered pins to the bar, making primers on the shotgun shells.

The concept was—you know that a mousetrap or a rattrap is spring-fed, right? And the idea is, instead of you having a trigger with a spring on it, the rattrap spring becomes the same thing as the trigger. So when you open it, it releases the spring, the spring slaps down, the two pins hit the two shotgun shells, and the shotgun shells blow your face off.

The Burning Bed. This was an Indian couple in Area Six. The husband was away, in India. For some reason, he wanted out of the marriage, but because of their religious beliefs, they couldn't get a divorce. So what he did, he had a friend secrete three gallons of gasoline with an ordinary electric timer, you know, the kind you use when you go on vacation, for turning your lights on and off. This timer was connected to a hot-plate coil. The idea was, when the timer comes on, this coil would heat up and it was gonna melt the plastic containers and once it spread, the fumes would ignite immediately.

So the friend put it all in the box-spring mattress of the wife's bed. In other words, she laid right on it. She was sleeping right over a bomb for days.

She called either the fire department or the police department on two different occasions, complaining of the strong odor of gasoline. They came out and didn't find anything. And finally, she called again and a district car came out and when they looked under the bed, they saw wiring. And when they lifted up the mattress, they saw the three containers of gasoline with the coil. Then we came out and, of course, just pulled the plug.

The other part of the plan was the husband was going to call the wife from India and make sure she was in the bed, or at least the bedroom, when this thing went off. If his plan had worked, she would have just been engulfed. You're talking three gallons of gasoline, it burns very rapidly—especially when one of them starts, it breaks the container, now it spills all over and runs. And he would have been listening to his wife die. And that would be his alibi—he was out of town.

There's the bomber equivalent of the pyromaniac and that's the serial bomber. We do get them. We do get them.

There was the Gay Liberation Bomber, he set off bombs in six states till he blew himself up in a car somewhere in Iowa—he was sitting in a motel parking lot and had a bunch of these bombs made up, in the trunk of this rented car, and one went off. He's still alive but horribly disfigured.

His whole idea was to mutilate people's groins. He'd leave paper bags with dollar bills sticking out of them on sidewalks—you'd see a dollar bill sticking out of a bag, you'd pull on it, and this would activate the bomb. His triggering device was a clothespin that set off an electrical circuit. Given the right circumstances, you'd squat down to pick that thing up and this device would go off and hit your lower body, groin area. It was all fragmentation stuff in there.

He went all through the Midwest: Chicago, Milwaukee, Black River Falls, Dubuque, Minneapolis. He planted some of the devices in parks, playgrounds. One woman got hurt—all the rest went off by themselves. He threw one from a train. He's currently a long-term resident of the federal penitentiary.

The big one now is the Unabomber. He's been driving us crazy since November of '79. He's a definite serial bomber.

He's done twelve or thirteen bombs throughout the United States. The first one was here in Chicago; he sent a package of explosives from the University of Illinois to Northwestern University. He killed a guy in Salt Lake City. They've been looking for him for about twelve years now.

His targets are universities and computer outfits. His M.O. stands out. I can't tell you what his M.O. is, but he makes all his devices the same. He always leaves his signature. He wants everybody to know that he's doing it. It's like he's saying, "Here I am. Find me." It's like a challenge. This guy is like, "Catch me before I kill again."

Every guy who makes a bomb has what we call a signature. There is something that he always does when he makes the bomb that the Crime Lab is able to determine exactly what he did. The Unabomber has his own signature. You get a criminal bomber, you know, *he* even has a signature because he becomes proficient at a certain type of bomb and then that's his signature. There's always a signature.

The bomb-maker, the way he puts his bomb together and makes his connections, it's the same way as handwriting. There might be three different bomb-makers, but the three different bomb-makers will make their connections and make their devices in three different ways. They'll use the same type of cords, the same type of everything, just because he was successful at it. Everybody's a creature of habit.

And depending upon the post-blast evidence we're able to obtain, we can probably tie the bomber into other bombs.

The problem is *anyone* can make a bomb. The information is available, the materials are cheap and readily available.

You could go around to your Radio Shack, to your local drug store, to a hobby shop—and build the most sophisticated bomb that I couldn't take apart. It's scary. It really is.

Most electronic components that bombers use can be purchased at any electronics place. We call these places "Bombs

'Я' Us." They're the bomber's paradise because everything you need to make a bomb is there.

It's no reflection on the stores; they're legitimate concerns. But what you need to make a bomb is there.

Like microswitches. Just a little switch. Fill up a box with explosives, put in a battery, a detonator, you open the box, the switch opens up, or you close something—you either open or break the circuit and boom.

There are books that can be purchased by anybody on how to make bombs. They advertise in magazines like *Soldier of Fortune*. You can send in for them. They're available all over—mail order, buy it at stores. They're available to the good guys and the bad guys.

You can buy bombs on the street. Sure. Not everybody knows how to make them, so a fellow who has the knowledge of how to make them starts to make and sell them himself. The Bureau of Alcohol, Tobacco, and Firearms has their agents on the street buying bombs all the time. The price varies, from about $50 to $250 a pipe bomb, whatever traffic will allow, whatever the maker thinks he can get out of you.

The most sophisticated bomb I ever ran into was made by a member of a motorcycle gang. He put this thing together and had it on the street for sale. It was radio-controlled. It wasn't completely assembled, but all the parts were there. It was a good one. They built another one and sold it to somebody who went on out to the suburbs and bombed a place, a restaurant. The informant said the bombs sold for about $250 on the street.

You can buy black powder, smokeless powder—it's made for reloaders. Gun shops. You can buy tins of it. You can buy it at hobby shops. You can buy hobby fuse; you can buy this rocket fuel the kids have for shooting their rockets up into the air. Like powder—you just go buy a box of shotgun shells, take the powder out of it. You can find any of that kind of stuff and end up with a bomb.

Anybody that makes a bomb is a crazy. You have to be a little bit loose to be making bombs in the first place.

The very concept of the damn things is that they're gonna cause mayhem, right? Now you're standing on top of it, putting something together that's gonna cause mayhem. Therefore, you've got to have a brain that's soft as a pound of mashed potatoes to do that stuff.

And that's why a lot of these guys get killed. The bombers. You go to a bomb scene and you find the bomber's mortal remains. And that's because he made some miscalculation. So you go around with plastic bags and pick up his fingers, hands, parts of his head—that's because the hospital wants to know if they can sew some of this stuff back on.

We've had this thing going on with dope dealers on the West Side. It's gone on for years. So far, we've recovered eighty-six hand grenades. We believe them to be made by the same person.

All of them are old World War II fragmentation grenades. They're used as practice grenades by the military. They have no powder and no primer. They're hollow, inert.

But somebody found a quantity or obtained a quantity of these inert military practice grenades and reassembled them. You can buy them in any surplus store.

Hand grenades have a delay fuse on them. If you ever watch the old movies where they pull the pin, they throw it in a building, they back up against a wall, and they go one thousand, two thousand, three thousand—a matter of four, five seconds, it goes off.

But now what this guy did, he replaced it all with smoke grenade pins, spoons, and primers. And he acquired a military fusing mechanism that's used on smoke grenades. And he used this in hand grenades.

But what he didn't know is *there's no time delay on a smoke grenade*—it's a momentary delay. One second. I mean, you pull the pin on a smoke grenade, it goes off instantly. The person who pulls the pin, there's no time delay. When he pulls

the pin and lets the spoon go, it goes off. He's ready to throw—
but he's never going to throw.

This all seems to be dope related. Drug dealers are using
them for protection and also offensively. There was an incident where we believe one group of drug dealers tossed these
grenades at another group of drug dealers.

While this has been going on, we've had to go and pick up
fingers on the West Side. The grenades aren't packed with high
explosives, but they go off strong enough that we have to pick
up fingers, parts of arms. One guy lost a hand. They expect it
to be like in the movies, like Jack Palance going back with a
grenade. It isn't.

We more or less think the person who made them didn't
know what he was doing. We got the guy—Undra Heard.
He was indicted this year on multiple counts by the federal
government. But we're still recovering his grenades.

Over the years, we've been called to a lot of scenes where
they've found grenades. And you can see the pin's come off;
it's ready to go. That's where your police star comes in handy.
You've got this nice pin on the back of the star that pins it to your
shirt? You stick it right through the hole in a grenade where the
pin's come off, it plugs it up so it won't go off. We've done that
lots of times.

Seventy-five percent of all bombs are pipe bombs. The most
common bomb out there today is the hand-ignited pipe bomb.
Very simple to make—black powder—powders are very easy
to obtain: take ordinary shotgun shell powder with plain ordinary
what we call cannon fuse, which you can buy in any hobby shop,
put it in a pipe, and you got one hell of a device.

With a pipe bomb, it's a mechanical explosion. The powder
inside isn't really exploding; it's burning. That burning powder
inside creates gases, those gases have nowhere to go—it's like a
pressure cooker that blows up when there's too much pressure.
The buildup of the gases by the burning of the powder creates a
mechanical explosion, shattering and fragmenting the container,
which is the pipe.

*   *   *

Pipe bombs are the Saturday night specials of explosive devices. It's just like with guns. If you're gonna kill a guy, it's a lot easier to kill him with a .22 because there are so many .22s around. It's a cheap, economical way to do something. You don't come out with some exotic hunting rifle that costs $2000 when you're gonna blow your neighbor away, right? So what they do is they use a Saturday night special.

With pipe bombs, you can take any type of container and confine the powders. No matter what kind of container you put it in, it does the same thing: It causes a lot of frag and it does a lot of damage.

Pipe bombs are like hand grenades: You initiate them. They're either lit like a firecracker or initiated electronically and that can be so varied, you're only limited by your imagination. You can initiate a pipe bomb with a wick, you can use a flashbulb, blasting caps, a chemical reaction. You can set them down and light them; you can light and toss them.

There was a guy on the South Side—he made a pipe bomb, had a buddy drive him by the house, and he lit the pipe bomb and went to throw it—and the wick was too short and blew his hand off. Turned to the guy in the car and says, "Would you drive me to the hospital?"

One of the most dangerous of all explosives is flash powder, which is used in ordinary fireworks. Fireworks, I feel, are probably one of the most dangerous explosives to handle because they're very sensitive.

Three military EOD [Army Explosives Ordnance Detachment] men several years ago in California died when they walked into their bunker that was loaded with fireworks. One of the men stepped on what they call a torpedo and it set off an explosion and three of them died.

We had a couple that would let their four-year-old little boy light their cigarettes for them. They let the kid light cigarettes. So what did he find? He found a homemade firecracker, an M-80, that his father made. He thought it was a cigarette, so he was gonna light it for his dad. Blew his face all off.

Certain explosives are more sensitive to heat and shock than others. Military explosives are the safest of all. Because of all the bouncing around they have to take, they're very safe. And what are military explosives made for? *Nineteen-year-olds.* They have very rigid standards: TNT, hand grenades, mortar shells—it's basically the safest stuff to handle.

You can bounce them off walls, chew on them—in Vietnam, they used C-4, which is a plastic explosive, to cook their meals or reheat stuff.

I read one of these books—they tell you how to make TNT on the stove. But man, you've got to be the luckiest guy on two feet if you ever make it on your stove and it doesn't go off.

The homemade stuff. Improvised explosives. Kitchen explosives. They're the most dangerous because nobody knows what the hell is in them.

I had a boss tell me, he says, "If you guys ever got a real bomb, you wouldn't know what to do with it." I said, "If I ever had a *real* bomb, I *would* know what to do with it. But when they start messing with chemicals and shit . . ."

There was a guy in 1969, Frank "Mad Bomber" Kulak, who terrorized the city on a many-months-long bombing spree and ended up holding about a thousand policemen at bay. He did it all with automatic weapons and improvised explosives.

This guy was an ex-Marine, a World War II veteran. He was an absolute, total loner; he was the neighborhood peculiar bird—he was always around, everybody knew him, he never said much to anybody, he was single and lived with his sister in a family three-flat. He was just one of these real quiet guys.

And then a rash of bombings started. A number of people were hurt, a few were maimed. One of the bombings that really got everything going was the placing of an explosive device in the toy department of a Goldblatt's department store. It was made to detonate when disrupted. A grandmother was killed; she opened the package. She was a complete, total, random, innocent victim. The majority of his devices were all activated the same way; he left explosive devices around town. There were more fatalities.

Bomb and Arson started receiving information from everybody who knew this guy as the frequency and severity of these bombings increased. Somebody got some information that this fellow may be the bomber. Some guys from our unit were out there that day when there was a call of a man with a gun at his home. So they went over to the house and so did district officers.

They went up on the third floor, at the rear, and knocked on the door and tried to talk to this fellow. There was a Bomb and Arson sergeant, a patrol sergeant, a bomb tech, and another arson investigator there, and this guy opened the door and just opened fire on the officers—he killed two instantly, the bomb tech and the patrol sergeant, and shot a third one in the chest. Then he started setting off explosives. He blew up the back stairs of the building.

It was World War III out there when the thing finally went down. There was a massive shoot-out.

He was firing off all sorts of modified military explosives: rifle grenades, hand grenades, mortars. He had automatic weapons. He fired thousands and thousands of rounds. He fought the Chicago Police Department to a standstill for better than five hours. This was the ultimate barricade. One man against probably a thousand officers.

When we could see him in the front window, I went up and got the bodies down to the second floor. They were both multiply shot.

I know people that—one of the first guys there couldn't get away from his squad car in front of the house because he was pinned down. The bombs going off gave him concussions and made him violently ill; it's like a gigantic hammer slapping you time and again. Noise and concussion just beat your body up—

everybody's shooting over your head and up into this house and he's shooting back down.

Kulak's intention was eventually to set off the ultimate bomb—he had one huge improvised device up there that he hoped to lure as many police up there as he could and then detonate it and take them and himself out at the same time. He never did do that and I believe the reason was that his sister was in the building and he didn't want to get her killed.

It went on for hours and hours and hours. The city actually ran out of ammunition at times. We had to send to the North Side to get more tear gas and ammunition because all the stuff was used up on the South Side. We wanted tear gas to get him out of there, but he was wearing a gas mask. He had it all thought out.

Sometime late in the evening, he surrendered to the hierarchy of the police department. We found fifty-one devices in his apartment, things that he *hadn't* fired at us. So after the firefight and after we moved the bodies out and tried to clear up the scene, we had a lot of military ordnance that hadn't detonated; in other words, they had dudded. And that's just as dangerous as handling a live one. They all had to be collected and moved and blown up.

This was a guy who had no criminal record, never even got drunk in the neighborhood tavern. He kept to himself. He was an honest person until he took these fanciful explosive things out.

You get a homemade device—God only knows how this guy made it. We have no idea what we're dealing with. We don't know if we're dealing with a sophisticated device or a simple firecracker device or an incendiary device. It can be booby-trapped. You can have a pipe bomb with a burned wick and you can say, well, they lit the wick and it didn't go off. When, in reality, it could be booby-trapped and have an anti-disturbance switch in it so that if you moved it, it's going to go off.

You have to stay keyed in. When you're talking improvised devices, there is no book on how you render it safe. Because it is—the key word is "improvised." So one guy can't say, "Oh, no, no. You cut the blue wire before the white wire." That's Hollywood. You have to be high on the sense which brings all of your senses into play very acutely on what you're doing.

You have no idea. That's why the hardest thing is to walk up on it.

Explosives are a mystique to many people. They don't know anything about them other than they'll kill you. They don't know how or why.

All somebody has to do is mention "bomb" and nobody'll touch it; everybody'll back away. A lot of our cases, especially in federal and government buildings, are suspicious briefcases inadvertantly left behind and packages on radiators with somebody's lunch inside. That's the majority of the time—but you don't know that going in.

Even other cops who are at the scene—their basic instructions in the Orders are—stay away from any suspected bomb and clear the people out of the area.

Everybody else runs away from them. You're the one guy that *can't* run away. You've got to go towards them. And you've got to decide what to do about them.

You're in a situation where something has to be done. It has to be done now. You can't defer it for twenty-four hours. You have to make a decision, whether it's dismantle it, remove it, or detonate it. But something has to be done.

The hardest part of the whole job is walking up on the device, because you don't know what you're walking into. Once you're there and assess the situation . . . But it's walking up on that little baby.

You don't know if it's radio-controlled, you don't know if there's a timing mechanism, you don't know if there's antidisturbance on it. You've got to walk up on it to see what you have. It might be nothing more than somebody's lunch, but you don't know that till you get there.

We had two cases at Police Headquarters. One was a Kentucky Fried Chicken container with a bomb in it that FALN placed in a planter right outside the entrance.

A few years ago, the former commander of Bomb and Arson found a brown paper bag in the washroom. He called in all the bomb techs. They went in there and found it was a half-eaten long john.

We had an incident at O'Hare Airport: a ticking package at the flight service center of a certain major airline. This is where the pilots go, the flight attendants go, for instructions and whatever. So here's this ticking package; they called the Bomb Squad.

Another guy and I went out there. We asked the woman who found the device what happened—we always ask, "What did you find? What did you do?" This woman employee said she was walking by the luggage rack in this flight service center and she heard a ticking sound coming from a suitcase. So she removed the suitcase, which she shouldn't have, put it in her office and surrounded it with filing cabinets. Called the police.

The police arrived, evacuated the area, cordoned off the whole area. The fire department was there. The airline shut down. They called the Bomb Squad.

We responded to the scene. We listened to this suitcase. It was not a ticking sound. To me it sounded like a tape recorder rewinding.

A bomb is a bomb until it is proven that it is not a bomb. We were ninety-five percent sure this was not a bomb. We decided to hand-enter. We went in—very close, very carefully, looking in there, and cut open—and here it was, a battery-operated dildo that had an orbital, pivotal motion. Somehow, I guess from moving it around and having the switch turn on, that's what the woman who discovered it heard—*whoo-whoo-whoo-whoo-whoo-whoo-whoo*.

On the dildo was inscribed SWEET LOVE TINA. Well, Tina didn't report to work till two o'clock that afternoon and I think she was fired.

Static electricity is the great danger in approaching a bomb. If it's electrically initiated, you can set a bomb off just by walking across the carpet, or having too much nylon on your body. We had a woman bomb tech for about a year; she could never wear panty hose. You try to wear crepe soles; crepe soles are best for crossing a carpet. We wear cotton coveralls because cotton doesn't generate electricity. And there's no metal on these coveralls at all, whatsoever. We have static wrist straps to take the electricity and put it in the ground. We turn off our radios when we approach a device.

We do not let the news media anywhere around when we're doing our rendering safe procedures. My answer to the news media when we find a device is either, "It was an improvised explosive device that functioned as designed," or, "It did not function as designed."

I do not describe it; I do not tell them anything else. I do not allow them to film anything we do, our equipment, or what have you. And this is standard throughout the bomb community.

A couple years ago, up in northern Illinois, they found a device. So the police chief gets on TV and he had the device all spread out in front of him on this table. And he says, "This is why it didn't work. Because of that." Now, he just told the bomber what he did wrong.

You'll get a device, let's say in an airport, a plane. You shut down the runway. Most airlines will say, "Hey, wait a minute! You shut down O'Hare Field for fifteen minutes, you got a backup up the nose, money . . . tremendous." But, if we don't do that, and the bomb goes off . . . it comes back: "Hey, what is the first thing you do at a bomb scene? *Secure the area.*"

We had a situation in a bank not too long ago. A woman walked in the bank with a package. She said, "I want 'x' number of dollars."

They gave it to her, maybe $20,000, I'm not sure, and she ran out. A police officer chased her. She pulls out a gun. "If you don't let me go," she says, "I'm gonna shoot myself." He says, "Go ahead."

So she fires once, the gun didn't go off; she fired a second time, it just went around her head. The package was with her there.

But the copper comes up to me and says, "That's not the package with the bomb. It's still in the bank." So I go in the bank, I ask one of the security guards, I says, "You still have the package here?" He says, "I don't know what you're talking about." Then a sergeant comes up to me, "Yeah, the package is up there in the front."

This lady bank robber left the package right on the floor in the customer service area, in one of the little cubicles. So I go up there and one of the bank officials had put a couple of like room dividers around it.

I say to the official, "I want everybody out of the bank." He says, "I can't shut down the bank." I says, "Okay, I'm leaving." "What do you mean you're leaving? You have to take that apart." I says, "Everybody has to get out of here." "I can't shut down the bank." "Well, then it's your device." He said, "Now you can't do that." "The fuck I can't. I'm leaving."

He decided to shut down the bank. I shut down Michigan Avenue until we determined what it was the woman had planted: it was some towels rolled in plastic garbage bags, some dresser doorknobs in there, with some wire—it didn't even look like a good hoax device.

Boy, I'll tell you, when you go up on a bomb, it's not being afraid, or being shook, or anything like that, it's really . . . intense, is the best word I can come up with.

You get into a tunnel vision thing when you get to a scene. I've felt this; other guys talk about it too. You lock in on what you're doing and everything else kind of fades. All you're thinking about, all your energies, are all going one way.

Say I'm dealing with another bomb tech maybe and he's dealing with me and we're saying, "Get this. Get that. What do we need? This, that. Get them out of here." And you become aware that you don't see other people, you don't see other police officers, you just glance around and see that you have the conditions set up, cordoned off and everything else, and all you're doing is you're channeling on this stuff. You see nothing else. You're not hyper, but your adrenaline is high.

Now this adrenaline high and low can be devastating; it can be very, very dangerous. A scenario: You're working on a device, an actual device, so your adrenaline is high. And you do something that makes you believe that you've rendered this device safe. The adrenaline goes down the drain. You come in there on an adrenaline high, but now you believe everything is all right, so you go to a low. And now you become lackadaisical. Except you *haven't* rendered it safe, because it's not rendered safe until it's completely disassembled. It's like you let your guard down, and that's when you can get killed.

Don't let anybody kid you. You are nervous when you're up on top of an explosive device because if it goes off, that's the last thing you're gonna see. It increases your heart rate quite a bit. But you can't be flighty or excitable.

The most dangerous thing a bomb tech ever deals with is a pipe bomb. Of all bombs, the pipe bomb is the most dangerous. You deal with them so much that you can't get any apathy towards handling them.

The reason that they're so dangerous is that they're very crude. Normally, a pipe bomb consists of a pipe, a cap at each end, and some kind of a fusing system. Well, when the person that made it, if he spilled any powder or if there's any black powder in the threads of the caps, the person *removing* the caps can cause enough friction to set off that small amount of powder in the thread—black powder is very sensitive to heat and friction—and all you have to have is that little bit of friction and the whole thing goes off.

So even the simple unscrewing of the end caps could mean your demise. That's why we never remove a cap by hand; we do it remotely.

Occasionally on a pipe bomb, when you don't see an external fuse, there could be an *internal* fusing device, such as a mercury switch. The person that picks up that pipe bomb, when he turns it over, the mercury in the little switch will cause contact with a small battery that will generate an electrical current that will set it off. So if you move it at all, if the mercury goes to either end, it can set it off.

A simple pipe bomb killed two explosives technicians in Los Angeles a few years ago. Their top two men. Two of the most renowned bomb experts in the United States—nationally known—died in West Los Angeles while attempting to render safe a pipe bomb. The United States government had sent these guys to Lebanon to look into the explosion over there that killed all the Marines—they thought that their expertise would help make a determination.

Yet these two guys died in West Los Angeles in 1986 taking a simple pipe bomb apart. Killed them both.

You never know for sure when a bomb is going to go off. There's no way of knowing. Unless you're working on an old-fashioned mechanism and you're looking at the clock. And you know you've got a wristwatch and you know when the hand comes around and hits a pin, it'll go off.

That's the way it's supposed to work. But you never know for sure. Even with a clock device, because they can set up a clock and it looks like you have fifteen minutes. But a small thing like just reversing the timer . . . Like a kitchen timer has an hour on it, okay? And you're looking at it, it says it's got forty-five minutes. You think you got forty-five minutes. Well, in reality, you only got fifteen, because it's running backwards. So, you never know. The last thing you might hear is *boom!*

That's why I don't like fireworks.

A bomb either works or doesn't work. We've had bombs malfunction because the switches on a mail bomb were bent because it was handled through the United States Post Office and they abused it so when the bomb was supposed to go off, the contacts didn't meet. Or the bomb had a bad solder joint. Sometimes the simple fact that on a timer watch, they didn't sand the shellac off the hands and so it didn't complete the circuit.

* * *

We've had dynamite that has gone off and because of age, deterioration, mishandling, and everything else, it hasn't functioned at one-fiftieth of its original design potential. But you don't want to be on top of dynamite, even in a weakened condition, when it goes bang. It's like the man says—when you feel the dynamite start to swell, all you can do is squeeze it and hope the swelling'll go down.

We've had devices that, when we looked into them, for all intents and purposes they should have detonated. The only difference in their exploding or not exploding was the thickness of a coat of paint on the side of a piece of equipment.

There's two ways to disarm a bomb. Either by hand entry or remotely. We try to stay away from hand entry. It's just very dangerous. Even the paper on a package can be wired so that if you fool around with the outside container, you can set it off. The bomb techs lift up a little corner and try to peek in there, see what it is and that in itself is one of the most dangerous things to do.

Hand entry was very common years ago but the devices were a lot simpler, less sophisticated. But nowadays, it's not true. And the technology is here.

Remote entry is the name of the game. Remote handling of suspect devices, mechanized machinery, and robotics, all over the place, that's the name of the game now.

Even with remote entry, you still have to walk up on the device, not knowing what it is or when it's gonna go off. Nothing will ever replace that, or the bomb tech's skill in figuring out what the hell he's got and what to do about it.

We've got a total containment vessel now. A hundred sixty thousand bucks. It eats bombs. A total containment vessel eats bombs. We can literally place a rather large charge—we don't want to say how much—inside of it and detonate it and it will safely contain the explosion and the frag, like from pipe bombs, hand grenades.

The days of a guy going up and working over the top of a device—I hope those days are numbered. Because, no matter what you do—if you sit there and watch a package for an hour, and decide, okay, now's the time to go up—you walk up to the device and at that moment it's the time that the bomber has designed it to go off—you're gonna arbitrarily pick a time to go up there, and what it is, is "But for the grace of God go I" because if it's the time, it's going to be the time.

We have a robot named "Little Frankie." We've had him since 1986. We named him after the former head of the Bomb Squad, Frank Kasky. And it is a track-driven robot, like a tank. It's just a little remote-control vehicle that has an arm and a claw. It has TV cameras on it that enable us to see, and sound equipment that enables us to hear. It runs on a tether up to a hundred and ten yards, three hundred thirty feet, so we can be a football field away from the device and send the robot up to look at it. It can carry up X-ray equipment, take an X-ray, and bring back the negative. We can look at the device, listen to it, X-ray it—all remotely.

You're operating this robot from a console. Like a video game. You have a joystick and different buttons that perform functions. But you must understand, when you're looking through a TV camera at a black-and-white screen, you have no depth perception. And you can only see what that TV screen shows you; you have no peripheral vision.

We can send Little Frankie up there with tools that will render the device safe or he can move it to a safe area. Or we can have him carry an explosive charge up there, drop the explosive charge; we can blow the thing in place.

If we can get Little Frankie to pick the device up and carry it over to the total containment vessel, he can put it in the total containment vessel, and close it, and then it can't get us at all.

* * *

Most bomb techs in the world agree that if you've got a device where you can't safely render it safe, then you destroy it, you blow out windows, you destroy property, rather than risk lives. You can always replace property.

We've got methods and equipment to help us, but nothing will ever replace the experience of a bomb technician; in other words, your brain, your eyes, and your hands are the most important tools. And all the equipment we have, from a screwdriver to the total containment vessel, is worthless without a good bomb tech.

The FBI has a Bomb Commander seminar every year. One year, they had a State Department psychiatrist who was going to give us the psychological profile of bombers. And he started off his talk, he says, "You know, guys, people who make bombs are very much like people who take them apart. You're all fucking nuts." So I turned to my buddy who runs the New York Bomb Squad, "Well, *I'm* not crazy." "Well, I ain't crazy, either." We're not crazy. We're not thrill-seekers. We're a unique breed.

You always have to look for the "What if?" situation. And you always have to look for the second bomb. Just because you found one doesn't mean it's the only bomb there. If you find twenty-three bombs, that doesn't mean there isn't any more. Depends what the bomber wants to do—does he want to harm an individual or does he want to harm the explosives technician—you know, what's the scenario behind his planning or placing the explosive device?

We do a lot of bomb sweeps. Big guys come in, presidential candidates, Jesse Jackson . . . Secure the area, see if there's any devices.

You can stick a device in a heating duct. You can stick a device in a microphone. Almost anywhere. A man can walk in with a device on his body. Metal detectors cannot detect some devices.

There's always the washrooms; they're always probably the best place; you know, women secrete devices in the private parts of their anatomy.

On a sweep, we go through every aisle, all the obvious places, but we concentrate on the public access areas mainly. A lot of these auditoriums and stuff are secure and they have security, so the only place an individual can place a device is in a public access area—washroom, stand-up ashtrays—those ashtrays are great places—anyplace they can secrete a bomb without being seen. It can be as simple a thing as leaving a briefcase or package.

Anything that does not belong. That's the secret to a bomb sweep.

You can go crazy on a sweep. You can keep thinking, What if, what if?

But it's not one hundred percent science. If somebody has a real sophisticated plan in place, chances are it's gonna be successful. It's like they say about burglars. If a burglar's determined to break into your place, you can't stop him. He's going to get you. Same thing with an assassin. When an assassin, or a bomber, really puts some effort into it, you're not gonna be able to stop him.

The Secret Service will tell you that—if somebody really wants the president, or the vice-president, or a dignitary, there's not too much they can do to stop him.

Our biggest enemy, when it comes to bombs, is not the general public—it's policemen.

They have a tendency to touch things, take things apart, without having any knowledge. When I talk to Bomb Squad commanders—invariably, invariably—there's two to three incidents a year where policemen will pick up a device, put it in the trunk of the car, and play with it, take it apart.

I had a guy one time, nine o'clock, a beautiful autumn morning. The guy had found a grenade. That was the call.

And there is this fellow, sitting in his squad car, reading his *Sun-Times,* with the grenade on the roof of his squad car, right above his head. So I walk over. "Hey, how ya doing?" "Okay. Fine." "What do ya got?" "Anhh, I got this grenade up here." "Where'd ya get the grenade?" "Well, a woman was sweeping the hallway, she found a grenade in the hallway. There's been some gang problems there."

I look at the grenade and I say, "Get out of the car, please." I say, "You in the military?" He says, "Yeah." "Know what kind of grenade this is?" "Yeah, it's a standard army issue." I said, "How does it operate?" He says, "Well," he says, "You got the spoon, you got the pin, you pull the pin, you throw the thing, the spoon pops off, it goes bang." "Fine," I said. "You look at that thing and tell me where the pin is." He looked at it. "Oh my God, there's no pin in it." "Yeah. Right."

What had happened was, this grenade had been around for a while. The spoon had rusted shut, somebody had extracted the pin and thrown the grenade to make it work as it was supposed to, but it never came loose.

Now the policeman puts this thing four inches above his head, sits in the car reading the *Sun-Times* . . . with this grenade. It could have gone off at any time.

I put the pin back in it; that's what I was there for—I used my star to do it. Took that same grenade out to the range, and pulled that spoon—remotely—and that grenade went off just like it was supposed to.

Bomb Squad:
Contributing Police Officers

LIEUTENANT TOM BRADY, explosives technician III, commanding officer, Bomb Squad. As head of the Bomb Squad, Brady is responsible for the rendering safe procedures for all recovered explosives and explosive devices. Brady's twenty-eight years in the CPD have encompassed sixteen separate assignments, including vice officer in the Eighteenth District, homicide sergeant in Areas Four and Five, aide to the Deputy Chief of Detectives, and federal-grant proposal writer for the CPD. Brady has also worked undercover in the Confidential and Corrupt Practices Section of the Internal Affairs Division and headed a surveillance squad on career criminals for the Criminal Investigation Unit. Brady served as executive officer, Bomb and Arson Unit, from 1985 to December 1989, when he came to the Bomb Squad.

EXPLOSIVES TECHNICIAN JIM BROWN has been a policeman for thirty-one years: five years on patrol, five years in Area Four Homicide, and twenty-one years with the Bomb Squad.

COMMANDER JOSEPH GRUBISIC, explosives technician III, head of Bomb and Arson Unit. Grubisic was in charge of the Bomb Squad from 1985 to 1990. His duties included responding to all bombing scenes, coordinating post-blast and follow-up investigations, overseeing proficiency practice, and supervising sweeps. Grubisic's thirty-two-year career in the police includes extensive work in the Intelligence Section of Organized Crime, the former Red Squad, which investigated terrorist activity, Gangs North and South, and Bomb and Arson since 1983.

EXPLOSIVES TECHNICIAN FRANK GUTRICH,

thirty-one years in the CPD. Gutrich has worked patrol, served as an evidence technician for the Crime Lab, handled homicide, robbery, and burglary as a detective in Area Two, and has been with Bomb and Arson since 1975—as an arson investigator for two years, and as an explosives technician in the Bomb Squad since 1977.

DETECTIVE RON HARRIS, explosives technician.

Harris joined the force in 1963, worked one year on patrol, four years in the Canine Unit. Harris has been a detective for twenty-two years: twelve in Auto Theft and the past eleven years in the Bomb Squad.

DETECTIVE HARRY SELLERS, explosives technician.

Sellers, who retired in 1989, was with Bomb and Arson ten years, working both arson and bombings: as a detective in the Arson section for four years and as a Bomb Squad member since 1983. Sellers joined the CPD in 1962, was assigned to the Area Two Task Force, worked as a Crime Analyst from 1965 to 1967, became a detective in 1967, and went to Area Two Auto Theft, where he worked until 1972, when he joined the Vice Control Section. He returned to Auto Theft in 1973. In 1979, Sellers came to Bomb and Arson.

ARSON

A lot of times, we'll get there and the bodies will still be there. You're digging around in the rubble while the bodies are laying there.

You try to think it's no different than a burnt couch. I mean, that's how you get used to it. A body laying in the corner, burnt up, is something like a burnt couch.

I start asking them, you know, "How did this one start?"

CPD arson investigator

It's a 104-degree August day. CPD headquarters. A phone goes off on a steel desk that's sweating from the heat. "Arson *Hot*liiine" sings a cop into the phone.

This is a much different voice than the one you usually get when you call one of the CPD's specialized units. Call the Vice Control Section, for example, and the way they say "Vice" makes you want to repent. And Violent Crimes—there's no sing-songing "Violent Crimes" into the phone; the unfailing way homicide detectives snarl "*Vi*-lent Crimes" when you call makes you know they're on to you and they're going to get you.

But this Bomb and Arson detective—"Arson *Hot*liiine"—is a cheery host, inviting all callers to open up, spill the secret of who's about to torch what. And he remains cheerful, optimistic, this black August day in an unair-conditioned side office in the middle of CPD headquarters, even after three calls in a row have been placed by callers anxious to know the latest sports scores. "No, you want the *Tribune*. This is the Arson Hotline," he keeps saying. Nicely, too.

The Arson Hotline is only a couple of digits different from the number for the *Chicago Tribune*, and it's flooded with calls about sports results and sports stats. One arson investigator says, "One day, I pick up the phone and this guy goes, 'Give me the results.' I say,

'What do you mean, *'results'*?"

The Arson Hotline also gets tips on arsons waiting to happen. Like the one from the security guard, horrified by his employer's suggestion that he go in at night and torch the boss's failing business, situated on the ground floor of an apartment building filled with small children. Arsonists have called, too. "We get calls sometimes from participants in arsons who feel afterwards they didn't get their fair share of the profits," says one arson investigator. "We get most of our tips around Christmas, when people think in terms of what the reward money could do."

The Hotline is one route to the solving of a crime that is extremely resistant to investigation. Unlike bombings, which usually make their presence felt, either by discovery or tragedy, arson may never be discovered. "Arson is unusual in that you must *prove* that it happened," says Lieutenant Tom Brady, former head of the Bomb and Arson Unit, current head of the Bomb Squad. "You don't have to prove a robbery; the victim tells you—'Hey, I was stuck up. A gun was stuck in my face.' A burglary, something is missing. But in arson, we must prove it occurred. And it is very difficult. Arson is *the* most difficult crime to solve."

The arson investigators in the CPD's Bomb and Arson Unit sort through the approximately twelve thousand fires that occur in Chicago per year, twenty-five hundred of which are found to be arsons. They come in on the aftermath of fire, just after it's been extinguished by the fire fighters, and search unsound structures for clues the fire itself may have consumed. They then interview witnesses, or anyone who might be able to connect a tossed match to criminal intent, hunt up suspects and, in the case of arson-for-profit detectives, embark on what can be years of elaborate paper- and suspect-chasing. Even the most straightforward arson case can take weeks, months, to put together to the satisfaction of the judge who always seems, they say, to want 110 percent proof on a crime that typically occurs at three A.M. when all potential eyewitnesses are asleep or otherwise dead to the world.

Arson is a crime that is easily committed, easily concealed, and that can easily rage out of control. . . .

We had an old woman who owned a restaurant that was going under. The neighborhood started changing and her business wasn't doing very well; she had a sick husband, a very sick husband—he was at home but he was on oxygen, life-support systems, and she was about seventy years old.

There was a family in the neighborhood that worked for this woman. A waitress and her brothers. And they were so close, it was like a family situation, her with these employees. At one point, she told them, "You know, I gotta get out of here, this building, you know, business is bad," and she just had to get out.

And she made a kidding comment that she wished the place would burn down. That would be the answer to her problems.

So one of the brothers in this family picked up on it. He said, "Do you really want the place to burn?" She said, "Yes."

So what he did is, he committed an arson out of love—it ended up as an arson-for-profit, to get out of a lease, or get out of the business, whatever way you want to say it—but it was not done for money, it was done more out of respect and love for this woman and her family.

This restaurant was in a multiapartment building. Many people lived upstairs. *Children* were living upstairs.

He went in there, he spread gasoline all over the place—not knowing what he was doing. Two five-gallon containers. He had towels spread all over, he spread them from one place to another. And then he stepped out of the room for a minute to let it saturate in the floor.

What people don't realize . . . when you use gasoline in an enclosed area, the room becomes—literally—a bomb. From the fumes.

He spread the gasoline on these trailers, we call them, to propagate the fire. He stepped outside, because he almost got overcome by the fumes himself. He stepped out for about thirty seconds. What he did was, he let the fumes build up in the room.

He opened the door, he went a couple feet into the room, he lit a match, and it was just like he was in the middle of the fire. It *surrounded* him.

It blew him out the door—on fire. His clothes . . . you could follow the trail of his clothes, going home. He ran down the alley, his shirt on fire—he threw his shirt into a playlot, screaming as he was running home.

He ran home. Instead of going right to the hospital, which was only a couple blocks away, the Cook County Burn Unit, probably the best burn unit in the city, he went home—and his family, they put him in a cold shower, which wasn't bad. They put him in a cold shower, but instead of taking him to the hospital then, they tried to hide this event. They doctored him for many, many hours. They did the complete opposite of what they should be doing—they covered his body with an ointment like Vaseline or a grease-type of thing, which is the worst thing you can do. That used to be the remedy. Now it's cold water and ice.

They kept him at home, but eventually they saw that he needed help; he wasn't gonna make it like this. They called a friend who was a nurse somewhere. The nurse said, "I can't treat him. You better get him somewhere." So instead of taking him to the Burn Unit two blocks away, they wanted to get all the distance they could between the fire he set and the hospital, so they took him all the way out to a hospital in the western suburbs, which didn't even have a burn unit. They came up with some farfetched story that the kid was hurt trying to fix a hot water heater.

We had a stop with all the emergency rooms, that as soon as a guy came in with a bad burn, to call us. So we went out there and I talked to the doctor. The doctor told me, he said, "This kid has a fifty-fifty chance of dying."

So what we did, we used a technique—that works—we told the kid that we're not gonna lie to him, he had a chance of being a fatality in this fire and that if he had anything on his conscience, he should come clean because we didn't believe his story; we knew it was totally bullshit that he got caught with a hot water heater with these kind of burns. And we told him he was seen running two blocks from his house, on fire.

Anyway, he confessed. Later, he implicated the old lady and they both pled guilty in court. And he went through several surgeries of grafting his skin. He was in the hospital for maybe two months. He was a nice looking kid, too. Now he's got permanent nerve damage, permanent scarring. This was a twenty-two-year-old kid, never been arrested, and a sweet old lady with a sick husband. Somebody's grandmother. They could have burned the building down, with all those children inside.

We had one downtown, an old flophouse at Erie and Dearborn. A lot of old people lived there. There were six dead in that fire.

How it started, this *dog*—and that is exactly what he was—fell asleep smoking. The manager, or one of the other people in the hotel saw smoke, knocked on the door—the guy's inside, trying to put it out with a glass of water. He didn't want to get blamed for the damage; he's trying to put it out. The guy outside said, "Should we call the fire department?" "No. Everything's okay."

Well, he lost control of the fire. What did he do? He ran out of the building. Checked into the Lawson YMCA. And the whole building went off. And six people died, six poor old people.

We grabbed him—he was sleeping on the Alcohol Rehab floor they have at the Y—we woke him up, dragged him out of there. And he said, "This is basically what happened, you know. I got scared and I ran out."

What can you charge the guy with? I mean, he didn't intend to kill anybody, but he got scared, and he ran out—but he ran out *knowing* the place was on fire. That's what I can't . . . that's what I can't understand. How could you not even try to call the fire department or not knock on doors? He just walked off like nothing happened.

What we're dealing with, there's two types of problems: One is ignorance, accidents, and the other type is criminal, malicious.

People think fire will be confined to where they set it. They don't understand fire. Fire does what it wants to do. People pour gas all over and it self-extinguishes sometimes because the windows are shut. Or one piece of paper takes down a whole building. There are just so many variables. Fire goes where it's gonna go.

In a lot of criminal cases, people don't really want to hurt somebody. What they want to do is get even and lash out. Or they *do* want to hurt somebody and they end up killing ten others.

The problem is, fire doesn't understand what the person wants.

Fire goes whichever way it's gonna go. The wind, the resistance, the humidity, what's burning, whatever.

We've locked up a lot of people where their intent was just to set a small fire, be they seven-year-olds running around with matches or gang-bangers tossing Molotov cocktails. And you just can't control it.

People who set a fire to lash out, they want to destroy a piece of property and not hurt somebody; it might work that way, it might not. Trying to get even by burning somebody's car or house, you might be killing the person next door. You don't know how it's gonna communicate.

A guy was rejected by his girlfriend. He had made a lot of problems; the management of the apartment building asked him not to come back into the building. He started a fire. The mentality was, "I'll get even." He wasn't thinking the whole building would go up; he just wanted to set a nuisance fire, show his girlfriend.

The bottom line there was, the highest-ranking black member of the fire department, a deputy chief, was critically hurt fighting that fire. As of this moment, he still lays as a vegetable. He wasn't supposed to live; he survived, but he's a paraplegic from the neck down.

The thing about arson is—usually the person they're after or the people they're after don't die. The intended victim is usually not the one that's killed. That's the real sad part. The intended victim is usually out; they just stepped out for cigarettes or something. It's usually the kids and the old people that die.

That's how we get a lot of arsonists to talk. Arsonists always say they didn't know it would cause death. Of course they all say that.

So we say to the arsonist, "Look, this was a small fire. We know you're not the kind of person that would want to hurt anyone. Let's hear your version." And they talk because they don't want people to think they attempted murder.

Many times, the person who discovers the fire is the one who set it.

The fire department at any fire scene takes photos of the building. And then they turn the camera around and take photos of the people in the crowd.

It's classic with arson. The person who sets the fire goes back to see it.

Not only do they go see it, they go back to play hero.

We had a guy, we charged him with murder, he burned down a couple of buildings. He sets the fire in the back, he comes back later and rings doorbells in the front, trying to play hero. He rang doorbells to try to awaken the people in the building, one of whom *died* in the building.

We see the same people all the time, every fire scene. They *all* look like suspects. They look catatonic. The scum of the earth turns up at a fire.

Large fires attract every nut in the city. You could arrest a lot of these people just on looks alone. I mean, you look around and it's like "He could be the arsonist" and "He could" and "He could . . ."

We drive around the city together; we'll look out the window: "There's a fire-setter." It'll be some mopey guy, walking along with his head down, wearing nerdy clothes. Mopey—dirty, scruffy, doesn't really take care of himself. They don't dress well. They don't bathe very well. Overweight, fat a lot of times. It's a definite type.

It's common for firesetters to be at the scene of the fire that they set, to help out, help the firemen, help the police, give information. They'll be rolling up hoses, offering all kinds of help. The fireman's friend.

I handled a fire where four houses were down. When I came on the scene, I interviewed the chief and he said, "I got an eyewitness. It's a male white. He told me he was driving down the street and he discovered the fire." The kid's rolling up hoses, helping the firemen. I went over and interviewed him, he said that he was driving along, saw smoke, followed the smoke, comes up on the burning house, and he runs in to see if anybody's there and he gets some of the occupants out of the houses on either side that are burning. "Did you see anybody suspicious?" "No." So I went around and interviewed other people.

A few months later, they arrest a kid for setting a couple of car fires. The name sounds familiar, so I go through my notes and it was the kid I had interviewed. Who do you think was the one that discovered the fire?

This guy worked as a security guard and he alleged that he chased two young black men out of the parking lot of the multistory apartment building where he worked—and he chased them away, but they burned two cars before they got away. Something didn't ring true with his story and we found out he set the fires himself. The hero syndrome.

He finally confessed to the one where he was a security guard, that he burned the two cars. And while he was confessing, he confessed to an arson three years before, where a mother and her five children died.

He was just one of those psychs that every time he had an argument with somebody, especially his girlfriend, he'd go out and set a fire. It was never at his own place.

We found out that he had set lots of fires. He used to work for a board-up service. And, at the scenes of the fires that he set he'd be out there, most of the time. He'd be out there, passing out cards to the victims for his board-up service.

It turned out they eventually fired him because they themselves, the service he worked for, suspected him—because he was calling fires in, he was calling the board-up people, on his days off. "Listen, there's a fire down here. You might want to get somebody out here real quick. I'll get out there with my cards."

He set the fires for psychological reasons, but he thought he might as well make some money on it.

Once you get one big fire, you'll get a big spurt of fires. Or you'll get a pattern in one area; all of a sudden there's a bunch of fires in one area. That's because people who were halfway thinking about it get inspired and they go ahead and do it.

We've handled tons of fire deaths. We've gone into buildings, seen old women sitting upright in chairs, totally burned. Children are the worst—in closets, in the attic, under beds; it's terribly depressing.

Most of the time, the bodies are gone. But if they're really burned bad, and they know there's no chance to save them— there's really no point in getting them to a hospital—they leave them there so we can take pictures. If it's obvious they're dead, they'll leave them.

They look like mannequins. They're just frozen in a pose.

I try not to look at it as a human being, because—how can anybody, how can something, or some*one* do such damage to a body? And then, you know, you see the kids, or you see a body and it's really bad—you can't eat for a long time.

You therefore don't look at it as a body. You look at it as a piece of furniture or a piece of debris, or another piece of evidence instead of it really being a person.

It's a very odd feeling. We're there, going about our business, and there was a tragedy there. And it's still there. The bodies are still there.

To know, you'd actually have to be in a smoke-filled building, to know what people who die in a fire go through, the panic they suffer.

I mean, we come in after. But we went—this is bullshit compared to a real fire—but my partner and I were in a factory once, on fire. This was an empty humongous factory where a phone company kept cables stored. And they had a small fire, a *real* small fire, and we got called.

We got inside the building. Now it started to smolder again. You're talking about like cables and chemical cables. The building starts filling up with smoke. You've got a flashlight—you remember where you came in the building. But once that smoke fills up, you're dead. You can't see nothing. You get so panicky. Where's the exit sign? What door did I come in? You're *lost*. I mean, I don't care if it's your own house. You are lost. . . . I had my flashlight, all my training, and I was just totally disoriented. You actually have to be in a room to know what I'm talking about, a smoke-filled room.

We had a fire at the Hilton a few years ago. They figure it was a prostitute left a cigarette burning. The bodies were found like two feet from an exit, a stairway. They were so close, but for the smoke, they couldn't see the door. So what the Hilton ended up doing is putting in a ten-million-dollar system where as soon as their smoke alarm system goes off on the floor, it activates a neon sign that runs the whole length of the wall and points to the exit. But these people—they died not knowing that if they had gone another *foot* they'd be out.

And for a kid . . . I mean, what's a kid?—the thing he's gonna do is run maybe for a window or probably for the closet, because that's where they're usually found, in closets or under the bed.

Most people die from the smoke—they're not actually burned; they're just partially burned. That's the only good part. Kids. They die from suffocation, usually within three to five minutes. So they don't die from actually getting burned up. You know, that's the only consolation you have when you're looking at the bodies of these poor kids.

We go in immediately after the fire is struck. That's the best time to do it. Because if we don't do it with a time frame fairly immediate, rain, snow, different things can change the scene.

If bodies have been left at the scene, it smells like you're walking into a barbecue. The smell is like that of roast meat.

When you walk in, there's still water running from floor to floor, hanging rafters, burnt rafters. We put on fire boots, our own police helmets.

Our guys wear steel-plated boots. Most people don't realize that when wood burns, it leaves the nails exposed. And when you step on a nail, you better have boots with a steel plate on. Every once in a while, we'll get a guy who thinks the fire isn't that bad and he doesn't put his boots on—and he gets a rude awakening when he steps on a nail.

We take shovels to the scene and we dig for evidence. It's hot, dirty, time-consuming work. You're looking for something, but you don't know for what. We collect our own evidence. Our detectives have cameras, they photograph the crime scenes, and they collect debris samples. We sift all the debris through metal sifters trying to determine if there's any additional evidence buried in the rubble. Matches. A lighter. A timing device. Evidence of a trailer. Signs that an accelerant has been used. You're digging up, trying to look, to uncover evidence. You find it, put it in the can, send it to the Crime Lab for analysis. On major cases, we work with the Crime Lab; they do their schtick, we do ours.

What you're trying to do is reconstruct the scene. Because by the time we get there, the fire department's been there, they've hosed everything down, they've thrown a lot of this stuff out the window, they've tossed everything around and when you get there, you're looking at this fire scene, and what you have to do is put the furniture back—try and place the furniture where things originally were so you get an idea—oh, this was here; this was here; it looks like the fire started maybe near the sofa or did the fire start near where the stove was at?

You gotta go out, sometimes, and bring it back in. You gotta be able to know where these things were, especially once you're talking to the offender and you get a confession, you want to be able to have his confession coincide with your cause and origin.

You start from the least amount of damage and work your way in to the most damage. It's like putting a puzzle together, backwards.

Once you're in the room, or area, of origin, then you work a little closer. You look for where the fire was set, what was used to set it. People might use wax paper, grease, charcoal lighter fluid, kerosene, paint thinner, grain alcohol as accelerants. Grain alcohol is getting to be very popular now because a lot of people are freebasing; grain alcohol keeps the flame going in the pipe.

You start looking for burn patterns—low burning, high burning, different types of patterns—low burning indicates a possible accelerant, or that the fire started at floor level, or that it could have been a secondary fire caused by a fire somewhere else.

Pour patterns. A big indicator of arson—not many fires start at floor level, so pour patterns show an accelerant was used. And wherever it's burned longest and hardest, that's where the accelerant was poured. Wood next to it might hardly be burned at all. It's called the line of demarcation.

The best indicator that you have an arson is multiple points of origin. That's the big one. If you have a fire on that side of the room and a fire on this side of the room and there's no fire in between—come on, how could it happen?

When they use gasoline, they play right into our hands. It's real easy to determine it's an arson if gasoline is used. The gasoline soaks in and not all the gasoline is consumed by the fire, okay?

What happens is, if you throw gasoline on the floor, what you'll have, it'll puddle, it'll form a pour pattern; if you have a concrete floor, it might go *underneath*. And after the fire, we take out a section of the floor and guess what? There might be gasoline on the other side of this floor piece that wasn't consumed.

And unless the place has gasoline, it's an intentional fire. If the grocery store owner says he never keeps gasoline, why would it be there? If you have a gift shop, and I ask you in our interview, do you store kerosene or gasoline or any kind of fuel and you say no, then how do you explain how the gasoline got in there? Somebody brought it in.

We can send somebody in with a sniffer, a hand-held vapor detector; it's like what the gas company uses—it detects the presence of hydrocarbons, anything that's a petroleum distillate.

We've got guys who've seen probably thousands of fires. They can look at gasoline and detect pour patterns—there are certain common denominators that are similar, pour patterns on a rug. They can actually read the pattern.

The patterns are the evidence of a crime. You don't get certain burn patterns and you don't get certain pour patterns on accidental fires.

Burn patterns. When wood burns, it looks like an alligator's back when it's completely burnt away. The depth of the alligator char will tell you how long this particular piece of wood was burning; the color of the alligatoring will tell you if an accelerant was used.

What burn patterns tell you—if you are lucky enough to have distinct burn patterns—it will probably lead you to the origin of the fire.

What you're looking for is direction—Where did this fire originate? One of the tricks you use, look at the light fixtures— a light bulb will expand and move into the direction of where the heat was coming from and it will tell you which way a fire came.

Also the window glass. The way that the smoke is pitted on the windows, from the fire, the degree of smudging, the blackening of the glass, that tells you if it was a slow buildup of heat or an extremely fast fire. If it's a fast fire, the blackening won't be even; with a slow fire, it's generally more even.

A lot of times, you go to a fire scene and you don't know if it's arson or accidental. You have no idea. The perfect example is a sofa or bed fire. How do you know if that was intentionally set or not, or just somebody smoking a cigarette on the sofa?

We had a case like that. The girl at first said, "I was smoking on the couch, maybe the cigarette fell out." She finally admitted, she was being evicted again, she was putting all her stuff out and, yeah, she used the cigarette to start the fire. And whether it's intentional you don't really know till you interview the person responsible for it.

What happens a lot is people accidentally burn themselves setting fires and get caught that way. You find out if an eyewitness saw somebody running away from the fire.

You ask a lot of questions. Of eyewitnesses. Of the suspect. And if something doesn't click, or there's a change in what was said, a red flag goes up. You talk to them and you lock in what they said. You remember what they said, because they might change it at a later time, especially when they're scared—you change your story a lot, man, especially when it's a lie.

It's real hard to make arson stick. Number one, the judge wants you to prove that it was arson and not an accidental fire. *Then*, they pretty much want a witness that saw the guy light the fire, or the guy's admission.

That's *awfully* hard. I mean, you can throw a cigarette, a match, anything like that, and be long gone before. . . . Or, intent, you can't prove somebody's an arsonist because you saw him throw away a match.

How's anybody gonna see an arsonist? Mostly, they go in at three A.M. when eyewitnesses are nil.

The weapons of an arsonist aren't illegal. It's not illegal to have a match on you, a lighter, a can of gasoline.

Even if you've got the guy's admission, by the time he gets to court, he'll say, "I didn't say that. They had me in there for eight hours. I was tired. I said anything they wanted."

But sometimes, if he can tell you exactly how he did it, especially if it's complicated, and if that matches what your investigation shows, sometimes that's enough for the judge.

There are a number of different classic profiles or motives for arson. There's arson to conceal other crimes. There's arson for revenge. There's terrorist arsons. Arson as part of the hero syndrome, vanity fires. Thrill seekers, pyros. Arson-for-profit. They all fit into these general types.

The biggest motive in arson is revenge. Absolutely. Most arsons are for revenge and jealousy. Those are very common. Very common.

Arsonists are sneaks. They're not the kind to confront anybody. Arson is a very sneaky crime. You want to get back at the person, but you have a good chance of nobody knowing you did it.

We've had fires—two neighbors are out drinking on the stoop of an apartment building, they get in an argument, one guy sets a mattress on fire in front of the other guy's apartment and it spreads and it kills everybody on that floor.

The way you get even with somebody in the ghetto is you burn their car or you put a rag under their door. The majority of fires in the projects, we have a lot of fires in the projects, are revenge-oriented. It might be gang-related, boyfriend-girlfriend, jealousies, or narcotics-related, whatever it is.

They take some garbage or some rags and start a fire by the door. The doors are steel, thank God. But you have to remember, in the projects there's only that door. There's no back door. So if that fire gets going under that door, you could have an asphyxiation type of case. A lot of people die; people die from somebody setting a small fire by the front door.

What happens in the projects—they're on the thirteenth floor; they see smoke; they think the fire department's coming—guess what? By the time they come, people panic and they jump out the window. You hear it all the time.

Most of the revenge arsonists, usually they break down, they cry, they show a lot of remorse. They really didn't mean for it to occur.

It's not unusual for an adult female to be involved in fire-setting. We get many adult females. Those are retaliation motives, usually, the spurned lover, the boyfriend—if I can't have him, nobody can have him; I'll burn him down.

The most common trigger for revenge arson is boyfriend/girlfriend. Second most common is evictions.

Three people died in an apartment house fire and there were numerous injuries of firemen and police because a guy set fire to a couch standing out in a hallway after his landlord evicted him. Three eyewitnesses saw this guy do it. The fire spread from the couch up to the fourth floor; you get these old apartments, the stairwells act as a flue.

We picked this guy up; it was sort of a cold night. He said, "Oh, I better get my coat on. It seems chilly out." I couldn't believe it. I said to him, "Three people are dead because of you and you're worried about catching a chill?"

We took him in. We showed him the pictures of the victims. I was yelling at him nose to nose. He never blinked. He knew the people that died and it never even fazed him. He had no remorse. He just didn't care. I'd have to say he was more ruthless than most.

We found out that he told the building manager that the couch left out on the landing was a fire hazard. I guess he proved his point.

Arson is used, often, to conceal other crimes. It's a panic cover-up. It's a scared reaction; it's not planned. If the offender executed a well-planned crime, he wouldn't need to do arson to cover it up.

*   *   *

We handled one where the arson was designed to lure the person out from his apartment so the offenders could rush in and rip him off.

This guy was going to rip off a guy in this particular building that he dealt with in the past with drugs. He knew that the guy was holding a lot of dope and probably a lot of money.

So what he and his buddies intended to do was rip him off. And the way they were gonna do this was to try to set a small fire in front of his door, panic everybody to get them out of the building, and when everybody fled the building because of the fire, they were gonna run in and grab his dope.

Unfortunately, the fire communicated and a guy died in that fire. He was in another apartment, this poor fifty-two-year-old guy, all dressed to go to work.

We get a lot of arsons meant to conceal homicides. It's an emotional reaction, especially in those cases where the homicide is the result of passion.

We had one one time where the guy killed his mother and, of course, became very excited, and realized he had to do something to cover this up and started the house on fire.

They think if they shoot someone and then burn the building down, that'll cover it up. Sometimes they don't even try to do that.

We had one—four guys, drug dealers, had gotten either ripped off or snitched on by the people they ended up murdering, three women and a man.

What they did was, they came over to the apartment, had an argument, and they shot all of them, the three women and a man. They put the man in a closet, they tied him up and threw him in the closet, poured gasoline or something on him and set him on fire. They tied the three girls together after they shot them, put them on one bed, poured gasoline on them and set them on fire. Two of them, we figured, were dead when the fire occurred. When we got there, we found the two girls, burned beyond recognition and tied up in bed and the guy in the closet.

The third one escaped. She was bound and gagged and shot and ignited, and somehow she managed to escape. She died eventually. But she had to go through all that hell—part of her statement was that it's the feeling of laying there, tied up, and seeing somebody pour gasoline on you and light you up and there's nothing you can do about it.

But she managed—they didn't tie her up real good—and she managed to get out and they took her to the hospital where she died a week or two weeks later.

We were at a scene once, a two-story brick building at the back of a lot. This was the Fourth of July; I'll never forget it. We came upon a body that was in the first floor enclosed porch, lying on his back, burned like I have never seen in my entire life.

His face was burned off. I looked at the chest cavity—his ribs were burned away. I could see his heart; I could see his stomach. The skin on his legs was burned off. The only parts of him that weren't burned were his two buttocks and the back of his skull. They were on the floor.

There was so much debris—everything was just around him, so we wanted to dig out the whole floor of the room he was in to look for pour patterns. So we would dig out as much as we could around him. Then we'd get it down to just maybe a little bit of debris, a little bit of soot, a little bit of dirt on the floor. Then we'd use brooms to brush off and then use water from a garden hose to wash everything down so we could see burn patterns on the floor very readily because it would be a clean surface.

In the process of digging him out, I shoveled up a foot. I didn't know there was a foot. It just came right off.

He had no nostrils or lungs left, so you couldn't check them for smoke inhalation. But one thing that *was* left was a hole in the back of his skull.

The coroner at the inquest determined that this guy was murdered before the fire. He had a fractured skull and was alive when the hole was put in his skull. It could have been done by a hammer, or a board, or a bullet. This guy was a Cuban dope dealer.

Arson to cover murder is a dumb way to do it. Someone will always know. You always can identify it.

* * *

Arson is used as a terrorist act in the narcotics business frequently. It's a message, generally. Pay up or your life is next. Or don't interfere with my area where I sell drugs, or you cut up the drugs improperly, or you're not giving the proper value—it could be any number of reasons.

When they actually murder, it's like an Outfit hit—the message goes out to everybody.

You'll have murder-by-arson. That's very common. We just had a policeman indicted for that attempt. It wasn't his wife; it was his girlfriend, but she had a baby by him. She was going into court to try to obtain support for that child.

And he spread gasoline both at the front door and at the back door while the girlfriend and the baby were asleep inside the house, about three in the morning. But the gasoline burned itself out. It was just for the luck of God it didn't actually get both doors going and then the woman and her baby would have been trapped inside without any way out. She woke up to the smoke and they escaped.

This was one of the few lucky cases that we can recall where there was a fingerprint that was lifted from the gas can. He left the can at the scene.

It's very common to try to kill somebody by burning their house down. You get both kinds: to send a message or to kill a person. Some people just want to send the message or scare them, but others, a lot of them, are the actual, intentional, deliberate, meaning to kill the person inside.

It's a different way of getting angry. Some people say, "I'm gonna kill you" and that's it. The fight's over. Other people say, "I'm gonna kill you" and they go home and get the gas can and *do* it.

With both arsonists and bombers, we find passion and rage in the person who does it immediately.

*   *   *

We got a call one night, two people dead in a fire. So we got there, the fire damage itself wasn't that bad, but the wife was laying in bed—she's completely torched—and the husband is laying by the front door. And his clothes . . . you could actually see the trail where he ran, throwing off burned clothing along the way, trying to get to the front door, into the hallway.

And on this one—I had no idea. Was this a murder-suicide? Was it a homicide-accident? I'm still not completely sure.

But the son, the son was about sixteen, seventeen, had been seen leaving the house about an hour before. So now we thought maybe he did it, so the homicide dicks were out there as well.

We questioned him for hours. He told us that his father told him he was gonna kill his mother. His version was that the father poured gas on the mother and lit her and some of the gas must have gotten on him and he caught on fire.

The poor kid didn't want to tell us this. It was like he didn't want to tell on his father, even though his father was dead. It ripped him apart to tell on his dad.

The weird thing was, a squad car was waiting outside the whole time this homicide-suicide or whatever it was was happening. The parents had split up and the mother was coming back to the house to pick up some things. Because she was fearful, she went to the police station and asked for a ride to the house. So a squad car was parked down the block, waiting for her to come out.

You can look for external marks on a body that's been in a fire to determine homicide. But sometimes external marks are not indicative of a homicide. When a body burns, the analogy would be a roast cooking. When the meat cooks, you sometimes get heat fissures. In a body, skin and tissues actually split open. Oftentimes, they look like knife wounds.

Once we get a dead body, it becomes the purview of Violent Crimes. To see if the person died in the fire, or before—if the person was murdered—one of the prime things they look for is smoke in the nostrils. They'll also be looking for an immediate blood analysis for carbon monoxide within the blood. Carbon monoxide is caused by the fire gases that the victim was in at the time. If he has no carbon monoxide in his bloodstream, that means he was dead before the fire—because he wasn't inhaling it to get it into his body.

People set vanity fires. Some are would-be firemen. Or they want to play hero. They don't get recognition in their work or their lives—this is a way to get some recognition.

You find a lot of vanity fires set by security guards. I guess it's most noticeable with that group. It's not the most exciting, engrossing type of job, you know. Here's a guy working at a particular place, he's on the midnights, there's never anything that happens, he's lucky he can even stay awake, he's always falling asleep. Boredom. He's never seeing any raise of any type. And he can't think of any way of promoting his own well-being there.

Some of these individuals in that type of scenario start small fires—and then detect them. This is what you refer to as a vanity fire. In other words, making themselves look good.

We've had firemen start fires, too. We had them start fires during the firemen's strike here. To bring attention to their cause.

Or you get guys who wanted to be firemen and never made it setting fires.

We had a series of small fires at a South Side church. Four fires in two months. The first one we investigated started in the sacristy and communicated to the church.

So I went there and I'm talking to different people and they're all talking about this one priest, how great he was, how he set up a security force after the fire, how concerned he was, how he's always out there on the job.

I'd gone through the seminary with this guy, but it just didn't click till I saw him—here was this short, very stocky little priest walking down the middle of the center aisle in this big, old church. He was coming down the aisle like he was God on earth.

And I said to myself right then and there—then it clicked, it clicked—and I said, "He did it."

Then I interviewed him and right away he starts complaining about the pastor, how he's never there and doesn't know what's going on, and all the responsibilities of the parish are on his shoulders, blah blah blah, just ripping into this pastor.

The next day I met with the insurance people. And they tell me that *they* suspect him, you know, for no real reason, they just had this feeling.

There wasn't much I could do. There was no proof. I set up a meeting with the monsignor who was in charge. I ran through everything. How a lot of the parishioners were talking about the priest—he was playing hero, he was always the one who discovered the fires. . . . He said, "Thank you very much." Hi, goodbye.

That week, there was another fire and another detective handled it and he thought it was the priest too.

Meanwhile, all the priests at the rectory are scared to death of this guy. Everybody knew he was goofy. But there's no one with balls enough to go to the archdiocese, go to the higher-ups, and say, "We want him *out*."

We get another call—another fire at this parish. We got out there and we're laughing on our way out there. The pastor had laid down about four-thirty, prior to dinner. Turned on his little electric blanket, put on his blinders, I guess they're called; he starts to doze off—he smells smoke. He looks down at the bottom of the bed—it's smoking. He sees flames. He jumps up, calls the fire department.

Can you imagine? This pastor is a very timid fellow and priests—I've known priests all my life—I can just see him, this poor little timid old guy, taking a little cat nap, putting his blinders on, setting his electric blanket, and then he smells something and his bed's on fire.

So by this time, we're laughing. I go up to one of the parish priests and I say, "You know who did it." I ask where [the priest] is and he says he's teaching the marriage class.

We go there and pull him out of it and Mirandize him. Then I say, "We gotta talk to you. We've been working on this, you know, now . . . it's getting too dangerous. Someone's going to get hurt. I know you're doing it. I know you're setting the fires.

I'm not out to hurt you. I've known you for years. But this has got to stop."

So his first line is, "I don't know anything about it." Denial. Then the next thing you hear is, "I can't tell you anything because of the Sacraments"—the confidentiality of the confessional.

So I just laid into him. "That's bullshit. You're lying to me. I'm not gonna put up with it anymore." I just laid into him like he was some kind of criminal.

He finally did 'fess up. He said he started all the fires, but he wouldn't 'fess up to the one with the poor pastor. He didn't show any remorse or anything.

We're interviewing him in his office in the rectory—I'm looking around and I see all these firemen's hats hanging on the walls. He tells us that he always wanted to be the fire chaplain for the fire department.

Don't forget this. We have a very select group of people that are sick. And they like to watch fires. Pyromaniacs. There are a lot of arsons committed to watch the fire trucks respond, to watch them roll out those big hoses, to watch the flames—it's a mental illness.

The textbooks' classic test: when you've got one of these people you suspect is a sicko, and they're intrigued by fire, when you interview them—light a match. Just watch their eyes. They get all excited—they might even have a physical orgasm.

Repeat arsonists are usually mopes. They're down and out. Their jobs are flunky jobs. Maybe they're overweight. They're the kind of guys you look at and think, "Gee, there's something wrong with that guy."

I've noticed repeat fire-setters like the sense of power and control. You interview them and they'll give you some of their reasons for setting fires. They say they feel they have to get rid of older buildings in the neighborhood, or abandoned buildings. They think they're like a clean-up campaign.

There was one guy who set hundreds of abandoned cars on fire. He said it was the only way he could get them out of the neighborhood.

They're doing a good deed, they think.

They enjoy the fire, the investigation, the attention. You know, "Gee, the detectives are talking to me."

You've got the for-profit motive. We check commercial fires closely to see if there's an immediate for-profit motive. Very difficult to prove, but it usually involves large amounts of insurance, changes in insurance—a policy suddenly goes up from one hundred thousand to five hundred thousand and a week after the change is in effect, the building burns down.

And you find out the guy's called three times during the week before the fire to ask, "Is my policy in effect now? Is my policy in effect?"

The two biggest motives for arson-for-profit are the failing business and competition. The failing business is *the* biggest motive.

There are more. How about just to get out of a bad lease? You don't have to pay rent if you have an arson.

How about your business has become obsolete? Say you've got a little Mom and Pop grocery store. All of a sudden the area's gonna come up for renovation and here comes a big food chain. How are you gonna compete? There's no such thing as loyal customers.

How about for speculation? How about in a changing neighborhood, to get rid of all the garbage? How do you get rid of old buildings? You burn it out. How do you get rid of all the bums? You burn the building out; they gotta move somewhere else. You still own the property, but now there's no tenants. And you've sold the building to the insurance company, which gives you the money to build when the time is right.

Buildings are very expensive to knock down. We're talking hundreds of thousands of dollars. So it might be cheaper to get rid of all the bums that are hanging out of the buildings—and defer the cost of knocking down the building; it might be a lot cheaper to have a fire in the building and destroy most of the building. And then whatever's left, the city will take down because it's a danger to the community. Arson for real estate speculation.

You get a lot of people who are bad businessmen and they're desperate. Or you have seasonal stuff—and you have a bad season. They're gonna go broke, some of them are gonna lose their life savings. And they reach a crucial point—they decide that they're gonna sell it to the insurance company.

We get cases with immigrants. They come here, they go into areas where a Dominick's and a Jewel won't go. They've got a limited amount of cash and they want to open up just a small business, like a Mom and Pop store, a grocery store, liquor store, something small that they can afford to get into.

What they do is, they pick areas that are very depressed because these areas are not likely to have the big food chains—you'll see the buildings that are closed: the old Jewel stores, the A&Ps. I mean, if I took you in the ghetto, you will not see these stores in existence.

So they open small stores in depressed areas. Most of their clients are on welfare or food stamps. They're not mobile and they'll pay exorbitant rates, two and a half bucks for a gallon of milk, to have the convenience of not having to travel. And the small grocery store owners charge astronomical prices because there is no competition, generally, because nobody else wants to be there.

Now you've got a possibility. You've got a guy that I think has good intentions. He's gonna work his grocery store, these people work twenty-seven hours a day, but he might be a bad businessman or he might not have figured what he's into, with insurance and everything.

They've got the dream, but it doesn't work out. Between the thefts and the robberies and the broken windows and the gangs— "Want to stay in business? Pay us." The dream comes apart. The bottom line is, it's not as profitable as he thought it would be. He's not making a go of it.

And what do they do? They either burn and collect the insurance and get out. Or they burn and get bigger. They use the insurance as a method of pyramiding. What we mean by that is, they have a fire, they collect their insurance, and they go out and get a better and bigger store. Business mobility.

We arrested an Arab grocery store owner. What he did was, he sets his store on fire. The place is completely locked up. It didn't go off that *much*; the mixture wasn't right. So he goes to the scene, the fire department is there, the place isn't totally consumed. It wasn't bad enough. So he locks up his business again, and leaves, and within a few minutes, another fire starts inside his store. This guy was determined, but not too bright.

I'll give you one that we *don't* talk about too often. It happens very, very often, but I don't even think statistics are kept on it. And that is, what happens when people get into car loans on cars and the car becomes a lemon or they don't keep it up well and they're into four- and five-year payments? They report the car stolen and it's burned. Guess who buys the car? Because you can't take out a car loan without insurance. They had a ton of those during the gas shortage when people had these big gas guzzlers. Who was gonna buy a gas guzzler in '73? Can't sell them so what do you do with them? Torch them.

This poor mope. Two security guards for this shopping mall were sitting in their car, drinking coffee one afternoon in the parking lot.

So they see this guy pull up, really neat little sports car. He parks in a pretty hidden place. The guy gets out of the car, takes the license plate off the front of the car—they're watching him—puts it down his pants. And then he sets the car on fire. What he did was, when he threw a match inside to burn it up, it burned his face.

They started chasing him—he ran—they caught him. We got that job. We take him in; we're talking to him—his mustache is burned off, his hair is singed—but this guy is like your next-door neighbor, he's married, he's got no police record.

And finally, what he said he did was—here's this brand new car, a $20,000 sports car, belonging to his brother-in-law, a Cook County sheriff. The brother-in-law was having trouble with the car and wanted to get rid of it. It was a lemon.

So they arranged for this guy to take care of this problem—he was a real nice guy to his brother-in-law. We called the brother-in-law. "Where's your car?" He tried to say it was stolen. "Well, your car's been set on fire." "Oh, really? Gee." "Oh yeah. *And*—we also have the guy who set your car on fire. We have him in the district. Would you like to come in and press charges?" He didn't want to come in; we talked him into coming in.

He came in and—until you make a claim, it's no crime. You can burn your own property. But once you file a claim, then it's arson-for-profit. It's called "burning with intent to defraud."

So he came in and we said, "We got the perp right here. We got him in lockup. Do you want to take a look at the guy, you know? He *says* he's related to you or something." He just . . . he just didn't know what to do. He *knows* it's his brother-in-law in there; he's a Cook County sheriff, and a brand-new one—he doesn't know what to say or do.

So we sat them both down and said, "Look, here's the bottom line. If you don't prosecute this guy for burning your car and you may not want to, he's your brother-in-law—if you ever make a claim on your insurance, you're gonna get charged with fraud."

So what he had to do was eat up three hundred dollars worth of payments every month for the next five years on a car he couldn't use. Can you imagine, for the next five years, paying for a car you torched that's just sitting out in your garage? That's justice.

Your actual arsonist is usually unsophisticated. Usually, the owner of the business hires somebody on the street, a bust-out. He takes some gas, spreads it around. Half the time, they set themselves on fire in the process.

I think people want to believe that torches are these slick, skilled, highly professional people. I really do. Some are. I've read about them, but I've never come in contact with them.

Most torches are junkies and bust-outs. Not much planning goes into it. You can burn down a building with a piece of paper.

They always say in burglary, it's like catching a ghost. That's what catching an arsonist is like. In arson-for-profit especially—because—number one, the businesses are generally closed, and second of all, if the owner is involved, he's probably supplied a key to the offender and they use these time-delay methods. In other words, the arsonist won't be there when the fire starts. He wants to be away from there for safety reasons and for being identified.

So they'll use candles, or they'll use battery-operated telephone devices, to give some heat to some gasoline or something, or they'll use trailers of paper—anything to give them some time to get away from the structure.

I'll tell you how they get away with it, too. The businessman who does this—most of the time they're in a bad neighborhood. So they go out, and they get to know some of the bust-outs in the neighborhood. They get the bust-outs. They say, "Hey, listen. I need a fire set. Would you set this fire for me?" And they say, "I'll give you a thousand dollars if you do it." Well, a thousand dollars to them is like winning the lottery, right? So he gets them to set the fire.

And if they get caught—he doesn't give a shit if they get caught. Because Mr. Businessman knows that the government, the state's attorney, if the bust-out gets caught and he says I did it for the owner, they're not gonna believe him. If he gets arrested doing the job, he's not even gonna have the money, because the businessman won't pay him till the job is done.

Yeah, they're not gonna believe he did it for the owner. Unless you get them on tape. And if you do, the owners are smart enough, they cut loose right away, because this guy doesn't mean anything to them. And who's gonna believe Tyrone with a record the length of his arm, even if he's the star witness in court, to prove that he did it for an arson-for-profit? Against this businessman? It's absurd. Look at it from the prosecutor's standpoint, is he gonna be believable? Are you gonna put some junkie on the stand as your star witness against the businessman?

So the businessmen use that. That's why it's very tough to prove an arson-for-profit. It's pretty effective. It's almost kind of foolproof for the owners to do this.

Most arsons-for-profit occur in bad neighborhoods. That's one of the reasons why they're getting out, because of the neighborhood, because business is going down. IBM doesn't set their business on fire. But these guys don't like where they're at. Maybe they got into that location because they felt they could make money in a poor location, but they don't like dealing with the problems.

You get a lot of arsons in lounges and taverns because they depend on novelties: we've had discos, we've had bucking bulls—all these things come and go. Every couple of years, something new comes in. When it does, a lot of times, these places go up in smoke.

Most arsons are on inhabited buildings. But with arson-for-profit, *most* of the time, they take care to try to get the people out ahead of time. That's most of the time.

We've had cases where people who were hired to protect the building perished. We had one case, where the motive was competition, these tavern owners *knew* their place was targeted, they hired a security guard to protect it, and he died when the building was torched. Now whether, in these cases, the arsonists made any attempt to get people out, we can't determine.

A lot of our work depends on informants. One of them, we happened to have a guard, a black security guard, who worked in a grocery store owned by Arabs.

This security guard calls me one day on the Arson Hotline. He proceeds to tell me about the plans of his boss to burn this particular grocery store. It wasn't a very successful store; they owned another store and, in fact, were slowly moving stock from one store to the other. He had been approached and offered money to participate.

He didn't want to participate, because above the grocery store there were apartments and there were children who lived in these apartments that he befriended when they came into the store.

He told us the plan. On the designated night, one of the owners was going to stay inside the grocery store, conceal himself in there, and wait till about three in the morning, and then start pouring the gasoline they had secreted in the back room, start the fire, then get the hell out of there, and go several blocks away to where the brother would be waiting in the car. Across the street from this place was a huge park, so they figured when the guy ran out this particular side door at three in the morning, there would be nobody to see him.

We went in there. We used a ramrod, broke the door down, caught the guy in there, and got the gasoline.

These brothers were going to do this when the people upstairs could be presumed to be sleeping in their beds. They made no attempt to warn them or get them out. His exact words to our informant about the people upstairs were "Fuck them." That's how he felt about the people upstairs. He didn't care.

I hate to think this, but it's entered our minds that there is a total disregard for human life. I just wonder if they have tunnel vision in collecting their insurance proceeds to the point where there's a complete disregard. I even question the regard they have for human life when they ask somebody to start a fire for them. Even the arsonist. I don't think they regard *their* life either—the arsonist they hire is just a vehicle, a tool to get to the insurance money. In the meantime, the businessman himself isn't starting the fire, for whatever reason, whether he's afraid or he wants an alibi. He's not doing it. He wants somebody else to do his dirty work. And the hired arsonist could easily get killed.

The most classic case of them all. Probably the worst case of arson-for-profit in the past fifty years, the Koreans and the failing business. What you have is a couple of Korean businessmen, their business was seasonally motivated, mainly a Christmas-type business. Business was way off; they had a lot of things on consignment, and it wasn't working. We have evidence that the suppliers were coming in to take their merchandise.

It just so happens they decided to sell the insurance company the building, or at least the contents, through arson. They arrange to have a fire started for their benefit. The fire was started with lighter fluid, the fire started really getting good, going good; the firemen arrived.

Three of them were up on the roof, venting, and fighting the fire using a very normal procedure. And the structure just became unsound. And they fell into the fire. Fell to their deaths, which isn't a very nice way of dying.

The businessmen subsequently took polygraph exams, flunked, and one member of this crew left the country and is now in Korea, and the other two were charged after giving admissions and flunking polygraphs. One's conviction was overturned and one was found guilty. And we have three firemen dead in an arson-for-profit.

You always look for motive in arson-for-profit. However, the most crucial thing you look for is preknowledge. Something that would show us that you knew this was going to happen.

People do things like, they have a dog to guard their house and they take their dog out. They don't have a dog in the house when it goes up. They remove items of sentimental interest, like photo albums. They raise their insurance within a short period prior to the fire. They move coffee pots, TVs, computers, everything else out. We had a guard agency where the boss gave the guards the night off the night he burned the place down.

There are a lot of red lights that tip you off the guy had preknowledge. One is where the fire was set. A lot of failing businessmen set fires where the records are kept.

Or say it's a restaurant or a fruit stand. The refrigerators have all been emptied out. The supplies are depleted. Or all the stock's at the front of the store.

You talk to people who live across from the store. They say, "Business has really been bad. They're always out of everything lately."

There was a string of bombings, pipe bombs, at Greek fruit markets a while back. With one of them, as soon as they discovered the pipe bomb inside, we went in and looked.

All the produce inside was rotten. We got the fruit stand's receipts out of the cash register. The receipts showed that the guy who owned the stand was just buying fruit in very small amounts from the Jewel down the street. Here's this guy *selling* produce. And he's not buying wholesale, he's not buying in quantity. He's shopping at Jewel and selling that. He does something like that, he's looking into the future.

Let's say you got a business where everybody the guy's doing business with is getting bad checks. And how come, lo and behold, all of a sudden he takes a certified cashier's check to the insurance agent to make sure his insurance is paid up? It's out of character. And then two days later, you got a fire.

You know who did it, but you can't prove it. Arson-for-profit is incredibly difficult to prove. Most arson-for-profit cases will not be solved in less than a year. Some go on for years.

Here's the key—most policemen are very aggressive and don't have the patience to wait two, three years for this. And if they suspect the owner, you know what they're gonna do? They're gonna come on strong, and it's a fifty-fifty chance the owner will either confess or deny it, and that's the end of the case.

Our thinking is—go in there and talk to them. Let him think that *we* think he's a victim. And, as long as he talks to us, there's a chance that he's gonna lie to us. And the more lies you tell us, the better.

In other words, why should I interrupt him and say, "You're lying. I bet you did the fire" and he denies it and that stops the communication? Our thinking is, let him talk to us three hours . . . then we go back over the lies, call him up two days later—Remember how Columbo used to do that stuff?—"Oh, by the way. Let me ask you about this."

All we're looking for is one more lie on top of another lie on top of this—and let him think he's fooling us. Let him think I'm dumb and he's smart. Play dumb. Play dumb. Let him think he's fooling you. And you know what? Remember the old story—sometimes you can't remember what lie you told? Six months later we're gonna go back to him, and guess what? He might tell a different lie the second time than he did the first.

No matter if you're a burglary detective, a homicide detective, an arson detective, probably the most important tool you have is your ears. If somebody wants to lie or give you something, you better be able to hear and take advantage of it.

Let's say it's a businessman we suspect started his own fire. You don't think we go into this guy and say, "Mr. Businessman, we suspect you." Because you know what he's gonna say to us? "My attorney says not to talk to you."

So what you have to do, you have to say to yourself, you have to treat him as a legitimate victim. Which he might be. And, again, he might not be. What we're looking for is either the truth, if he is a legitimate victim, or what we call "certain lies." Damaging lies. We have to prove them.

He says to us, "Business is good," and we find out he's been floating bad checks. Or let's say he says he was home and we come up with a witness who saw him come out of the business just before it went up. "Do you keep gasoline in your grocery store?" "No, I *never* would keep gasoline in my grocery store."—There's a lie. "My store is fully stocked"—and you go in and the shelves are empty.

The big thing is preknowledge. We find out from an employee that the guy had a twenty-seven-inch Sony color TV in the back. And we say, "By the way, did you have any personal property in the store?" And he says, "Yeah. I had this and I had that and I had a Sony TV." "What happened to the Sony TV?" "Well, it was consumed in the fire." That's great, because the cashier told us that the day before, the businessman took the TV out for repairs.

There are certain circumstances that cause a fire to be committed on a certain day. All of a sudden the last thing on the businessman's mind, destroying the business, will come to the forefront.

Like with the Korean case where the firemen died—we did the financial background—the people that had camera equipment on consignment notified the owner that they were coming in within a matter of days to take the equipment out. In other words, you can't keep a business going if you don't have a product. What are you gonna sell?

I handled another case, where the bank was going to foreclose on the property. He had a contract to buy and the note was due on Monday. He owed $140,000. The place went up over the weekend.

It's like "I can't wait no longer." You've got the creditors at your tail, the barking dogs are snapping at you. You know. I'm not making a defense for them, but looking back, it's easy to see how certain people get a feeling of helplessness—you know, they've had a business for five, six years, poured their heart and their money into it, and the thing's not going—and they'd *like* to make it go, but, you know, rent and banks and business and no help and competition—there's this feeling of, What else can I do?

The arsonist we usually see is not a criminal. He has no record. It's a one-time crime. He'll never do it again. He's a businessman who failed. And he can't admit failure, he can't face it, so he burns his own building or business. We almost hate to arrest these guys.

That doesn't make what they do right. They can burn a building and firemen die fighting it. Or it communicates to the building next door. . . .

It's a horrible crime, but you have to feel kind of sorry for these guys. They've got families, they've worked their asses off trying to make the dream come true, and they failed.

* * *

The biggest arson case ATF has ever handled, without a doubt, was a Greek arson-for-profit ring that was masterminded by a guy called "the Greek Godfather" who had his headquarters here—he owned a restaurant on Rush Street. This was the largest arson ring ever in terms of stretching out across the entire country.

The manpower involved . . . It took years to crack. It was a paper chase: business records, phone records—unbelievable how many phone records we had—credit card records, car rental records, hundreds of subpoenas.

And you know what broke it? Two things. A beat copper in Area Six making a traffic stop, and going through a guy's garbage several times a week.

The Greek Godfather worked this way. He had a lot of contacts in the city and across the country and he'd be able to get information about people in the Greek community who were in financial trouble—and offer his assistance. Or he'd find out which ones had particular habits that were expensive and they were in desperate need . . . their business could no longer support their habits. And he'd make it known through some of his underlings, his lieutenants, and they'd arrange to dispose of the restaurants by fire or explosives. Then the owner would collect the insurance money and, of course, he'd have to give a certain portion of it back to the Godfather.

There were two types of profit involved. One type: They'd muscle into a business, take over a business, bleed it as much as they could, and then burn it. The other type of crime they were involved in was someone in the Greek community, their business is doing bad; they're about to burn it, they come to the Godfather and say, "We'll pay you a fee. Burn our place for us." They were doing them a service. So the arson was either as a favor or as a threat. This went on from seven to ten years, from the mid-seventies on; it could have gone back much farther.

They had an individual that was solely a bomb-maker. Primarily pipe bombs. He also manufactured elaborate timing devices to start fires. They had another guy who was a muscleman, a tough guy, who'd do the extorting.

The bomb-maker posed himself off to be of Italian extraction and a member of one of the more noted Mafia families. He would use an Italian name—to act rougher, to give the impression that if they didn't cooperate, some bad things would happen. It has more effect to say "My name is Vito" than to say "My name is Joe."

The way we got onto this, there was a distinct similarity in the bombings. A person who makes a bomb is like a person who builds a house—he has his own M.O. These bombs all had the same kind of chemicals, pipes, caps, wicks.

So we're picking up on this bomb-maker's signature. And then a very, very lucky, fortunate incident occurred in Area Six, in the Eighteenth District. An individual was stopped by a beat car. It was over the theft of a telephone in a nearby building. He and his car were seen leaving the scene, so he was stopped. This guy turned out to be the bomb-maker; he stole the phone—he's a career criminal, an opportunistic thief.

The beat officers conducted a lawful search of the vehicle—opened the trunk of the car and found a suitcase in it. The suitcase contained a lot of tools and chemicals in jars. It was the bomb-maker's bomb kit. The beat officers didn't know what it was, but they knew it wasn't right, so they notified Bomb and Arson.

The guy couldn't explain satisfactorily what he was doing with all these chemicals in jars, so they were seized and inventoried and sent to the federal laboratory. These chemicals—along with the bomb remnants the bomb techs had recovered at the scenes—were examined at the ATF lab. And these tools and chemicals were the ones used to make the bombs.

ATF was acting as central collection and storage for the devices and remnants found in bombings around the country. And when this kit came through, this guy made his devices in such a recognizable fashion that the lab could say without question that the devices throughout the country—they didn't just say it was similar—they said that they were all made, identically, by the same person.

That was the big break. From a beat car stop over a small theft. So then our investigation centered on *him*. We started a surveillance on him. He didn't have any real occupation; he visited a number of places.

We used a variety of surveillance techniques. We had people follow him around at various times in a single-engine plane and different types of automobiles. We got permission for phone surveillance and got phone numbers for individuals who were repeatedly called. At one time, we must have had twenty, twenty-five machines going, monitoring telephones.

We developed what they call a link analysis, where you're actually linking individuals in a conspiracy together. Thousands of phone calls were analyzed between the nine codefendants we ended up with, linking them together and they all led to the Godfather as the center—the calls were coming in to him and then he would turn around and dispense the orders for bombings and fires.

One of the other techniques that we used is we checked people's garbage. A few times a week, going through some individual's garbage, to see what we could come up with, which is totally legal. The Supreme Court has ruled that it's public domain when you put the garbage out. We concentrated on the bomber's garbage.

I'm talking about police going out in the middle of the night, three, four in the morning, three, four times a week and taking the garbage out and going through it. We got on to the idea that this man was in different parts of the country at certain times, right? And he has five different names. Now how do I go to American Express or how do I go to MasterCard and find out this guy's card number so I can subpoena it and find out where he's charged things? You know how I did it? I went in his garbage and found his old bills and got his credit cards and his phone records and we turned around and found the account numbers and then we issued subpoenas for those card numbers and we found billing for those for the past couple years. And based on that we put him at certain crime scenes within a matter of days. He couldn't deny it. That's what the garbage led us to. The bottom line is, garbage is one of the best sources of information.

One night, one of the other guys couldn't make the garbage run. You gotta do it at some god-awful time, like three, four in the morning. This two-flat on the Northwest Side. I went up to the garbage and it just so happened that that particular night I was able to find the remaining components of flares, which were some of the chemicals this guy used in his pipe bombs.

In this particular case, the bomber, the things that we found in his garbage led to an arrest warrant being issued in federal court. The proof that he was buying bomb component parts was found in the remnants of his garbage.

We had the bomb-maker, but he was the lowest member of this whole ring. We still had the problem of how to get the head guy. A lot of eavesdropping, a surveillance camera, we had body wires, all kinds of sophisticated electronic equipment. The guy who didn't want to cooperate with them out in L.A. became an informant. When other incidents occurred throughout the country, things were all set at the ATF central lab to match against any other one, like you would do with ballistics in a gun case.

Finally, we were able to link the bomb-maker and the God-father together because it was proven they were in on the extortion in L.A. together. And all our phone records and credit card records linked the bomb-maker, the Godfather, and the seven others we eventually arrested.

There was no flipping. Usually, you get one flipping on the other. We didn't get anybody on this like that. I mean, usually, when you plead guilty, especially in federal court, you plead with the idea of knowing that a deal might be reached. These nine people did something completely different. They said, "We're gonna plead blindly. We're guilty, we're pleading. No talking. We're not talking to nobody. We'll take what we get." And that was the end of it. This was a close-knit group. The bomber got fifteen years. All the others got ten, eleven years.

We were kind of disappointed that when they pleaded guilty, they weren't going to try to save their skin. All along, we felt there were other bombings and fires they were doing we had no idea of. The bomber was in his fifties and got fifteen—he'd have to do a little more than seven and a half. We were kind of thinking that these years would be valuable to him and being the only member that wasn't Greek, that he'd try to save his skin and flip on the others. He was hired for his expertise. He was better than average, probably, but he got caught. So how good could he be?

Everybody gets caught sooner or later. Especially if you're gonna commit more than one crime. You can get away with one, but when you start doing the same thing over and over, you're opening yourself up to more chances of apprehension and convictions.

You do a lot better in life getting a nine-to-five job, five days a week, going to work every day, and knowing what you're gonna get. You do better than going out into the street and trying to find ways to make money.

And with this particular guy, the bomb-maker, with everything—when he was arrested—he was arrested early in the morning, I happened to be there—just a little modest house, modestly furnished—and he was arrested while sleeping on the floor. Mattress on the floor. So crime doesn't pay. So you know—the end results of all his activity ended up with him sleeping on the floor like a dog.

Arson:
Contributing Police Officers

LIEUTENANT TOM BRADY, commanding officer, Bomb Squad; explosives technician III; former executive officer, Bomb and Arson Unit, 1985 to 1989; certified arson investigator. As executive officer of Bomb and Arson, Brady was responsible for all Bomb and Arson field investigations and administrative matters of the Bomb and Arson Unit. Brady's twenty-eight years in the CPD have encompassed sixteen separate assignments, including vice officer in the Eighteenth District, homicide sergeant in Areas Four and Five, aide to the Deputy Chief of Detectives, and federal grant proposal writer for the CPD. Brady has also worked undercover in the Confidential and Corrupt Practices Section of the Internal Affairs Division, and headed a surveillance squad on career criminals for the Central Investigations Unit.

COMMANDER JOSEPH GRUBISIC, explosives technician III; commanding officer, Bomb and Arson Unit. Grubisic is responsible for all Bomb and Arson field investigations and administrative matters relating to the Bomb and Arson Unit. Grubisic was the head of the Bomb Squad from 1985 to 1990. Grubisic's thirty-two-year career in the CPD includes extensive work in the Intelligence Section of Organized Crime, the former Red Squad, which investigated terrorist activity; Gangs North and South; and Bomb and Arson since 1983.

SERGEANT WAYNE MICEK, Traffic Safety Division; former arson investigator. Micek has served thirteen years in the CPD. Micek worked patrol in the Twentieth District for two years, and served ten years as an arson investigator. Micek was promoted to sergeant in 1990.

SERGEANT EDWARD O'DONNELL, supervising sergeant, Bomb and Arson. O'Donnell has been a policeman since 1977. He worked patrol and tac in the Fifteenth District from 1977 to 1981, and worked in Bomb and Arson for eight years as an arson investigator, before being promoted to sergeant.

DETECTIVE TIMOTHY O'MEARA, arson investigator. O'Meara joined the CPD in 1969, worked patrol for ten years in the Austin district, and was an aide de camp to Deputy Superintendent John Byrne for eight years. In 1986, O'Meara was promoted to detective and assigned to Bomb and Arson.

DETECTIVE LOUIS ROSEN, arson investigator, assigned to the Arson Task Force of the Bureau of Alcohol, Tobacco, and Firearms (ATF). Rosen and his partner, Ron Sacolick, joined the force on the same day (September 8, 1969), their police stars are one number apart, and they both began patrol at the same time in the Town Hall District. Rosen made detective in 1972 and worked Area Five Burglary until 1983. Rosen was assigned to Bomb and Arson in 1983, worked as a cause and origin investigator for six months, then began working with the Arson Task Force.

DETECTIVE RONALD SACOLICK, arson investigator, assigned to ATF's Arson Task Force. Sacolick worked on a tac unit and a vice unit in Town Hall from 1969 till 1973, when he was promoted to detective. Sacolick then was assigned to Area Four Burglary for five years, joined Bomb and Arson in 1979 and investigated cause and origin for approximately one year before becoming one of the original members of ATF's Arson Task Force.

SERGEANT JAMES SANDOW, Area Three Property Crimes. Sandow was assigned to Bomb and Arson in 1978 and was a supervising sergeant for all Bomb and Arson personnel from 1978 to 1989, with specific responsibilities for the arson-for-profit team from 1980 to 1984. Sandow came on the force as a police cadet in 1965, became a sworn police officer in 1966, served in Vietnam from 1967 to 1969, was promoted to detective in 1971, assigned to Area Five, General Assignment Section, which handled everything not covered by the robbery, homicide and sex crimes, burglary, and auto theft detectives. When Sandow was promoted to sergeant in 1977, he worked in Eighteen and Loop Traffic. Sandow was assigned to Area Five Violent Crimes in 1990 and, later that same year, to Area Three Property Crimes.

SERGEANT STAN SURDEJ, Nineteenth District; former arson investigator. Surdej has been on the force for twenty-one years, the first ten of which were spent working Cabrini-Green, and ten as an arson investigator. Surdej was promoted to sergeant in 1990.

PROSTITUTION

Everybody's out there—judges, lawyers, school-teachers, priests. It's an absolute cross section. There's no typical john. I can understand the sixty-three-year-old bald guy going to a prostitute. But I can't understand the twenty-three-year-old, well-scrubbed, well-muscled, fresh-out-of-Yale guy who goes to a prostitute.

For the life of me, I can't understand it. It's danger-ous. It's not at all romantic. It's degrading. And it costs money.

Sergeant Ted Faulkner
Vice Control

Where's the romance?" asks an off-duty vice detective as we watch two men walk into the middle of a vacant lot off West Madison Street. I know I'm looking at two men because the vice dick has *told* me I'm looking at two men—otherwise, I'd think the tall, skinny one in mime-loud makeup, a fringed brown leather vest over a bare chest, brown leather shorts, and black garter belt with dangling clasps—the one who, on the corner moments before, was spreading the vest wide open, baring two tumor-like breasts—was a woman.

The guy's a gump, street for male transvestite prostitute. Male transvestite prostitutes represent approximately 60 percent of street whores, according to vice cops. "That's what has surprised me the most in prostitution," says a fifteen-year vice veteran. "How many men are on the streets. Even with AIDS, it's a trend that seems to be on the increase."

The two men have now reached the middle of the vacant lot. Nothing—not a billboard, not a line of trees, not a row of houses—blocks them from view. The blighted lot upon blighted lot moonscape of West Madison leaves them exposed. The gump sinks to his knees. The other man stands scanning the lots, the streets, a lookout for himself.

"Where's the romance?" the vice detective says again as he watches the couple. "I'll tell you what's romantic today. If the whore swallows your come. That's about as romantic as it gets."

He starts the car again; we inch west on Madison. A gump on the sidewalk brandishes his tiny breasts at us. Others stare hard at us, perhaps thinking they've got two kinkos cruising from Yuptown or the 'burbs, and lick their lips. Some come up to the windows, their made-up faces seeming to swim in at us. "Don't look away—don't look away—you've gotta see this stuff. Jeez, will you look at the *arms* on that one! You'd want to mess with somebody who's got arms like that? You know who really goes for gumps? Guys who've been in prison. They like these queens. Doing hard time changes a lot of guys. Maybe they think they're not really gay if they like men who look like women.

"Last month, I think I arrested one female prostitute. Everything else we picked up was a man.

"And the women streetwalkers . . . You know, if you work in Prostitution, coppers from the other units are always saying to you, 'Whoa! Prostitution! You got it made. You must be getting laid all the time!'

"I wouldn't want to touch anything I see out here with a twenty-foot pole. You have no idea how scuzzy these whores are. And filthy—you want to take several baths in a row after looking at street whores. The cops who think we got it made think all whores look like Angie Dickinson. They don't see what we see."

The cops who see the full range of prostitution as it's really practiced, from call girl to street whore, without the Hollywood/TV gloss, work undercover, citywide, in Vice; more particularly, in the Organized Crime Division, Vice Control Section, Prostitution.

Vice cops concentrate primarily on busting pandering operations, since pandering, legally defined as compelling someone into prostitution or arranging an act of prostitution for money or for anything of value, is classified in Illinois as a felony, whereas prostitution itself is a misdemeanor. The line between pimping and pandering is fluid and frequently crossed over; one vice cop explains it this way: "A pimp is anyone who accepts money from an act of prostitution *knowing* the money came from prostitution. That's a misdemeanor, though it may become a felony on the second offense. If the girl's on the street doing all the arranging herself and gives the guy the money, he's a pimp. If the pimp also arranges the act of prostitution, he's a panderer. You can have a pimp that's a panderer and a panderer that's a pimp."

So the vice cops target the arrangers, the panderers—people who meet runaways at bus stations, for example, and coerce or seduce them into prostitution; people who run straight and gay escort agencies; or bars with prostitution on the premises, and places people go to have a bad time, like the bondage chambers and domination houses.

They find out what's going on in this most secretive of professions through the Yellow Pages (you can find whores listed under "Escorts" or "Entertainment"), through ads placed in gay papers, and through ads in the alternative press, like the Chicago weekly called *The Reader,* which offers free advertising. "*The Reader* is our bible," says one vice cop. "We'd be lost without it." And Vice relies on people who, for whatever reason, are eager to give information on others—informants.

"There's a million ways somebody can drop a dime on you," explains Sergeant Dan Fontanetta, a long-time undercover vice detective. "Reformed prostitutes often have a compelling need to clear their conscience, for example. Or you make an arrest and the arrestee cracks. They loose lip. They're just making general conversation and they tell you things like, 'I used to work for a woman who . . .'; they give you leads on people you never even heard of. Or someone just wants to be an informant. There are people who like to tell you things. It could be an anonymous phone call, a neighbor complaining about the steady influx of people to a certain apartment. It could be a former client. It could be a girl's boyfriend or husband who's found out about her sideline. And the tip could just be a crank or somebody who's got a grudge. We investigate them all."

Once they've checked out the ad or determined that the tip is legit, the undercover investigators, working in teams of two or three, decide what role to play— for example, one goes in, playing the role of a college student interested in working his or her way through school by whoring for an escort agency, or an out-of-town executive looking for room service, and the two on backup wait, either to help make the arrest or to bail out their partner if things go haywire.

The object of the game is called "getting all the elements"—getting the panderer or whore to make it so blindingly clear that this is, indeed, a premeditated arrangement of sex for money that the case will stick in court.

The game is played as close to the edge as possible. The most common scenario is this: the decoy goes in without a badge, without a gun, without a radio, and the backup waits, hoping they don't lose the decoy, or miss the signal, or come in too late. "A lot of these people, they find out you're the police, they're not gonna think twice about killing you," says vice cop Jim Dillon.

The officers who work Vice Control, Prostitution, have all worked backup and they've all played decoy: the women, looking lost at bus stations or posing as escort service hopefuls, porno movie candidates; the men, as straight and gay bar habitués, call girl referrals, bondage chamber devotees.

Most of the activity, the vice cops say, is centered in Area Six. "The West Side may have more female street-walkers and a fair share of gumps," says one detective.

"But you got all the high-lining whores and all the kinky stuff in Area Six. Sometimes we think people sit around just trying to dream up things nobody has ever tried before, but somebody's always beat them to it."

Everybody thinks of a call girl as a very glamorous-looking female. But actually, a call girl is any female that operates through the phone. I might make out a case report on a call operation. "I received information, I called this number, offer of prostitution was made." This is a call girl.

I might have gotten her number from my truck driver buddy who's going down Madison Street, sees some whore and says, "I can't right now, babe. Give me your phone number." She wants to take this guy on for fifteen bucks. She says, "Call me anytime, honey." She is now a call girl. Why does she have to be a $500 call girl to be a call girl?

The conception of a girl picking up a phone and answering it and being a prostitute—I don't see that happening. But there can be a girl that lives in a low-income area that may be working the street and has her phone number out and she might be willing to commit an act of prostitution for fifteen dollars.

All whores have beepers. That's a definite. With all the heat on prostitution, they want to be on the street as little as possible. So they give their number to johns. "Next time, just beep me." That's how some whores graduate themselves up to call girls.

We've come across some male call operators. Males for males. Last month, we arrested two guys running a call operation—fifty and fifty-nine years old these guys were. Not what you'd call well preserved, either. Very scraggly guys, but they're getting business.

I've been in the unit eleven years; I've been a policeman for twenty-three, and probably in those eleven years the real, real, real, real good call girls you could count on your hands. I mean the *real* expensive ones. I mean the ones that won't take a client unless he owns a business or one of her regular clients gives him a real solid recommendation. The most I've ever come across was $500 an hour. I just hope that customers that pay that get what they pay for. When you find those, those are good. Those arrests give you a lot more pleasure than pinching the run-of-the-mill prostitute you happened to chance upon.

The true call girl is so removed that to get to her you've got to lock up somebody with some status: a judge, a lawyer, a doctor, someone who's willing to pay $500 just to come to her place, and take her out, wine her and dine her, and then, of course, have himself be relieved. A blue collar worker can't even come close to meeting this woman. Ever.

Most call girls work steady jobs. They have a select clientele. They make enough extra money from their clients so they can live somewhere downtown on the seventy-ninth floor, close to their clients, and they can afford to take a day job that may be glamorous, or creative, but doesn't pay a lot of money.

I don't know how anybody becomes a call girl. They probably meet someone who gives them the idea and they start out slow. Somebody at a party who might say, "Look, I know this guy who's interested in you. He's willing to pay big for your company." There isn't a proven path. It's not like becoming a brain surgeon by going to school.

A lot of high-lining whores live on the Gold Coast. The Gold Coast is whore heaven. It's close to the best shops, the best restaurants, the best hair stylists. It's convenient for the customers, too. They can drop by on their way back to the wife and kids in the 'burbs.

A few years ago, I arrested a woman in her fifties who ran a big call girl operation. She had trick pads in about five condominiums in really exclusive buildings downtown and on the Gold Coast. The girls that worked for her were just very, very attractive. They'd be sent to these apartments to meet clients.

We got on to her through security at a Lake Shore Drive condo. There were just too many girls going in and out of this one apartment in the course of a day. They told me that a guy who worked in the building was involved with the owner of the apartment and that she told him she had a bunch of girls working for her. I told security to have this guy give one of my covert phone numbers to this woman. I passed myself off as a businessman who constantly had clients coming in from out of town and that I was looking for girls who would commit acts of prostitution to entertain my clients.

The very next day, this woman called. She says, "I got your name from a friend. I understand you need girls for your business clients." She told me she had apartments all over the city, anywhere I'd need to entertain. And she told me she had girls who were models, fantastic-looking girls, living in these apartments, and, if I was so inclined, she'd send one of these business clients of mine to one of her apartments and she'd make all the arrangements.

I told her I was interested in sampling the merchandise myself first. She told me it was $150 an hour and all I had to do was tell her what type of girl I wanted and she'd send me to an apartment and arrange to have that type of girl waiting for me there. I said I wanted two girls, young, attractive. She said, "Go to 211 East Ohio, twenty-fifth floor. Be there at noon tomorrow."

I went there. One girl let me in. It was your basic trick pad—not furnished to the teeth, just a coffee table and couch in the living room, a bed and small TV and VCR in the bedroom. It was a very clean place.

The girl who met me at the door was extremely attractive, blond, a bit of a Southern accent. Another girl was inside; she said she was from South America. She was dark-skinned. Exotic-looking. They said they'd charge $150 each.

I got the deal down. I asked them what the $300 covered and they said sex with me. Then I asked if they'd *do* extra *for* extra. They said, "We'll do anything, but you have to pay." So I said I wanted to watch girl-on-girl first and then I wanted both of them to have sex with me. It came to $400 total.

I went in the bedroom. One girl came in. I said, "Hey, I've got some marijuana in a bag outside. Why don't I go get it?" So I went into the hallway and let my backup in. There were four of us now and we all went back in the bedroom and arrested them. They cried. It was a first arrest for both and that's always a little scary, I guess.

Then they did this funny thing that people do when they're arrested. Anybody. They start doing gallows humor. Suddenly, they're cracking jokes and saying, "Ha, ha, when you walked in and said this, I should have known, hee hee." So these girls were having laughs over the arrest. We brought them to the station and one of them spilled the beans on the woman running this operation, including her address. We got her. She had a trick book in her condo that had pages and pages of girls' names, what they looked like, and what they'd do.

When it got to court, the State felt there were no reasonable grounds for arrest based on the phone conversation and what the girls said to me, so they dropped the charge. The girls were given guilty with supervision. Everything that had been seized was given back. Six months later, this woman was pinched again.

Call girls don't suffer the same traumas that streetwalkers do. When streetwalkers can't turn tricks anymore, for whatever reason—because they're too wasted or beat up or nobody even wants them on the street—they're through; they're dead.

With call girls, theirs is first and foremost a thing of beauty. When the beauty passes, they practically always go into other lines of work. You find lots of old call girls in sales. They are usually still very nice-looking, but not as stunning, and they have developed very fine personalities to go along with it.

Many of the call girls marry well. They marry out of it. I have known many who have gone on to marry customers. Or they find a guy through other avenues. They meet a nice guy who's got a lot of money, they go ahead and get married and never let him know about the past.

Each and every escort service is a front for prostitution. Without exception. Some people think they're for out-of-towners who want somebody to go to some business function with them or want a dinner companion because they don't like to eat alone. They're wrong. Who's gonna pay $300–$400 for a dinner date? Nobody's that good a conversationalist.

Going to an escort service and expecting just a dinner date is like going to a massage parlor and expecting just a massage.

The escort services send girls over to business offices all the time. I always wonder what the secretary must think is going on in there. Commodities traders seem to use escort service girls more than anybody else. The Board of Trade is crawling with these girls. A lot of these guys don't have time for relationships, so they send out.

Lawyers have girls sent to them. Judges. We've seen the names in the books—we do arrests and searches and seizures in escort agencies and in their books are names of judges who have girls sent to their chambers. Or during a recess, the judge goes out and meets a girl at a hotel. Judges are pretty kinky. A lot of them go in for very bizarre fantasies.

Every escort service makes sure of one thing, that the girls always wear conservative business attire when they go in. Two- or three-piece suits, conservative dresses, simple hair, nothing at all to make them look like they're working girls. It's the clothes underneath that are wild. Once they get into the room, they take the business suits off.

You would never know. *I* never know. I work security part-time at a hotel and I don't see them coming in and yet I pinched a service that tells me they've been at my hotel all the time. And I think, God, where am I? I don't see them come in at all. Because they don't look the part.

Guys with money aren't picking up the girl on the street any-more. They're calling them through a service because they figure that if they pay $150, $200 for it, they're getting a *clean* girl.

And are they? Heck, no! Heck, no! I mean, what's clean? Maybe they're not getting so much a drug user, an intravenous drug user, but they're getting somebody who's had sex with a lotta, lotta men. A *lotta* men. And—you know what?—they might be getting a street whore anyway, a girl who's graduated herself up to an escort service.

Most escort service girls are ex-streetwalkers. You get a few college students, a few housewives, but mostly they're street hookers who see this as a better way of life.

There are escort services that advertise—the better ones use the Yellow Pages; the gay or kinky ones use gay papers or the free weeklies. The very cheapest services charge about $150, $200 an hour. That's rather cheap. The guys who go to these could be regular Joe Schmoes.

Then there are the services that don't advertise. We're talking multibuck, high-line, doctors, lawyers, judges, all Gold Coast. You don't get in unless you know somebody. Period. They bring you in.

Most escort agencies have two categories of whores: the ones billed as "Models" and the ones billed as "Actresses." "Models" cost about $300–$400 an hour. "Actresses" run about $400–$500 an hour. The usual phone pitch is: "Our models start at three to four hundred an hour. Our actresses start at four to five hundred an hour." The actresses are supposed to be much better-looking, the elite. I believe they're the same girls; you can get the same girl for a cheaper price.

The split between escort agency and prostitute, if the rate is $150–$200 an hour, is generally sixty percent to the girl, forty percent to the service. The higher the price, the bigger the cut for the agency. At $400–$500 an hour, the split is usually fifty-fifty. But if it's a repeat customer at Actress prices, the split becomes sixty for the girl, forty for the service.

Most of it's done on American Express, Diners. The girls are all given—I have one at work—a little credit card imprinter. You put in the card and then you rub it with a spoon. For American Express, you have to add a fifteen percent surcharge. It's written off as a business expense for the man.

The girls are instructed to write down "an expensive piece of artwork"—that's the code in Chicago. That way, the wife doesn't know when the bill comes through, or the company doesn't know. The guys with the major expense accounts, those are the guys who get the girls. A *lot* of corporate money goes to escort services.

Escort services are very organized. They're not like call girl operations where you've got basically one girl going freelance. She's working off the phone; she's all by herself. The services— they're very organized; a lot of women, a lot of money.

We pinched a service. The guy who owned it, a very big service in the city advertising in the Yellow Pages, he made $399,000 in June and July of last year. Cash. Three hundred and ninety-nine thousand dollars. This is standard. There are a lot of them making that kind of money. Now granted, that may have been a good month, but how bad could a bad month be?

Is it stressful? Hell, no. Maybe they do a little too much coke . . . but they are pampered like you can't believe. They don't work all day. They have their hair done on Oak Street, their nails done on Chestnut. They're getting a massage at four; they're getting a facial at five; they're turning two or three tricks a night and they're making $800 to $2000 a night. You got a busy night going? Darn right you make that much. It's only four, five hours work. That's stressful?

And generally if the guy's gonna pay that much for it, he's not a kink. Anybody who's gonna pay four, five hundred dollars for a girl, he's not a kink. So I mean it's not like you're walking the streets getting in a car with you-don't-know. They're going to the Ritz-Carlton; they're going to the Hyatt House. Maybe they have one or two too many cocktails, that makes them feel stressed, but for the most part, their life is a breeze.

*   *   *

What amazes me is escort service girls aren't all that good-looking. I haven't found anyone show up from an escort service that I'd look twice at on the street. But these are expensive girls. If I was a businessman and I was spending that kind of money, I would want stunning. There's one girl, she's been arrested by us a number of times, everybody knows her, I swear she'd scare a bulldog off a meat wagon. *Really* homely. She makes $150 an hour.

I've seen a few escort girls who have track marks all over their arms. I've seen them with real scraggly teeth and hair. Some look like they're forty years old. Usually, they at least have to look presentable, but rarely are they good-looking girls. I wonder why.

I went on an interview once and there was this woman there. I was sickened. She had to be fifty-five. She had really, really, really heavy makeup on. And when she left—everybody laughed. They all laughed about her. But she was working.

We get a lot of suburban housewives who come in. Or women from Michigan and Indiana. They work two, three nights a week. They tell their family they're coming in on a business trip. A lot of them follow the conventions from city to city to city.

They're making a heck of a lot more money than I could working a legit job—they're making $600, $800 a night. They're working Tuesday, Wednesday, Thursday and then they go home to their families, to their kids.

We go into interviews for these escort agencies. We make up different names when we go in. My ID is burned out. The police department gives you one false ID. I've used mine so much I can't use it anymore. I pray they won't ask for any ID. We take every scrap of our real identities out of our pockets and purses. You can't have anything that remotely links you with the police. You have to keep reminding yourself what your phony name is so you won't ignore them when they call out your name.

When they interview you, normally, they'll ask you what you'll do. "Straight?" "Oral?" "Greek?"—anal sex. "Two women?" That's for the guy who wants two women sent over; he wants to watch them. There's water sports: golden showers, brown showers. They ask you all this. It's standard with all the services.

When we bust a service, many times, the interview alone will supply the elements. But we also go on "dates" to gather more evidence, because state's attorneys always want more evidence. We don't arrest the clients, usually; they're just stepping stones to the panderers.

When we go on dates, the routine is this: Walk in, get the money, call the service, tell them I'm there, tell them the guy's okay, I'm gonna stay. Then I open the door and let my backup in. You don't arrest the client; you just say, "We're the police. We're handling a grand jury investigation. If you call the service and tell them the police showed up, you're gonna get locked up." Usually the guys start to cry. They beg you not to arrest them; not to tell anybody. It's pitiful. They get freaked out.

You remember the Mayflower Madam? Right after the book came out, I saw an ad in the paper: "American Executive escort service looking for pretty ladies." So I called for an interview. I go to this very nice condo and there's this woman there, she has a computer set up in an office and everything, and there's five of us, five girls waiting to be interviewed for this escort service. Just like in Mayflower Madam, the way they had it set up.

The girls came in, business suits, nicely made-up, hair real nice, painted nails. They looked professional. Most of them were students. College students. They all looked so naïve, so young. A couple of the girls were nineteen years old. I was sitting next to this one girl and I asked her, "Why are you looking for this?" And she said, "I need a part-time job because I'm going to school. I wouldn't tell my boyfriend; he doesn't know I'm doing this. I just need some extra money." And I thought, Okayyy. . . .

The lady in charge portrayed herself just like the Mayflower Madam. She was just so nice, so sweet. She goes, "Oh, girls, you're all so pretty. You've got to think of yourselves as professionals. You can't think of yourselves as dirty. You're not dirty. You're not whores. We're out there to please men. Give them a good time. Make them feel like real men. This is a business, this is a job, but this is really acting." This is what she's *saying*. She goes, "If you really don't want to have sex with them, don't. Tell them that you don't feel like it this time, but you will next time. However, they still have to pay for your time. They still have to pay the $150 for that hour. And, girls, they can only come once. If they want to come again, they have to pay again." That's common with the services.

This lady goes, "Sweet-talk them. Make them feel good. That's what you're there for." I'm thinking, I don't believe this. She tells them exactly what to wear, what to say to them, what to have in their purse—"Always bring condoms," she says. "Check to see if they have American Express."

I was hired by this woman and I went on a date. This guy said he was a lawyer and he lived in the suburbs. This guy told the woman on the phone, "I have a trailer home. I can bring my trailer into the city and you can send the escort to my trailer." I guess he wanted to avoid the surcharge for having a girl sent out to the suburbs.

So he brings it in and parks it right around Peterson and Cicero, right on the street. So I came in, he was a nice guy, he offered me a drink—"Take off your shoes; make yourself at home." He showed me around. "This is my sink. This is my bathroom. This is my bedroom. This is my stereo. This is my bed." I couldn't stall him much longer. After about fifteen minutes of conversation, it was like, "Well, let's go in the bedroom. Come on. Let's get out of here. I have an hour." That sort of thing. But he wasn't saying what I needed him to say. I wanted him to say, "Yes, I want to have sex with you"—to commit to an act. And the reason why I had to have him say that is because when I got hired as an escort, that woman, because she was *so* professional, her thing was, "Listen, you don't have to engage in sex if you don't want to. If the guy only wants you for a drink, or for dinner, or for conversation, then that's all you do. But he has to pay you for that time that you spend with him." So that made it very fuzzy in terms of the elements that we have to get. So I had to go out on this date and see what was gonna happen, see if the guy would say, "Look, I want to have sex or I'm not gonna pay."

And that's exactly what happened. Finally he said, "Let's go to the bedroom. I want to have sex with you. Look, you're a pretty girl. I really need you." That's when I said, "Uh, well, wait a minute. I don't do this on the first date." That was my line then; I didn't know what to say. "I don't do this the first time out; the second time I will, but, you know, the first time, let's just talk, have some drinks, have a conversation, you know, just to get to know each other. . . ." He goes, "Well then, I want my money back. This is ridiculous. I gotta have *some* service." So I say, "Okay. Here's your money back." And I left. And that was that. He never knew I was the police.

I went back to the agency and I said to the woman, "Hey, listen, this guy demanded that I have sex with him. So I gave him back his money, even though I spent the hour with him because I didn't have sex with him the first time out." And she said, "Well, why didn't you?" "You said I didn't have to. I didn't feel like it." And she goes, "Well, really, you should have. But, anyway, why did you give him back the money? You should have kept the money. And if that's what he wanted, you should have done it." So she gave me all the elements we needed. That's how I got her.

We're all actors in this unit. Anyone working undercover has to be. We have to think fast, when we go on these interviews or into some of these places, because if they find out we're the police, and we're in some room with a panderer and our backup's lost us, and they've just found out we're not who they take us to be, yeah, we could be in big trouble.

I did an investigation one time in a tavern, years ago. It had live dancers in the bar. The dancers would also do acts of prostitution in the bar. They had a table where they put a curtain in front of it. Our unit busted this place a few times. We'd go in there and we didn't have our guns, and we didn't have our stars; we had nothing on us that said we were the police, because before they'd let you go with a girl, they wanted to search you, they wanted to check you out.

So I was in this bar and struck up a conversation with the bartender and convinced her I wasn't the police. There are patrons in the bar watching these girls dance nude on the stage. And the bartender comes around from behind the bar and she pats me down, I mean she literally pats me down in front of everybody, you know, my sides, patted my crotch to make sure I didn't have a gun there, everything, my God.

So when she was convinced I wasn't the police, she asked for $150—$100 for the bar and $50 for the girl. She got me a black girl. I bought her a drink. The bartender took me and the girl into a back room; you had to be buzzed in. In the room was a booth and a table. She gave me one of those little three-dollar bottles of champagne. She gave me a flashlight; she said, "It's gonna be dark in here. So if you want to see what you're doing with this girl, you can shine the flashlight on yourself." I said, "Okay." She said, "When you're done, you gotta bang on the door real hard so I can hear. I'll buzz you out." So I said, "Fine."

When I went into this bar, my backup said they'd give me two hours. And in two hours, if I wasn't out, they knew the arrest was down and they were gonna have to come in. My backup was gone. They were nowhere near. They weren't coming back for two hours.

The problem was, everything went so smoothly, I was in there a half an hour and I already had a girl in the back room. I paid the money, the deal was down, and now I had an hour and a half to kill before they were going to have to come in.

So I told the girl, "Hey, listen. Turn me on a little. Dance nude for me." She said, "No, no. I got other customers that have to use this room. I got to make more money. Pull your pants down and let's get it on." So I said, "No, no. I can't. You're rushing me. I can't, I can't get excited." She said, "Well, come on. Let's go. We gotta do business. I got other guys out there. I gotta make some money." So I said, "Well, I tell you what. How 'bout if we do this? You rushed me and now I can't get excited anymore. How 'bout if we wait till after the place closes and I take you home with me?" "Well, all right, but I'm not giving you your money back." "No, no, that's fine. Okay." So she said okay.

So I bang on the door, the bartender lets me out, so I walk out from the back room into the bar and sitting at the bar is a guy I had arrested about a week earlier. He says to everybody, "Hey! That's the guy that just locked me up!" The girl I was with goes out a side window, the bartender goes over the bar and out the front door, the girls dancing on the stage go behind the curtain; there was a door that let you upstairs to the apartment upstairs— everybody runs. And I'm by myself.

Now, in the bar there are some guys that have been sitting, looking to get laid in the back room, that have been buying these girls drinks for who knows how long. They are not too happy that the girls have left as a result of me. So the guys at the bar are getting real ugly. They're saying, "Hey, you're the police. Let me see your identification. Got a gun, asshole?"

Now I got no gun, I got no star, and I got no backup. So I bluffed my way through. I started shouting out orders and stuff like that as I ambled toward the phone to dial 911 to call for help. But I think to myself . . . that's the closest I've ever come to . . . I mean, I could have really, really gotten hurt. Only because there was no way I could protect myself. There were six or seven guys at the bar that wanted a piece of me. But I was able to dial 911 and in a matter of seconds the police were swarming all over the place. But I lost the girl, I lost the bartender, I lost the other girls. And that's nothing to what happens to other police. But, in this unit, that's the closest I ever came to getting beat up.

There was a guy I was trying to get for a long time. He runs three escort services. I've locked him up twice since, but locking them up doesn't mean they're gonna go out of business; it just means you put a crimp in their style for a while; they're a little more cautious, that's all.

I got an interview with this guy. "Meet me at a restaurant." And he was really, really cautious. Before he'd meet me, he got my home phone and he'd call me at one in the morning to see if

I was sleeping there; two in the afternoon; he'd call me at all different times. I wanted to get him real bad. He was so disgusting, real blatant.

The very first time this man met me, he drove into a motel on Sheridan Road and he said it was gonna cost him twenty dollars to see if I was the police, meaning he was gonna rent a room and have sex with me. "It's gonna cost me twenty dollars to find out if you're wired," he said. "The hell you're gonna rent a room, buddy," I said. "I ain't going nowhere with you."

Then he wanted to meet me in a restaurant. I went with my partner and two guys from the Twenty-fourth District tactical unit. We didn't know where he was going to be taking me. They gave me a panic button; it's an alarm button; the other half is with your backup. It looks like a key chain, so I had my keys on it and I had it in my purse. And it was supposed to be that when I had the deal down, I'd press the button and everybody would come rushing to my assistance.

So this man made me drive him from the restaurant to an apartment on Sheridan Road. He takes me into the apartment and in the back of the apartment is an office with a woman in it. He tells me to take my dress off for the woman and he leaves the office. So I take off my dress. The woman's checking me for wires. She's going through my purse. She tells me I can't get back into my dress and gives me a pair of shorts and a T-shirt to wear.

And then they talked to me, asked me what I'd do, what I wouldn't do, and they set up a date for me at eleven o'clock. Now this is about nine o'clock at night.

So now I'm thinking, I don't want to wait till eleven o'clock, so I go in the john and I go into my purse and I hit the panic button. I go back in and sit down on the couch. My help's supposed to come in. Now it's nine-fifteen. Nobody's knocking down the door. So I go back in the john with my purse and hit the panic button again. So I go, well this is crazy. I have no gun, no star, no nothing. I'm sitting on the couch watching TV with about three working girls and this guy. So I said to him, "Hey, Howard, I want to get my gym shoes out of the car. You wanna walk outside with me?" Because I thought well, maybe they're outside and they don't know what apartment I'm in. They'll see me walk out and it'll be fine. We'll just go back into the apartment and lock everybody else up.

Howard says, "Sure, no problem." We walk outside and nobody comes to my rescue. I'm like, wait a minute! where is everybody? We walk to the undercover car I had, a Camaro. Howard says, "Come on, get the shoes out of the trunk." I didn't *have* any shoes in the trunk. So I say, "Howard, let's move my car." I figured, I'd get him in the car and I'd start driving around the neighborhood looking for my backup. With the bad guy in my car.

So he gets in the car and I say I want to move it closer to the apartment. We drive on a little. About a block and a half away, there's my partner. I pull up right alongside him and Howard's saying, "Where you going? Where you going?" I look at my partner and I say, "Where have you *been?*" And he says, "Where's your *dress?*" And the two tac guys are saying, "We saw the guy walk out and we said there goes some girl now with the guy." They didn't even know me.

Doing backup is nerve-wracking. Even though we talk it over beforehand, we decide what she should do, what the safest route is, what the signal for the arrest should be, you never know what's going to happen. It's scary.

And what also drives you crazy is there's no way of knowing when you're going to be called in. Somebody could want to hire her for an escort service, but not give you the elements of the offense for pandering for two hours. They might be making small talk. And now the backup team is waiting for her signal for hours. And, I mean, that's absolutely mind-wracking. Because you just think—what's going on? Should I knock? Should I check? How do I know she's all right?

You have to pay attention every moment. Can you imagine how it might be, standing in a hallway and it's not air-conditioned and it's 100 degrees, just standing there for two and a half hours looking around a corner, watching a door down the hall, waiting for someone to tell you, "Come on, let's make the arrest"?

You watch. You just watch. You find yourself listening for everything. You find yourself listening for a shriek, listening for someone to say, "All right. You're under arrest"—you're always listening for anything that lets you know your partner may be in trouble or the arrest is being made. Normally, there's a signal. But in addition to the signal, you're always listening for something else. You're always watching the door or watching the building or watching the car or watching her if you can see her. You're just waiting.

I was hired as an escort once and they sent me on a domination date. When I got to the service, the phone operator said, "This guy gets off on being spanked. He's all ready and he'll tell you what to do."

So I get to this guy's apartment and it's a pigsty. It stinks. Porno magazines all over. And he's got these whips and paddles hanging on the wall, all over the place. And he's laying on the bed. Just a robe on, no clothes underneath. He opens his robe and goes, "Pick your paddle. Beat me." And I went, "Okay, I've had enough. That's it. I'm the police." And my partners come in; they look at him, and they're like, "Oh my *God*." And you know what this guy's defense was when it got to court? "I was just kidding."

There are gay escort services, men with men. There are about five of them in Chicago. And they have services now, which really is like a breakthrough in prostitution, women with women. Lesbian escort services. I've gotten involved with a company that advertises in *The Reader*. I gave them a bogus name and a bogus address and they send me all kinds of literature: "In your spare time, we can fix you up with this girl." They get your general application and the whores send you letters and pictures of themselves. Now I've got a pen pal. She sent me a letter with a picture enclosed and here's this lady standing in front of a mirror, naked. I'm gonna lock her up for prostitution.

There are escort services, males for women. This is new. Women have had gigolos before; that's not new. That's been around since the beginning of time. That still goes on. But what *is* new is that women are just paying for the act of sex now.

I can't figure out what sort of woman would have a man come over to service her. It's very dangerous. You never know who's gonna walk through that door. It seems like the ultimate in looking for Mr. Goodbar.

I called a male escort service. The guy who answered the phone said, "Well, we've got two or three guys who can be your escorts. What do you want?" And I said, "Well, I'm not particular." He said, "I'll send over a nice, handsome guy. He'll meet you at three o'clock at Thirty-ninth and Western." So I go over there and I'm sitting in a Church's Chicken. Three o'clock comes. He's not there; he's late. Ten after three, a guy gets off the bus—I don't know it's him, but my partners are watching from the car—here's this guy, raggedy khaki pants with holes in them, dirty, filthy, looks like a mechanic, a raggedy T-shirt, he's got missing teeth, walks with a limp, he's got Converse gym shoes, shoelaces untied—he walks into the restaurant and says, "Hi. I'm your escort." He wanted seventy-five bucks an hour. I'm walking out of the restaurant with this guy with a limp, and my partners are sitting there laughing their guts out.

I have yet to meet a handsome escort. They're usually plain, scummy-looking; sometimes they try to dress nice, but they're still . . . plain. They're *not* nice-looking.

I remember the very first guy I got. I saw an ad in *Gay Chicago*—"Gorgeous, blue-eyed hunk. 6′ 2″, 180 pounds, 32″ biceps, 24″ waist, 8″ penis." I mean, this man was like a dream. I told my backup maybe they should wait an hour before they came to my rescue. I'm at a hotel. I called him up, "Can you come over?" He had no problem. He described himself a little more over the phone. Blond, blue eyes. So he comes over and I open the door. He was an albino black man. I almost had a heart attack. I almost had a heart attack. "You weren't what I was expecting," I told him. He was a scary-looking guy, too. Big and scary. I remember thinking to myself, What if I was legit? What if I wasn't the police and I opened the door on this guy? You'd have to be scared to death.

The hardest part of what we do is going to court. The judges are so thick. They want us to get these escort service operators to say, "You will have sexual intercourse—let me explain, that's S-E-X-U-A-L I-N-T-E-R-C-O-U-R-S-E—for $150— sixty percent goes to you and forty percent goes to us. You will perform oral copulation if the client wants you to" and they better say "Now that means a blow job" in case the judge doesn't think "oral copulation" is enough.

But it's all inference out there. It's all innuendo. They don't say, "I'm a panderer. Will you perform sexual intercourse for us for money?" It's all "Now, when you're working" or "When you're partying . . ." These people are street-smart. The only ones who aren't street-smart are the judges.

You get a lot of kinky things. There was a mayor's complaint that prostitution was taking place in a leather bar on North Clark Street. I go in. I'm wearing a leather jacket, a pair of riding boots that I had from when I was in the Mounted Unit, and jeans. The majority of the men that were in there gave an aura of being very macho, very into leather, very masculine. They're all into motor- cycles and they had vintage motorcycles bolted to the floor. It must have been "Jock Strap Night" because most of these guys were just wearing jock straps and nothing else.

So I go in there and I'm watching a group of these men walk around and it's weird. They're just milling around, just milling around, walking around like in a daze. And I was confounded as to what it all meant because in your straight bars, you don't find this. So what I did was, I emulated them, of course, so I could feel like I was part of them.

And there were two Oriental kids. And they walked to the rear of this bar, this particular room. Then they began to give head to whoever walked over there. And finally it got to the point where they were getting sodomized and—fucked.

If you will, it was like a feeding time for sharks. The frenzy that they would go in. All of a sudden, all these men went crazy.

They all did. First they were just milling around, like for a couple of hours before it started. They were waiting for something to happen to somebody, for something to break the ice. Once it started, they went *nuts*.

So while this is going on in the back, there's this guy about my size, very stern-looking, muscular-type, with a Fu Manchu mustache and a T-shirt with a German emblem on it from the Second World War that was only issued to the infantry which means, "I eat nails for lunch." And he was wearing a biker's cap and leather chaps—no pants on underneath—with a medieval type of thing, a shield if you will, over his penis. And he's walking around pounding one of his fists into his palm; all night long he's doing this.

So finally, when this frenzy gets started, he walks up to me and he stops in front of me and he's standing there pounding his fist in his palm. And he points to me. Now, I don't have any idea what he means by this, but I don't like it. All I know is our backup is outside; I'm with one guy I work with sometimes; I'm waiting for my partner to come in. He comes in; he starts to laugh. I tell him, "Shut up or you'll fucking get us killed." And I tell him to pretend he's with me so this guy doesn't get any ideas. So the guy with the leather chaps takes off.

At that time, being the officer that was gonna make the initial arrest, I made sure who the players were who were gonna be locked up and for what charges. I then told my partner to go outside and bring in the rest and call the police. There were four of us undercover; we needed more than that to make the arrest.

Meanwhile, two men standing next to me start to masturbate each other. While that's going on, to my left, there's another guy who, with one motion, drops to his knees, unzips another guy's fly, and begins to copulate him. And I've gotta remember who's doing what to who for court. You gotta remember this guy is doing that to this guy, while this guy is bopping that guy, without taking notes. It's real strange.

So now, finally, it's revealed to me by this one guy that was walking around clapping his hands, looking for a victim, that I was going to be the recipient of what they call a fist fucking. There was a cradle all set up in the back room, you know, this canvas sling you rest in while you're getting reamed. All they needed was someone to be a volunteer either willingly or unwillingly. So I have one of the guys there with me go outside and tell the backup to call for some uniforms to help us take the bar down.

We took the place down; nine of these guys were arrested. When I saw them in court, at first I thought they were all attorneys. If you had been accosted by all nine of these guys, you never would have been able to pick them out. They were all extremely well dressed, expensive three-piece suits, well mannered; their demeanor was just overwhelming that they were someone to be reckoned with. They hired an attorney who came over and she wanted to cut a deal. She said, "Come on. You don't really expect me to believe that you were able to witness this and know exactly what each one was doing?" I said, "Well, I can surely tell you that I did see everything I reported. And I have two other police officers as witnesses." She goes, "Just a minute," walks back to the nine guys, and they all took a plea of guilty.

I received some information on a queen who used to do bondage for an escort service and now was out running a house on her own. This house was one block away from Area Six police headquarters. I contacted her and we made arrangements for me to come over.

She came to the door and invited me in. She had a rough face, like a woman who's been around a lot, like an Eastern European face. I'm acting meek. My posture was that of submission. My vision was most of the time cast to the floor; I never looked her right in the face, and when I did, I looked at her with extreme humbleness.

She gave me a questionnaire to fill out. Name, address, phone number, age, what I enjoy doing. Then there was a list of things, with boxes to check off, from the most exciting to the least exciting: Dildo training—that's where they take a dildo and stick it in your anus and train you that way. Oral servitude—that's where they give you commands. Body worshipping—you worship their body to no end; just touching it—like "oh, oh, oh," putting it on a pedestal. The questionnaire also asked if you were a novice, a beginner, an intermediate, an expert and what degree of pain you were into.

So while I was sitting there filling out the questionnaire, the dog came in. A German shepherd. And I go, "Oh, God! Please, mistress! Take him away!" I'm jumping out of my skin. "I got bit as a little boy and I'm really afraid of dogs, so please take him away." "Oh, all right"—takes him away.

When she comes back, I say, "You know, I've never . . . Can I see the dungeon?" So she takes me to her bedroom and there was a makeshift stockade and a rack, several mirrors, whips and chains hanging from the wall, several dildos. And as soon as I got in, I gazed at the room with wonder in my eyes. I'm just awed. And I go, "Oh, oh, oh." "What's wrong?" "I've never been in a place like this. It looks so good."

Then she opened up the closet door and inside the closet was a whole array of leather goods, different getups for her. This is when I found out she was a man, because as she reached to get something from far in the closet, her robe fell open, revealing her penis. So now I'm more apprehensive. I'm dealing with a man.

She asked me which outfit did I like. I said, "Whatever pleases you, mistress"—which she liked. I said, "What about the money? Do you want it now or later?" She had me put it in an envelope prior to coming to her house. So in front of her I pulled the money out of the envelope so it could be ascertained that there was money in there—so she couldn't say later that it was just an envelope. And the act we decided on was, she was going to shove a dildo in my ass for $125, because that was the easiest to talk about without it looking like I was trying to build something. You have to remember you can't appear street-smart, or else why are you asking all these questions?

She asked me if I wanted to see a movie while she got ready. I told her I wanted to see some kiddie tapes, because that's a felony right there, just for possession of child pornography. But she just had some ordinary porno tapes.

So now, I've got all the elements down, and I'm thinking how can I get out the door without her setting the dog loose on me? I saw I had a clear shot for the door. I made for the door and opened just the front door, because there's two doors—the outside door and the doorway into the house. I opened the doorway into the house; my backup was just outside, waiting for my signal. Then I came back and sat down. And she came in, now she was fully dressed in her leather attire and said, "Now I'll take you back to the torture chamber." And I said, "I think you left the door open." "Oh, no I didn't." "Well, I don't know, but I think it's open. You better check. I'm afraid. Please, mistress." She goes to the door, and she opens it, and she seemed sort of startled that the door was unlocked. She steps into the hallway to look out the window. When she did that, I stepped in front of her. And then she looks at me. "You better open the door, motherfucker, or I'll tear your throat out." No more Mr. Meek.

Women aren't into bondage and domination. Men are. I've come across houses where the men pay to subject themselves to taking the most servile orders. "Get my shoes." "Wash my feet." And they pay *well* for that. They pay anywhere from $100 to $300 for a thirty-minute session.

The men who are into bondage and domination the most—and I mean by far—are men that are in a position of power, men who constantly in their everyday life are making decisions of who's gonna stay in the company and who's gonna get fired, who's gonna go to jail, who's gonna get the big order. When they go to this place, they're looking for an outlet to vent their anxieties and their frustrations, maybe their remorse as to having to fire somebody on Christmas Eve. So they go there for penance.

There was a place in Twenty-three, right near Wrigley Field. We had a report of a house of prostitution. We got there; it's a very nice townhouse; two pretty girls answer the door. We ask what kind of business they're running and they stumble around. We have a warrant, so we look through. And here are all these big, huge maids' uniforms hanging in a back bedroom. I mean huge, like four women would fit in. And it turns out this is a domination house. The girls tell us that men come in, put on the maids' uniforms, and they clean the house while the girls order them around and yell at them. It costs $200 an hour for these guys. And the place was *spotless*.

A woman or a queen runs the show in a torture chamber. And there are some ugly ones out there. I mean ugly. You don't have to be pretty to be a dominatrix.

What's standard equipment? Dildos. They're big on dildos. Dildos, whips, chains, cock rings, leather goods for the dominatrix to dress up in, saw horses, racks, stockades—they're flimsy; you could break out of them just by standing up, but it's just the fantasy thing of being in a stockade. I don't know. I don't understand it. Talk to a psychologist on that.

They hang whatever they can, whips and chains and dildos for instance, on the walls, and it's the visual effect of this that gets the guys all turned on. They call the room with all this stuff the dungeon—it figures—or the playroom, but that's a more general term for any place with sexual toys.

They use a lot of Saran Wrap too. These guys like to get all wrapped up in cellophane. Mummification. They like to have their pictures taken like that.

We got this one guy who hung people up in his attic on Wolfram. He had one customer who'd fly in special from New York. He had a great sound system; he'd play anything you liked while you hung there. What he did was, he had big Marine boots fastened to a board. He'd strap you into these, and hoist you up to the ceiling with this pulley he rigged up, he'd hoist you up there upside down, you're hanging upside down from the ceiling, naked—and then he'd leave. He'd leave the house. Him and his roommate would leave, go out for dinner. All I can think is, What if there's a *fire* in one of these places and you're hanging upside down from the ceiling?

Bondage houses are very hard to find. They might advertise, but with a code. They change locations all the time. They're rare in the sense that not everybody wants to be beat up, but they've got a fiercely devoted clientele. Guys who have found someone who satisfies these whims will never leave until their mistress leaves or she sends her slave away—and she never does that, because that's her meal ticket.

These places will do anything you want. What they tell you in bondage is: "Tell me when enough is enough." I had this guy who ran the attic tell me that he had a guy up there one time who wanted a girl to beat on the head of his penis with a hammer. And they did it. Because the guy was willing to pay for it. That's how this guy got off.

What bondage places will do sometimes is have the client pick a code word ahead of time that indicates when it gets too painful and you want them to stop. Because sometimes, as part of the fantasy, you might yell, "Stop. You're hurting me." But you don't really want her to stop. So, as a safety precaution, you pick out a word like, say, "tin can." Now if you yell out "tin can" the queen knows that you are really hurting now and that you wish the session to stop right now.

We cracked what I thought was the ultimate bondage place on Division and Dearborn a few years ago. This was a $1600-a-month condo; two stories. You went in the main living room, that was the torture chamber, the dungeon, and then they had bedrooms upstairs—that's where I never got, that's where they had the snakes.

I came in by myself. My glasses on. My dorky look. Meek. You gotta act real meek when you walk in these places. This woman meets me at the door. She had on what I consider erotic clothing: nylons, a garter belt, with heels, and like a half bra. I knew I was in the right place.

She introduced herself as Mistress Jennifer. "Follow me." Leads me in. She takes me into the playroom/dungeon/spare bedroom. In this room she has typical toys: a rack, stockade, dildos, whips and chains on the wall, lubricants.

I try to get the deal down. That's all I want to do, is get the deal down. Because my guys are worried about me; you never know if the pimp's gonna be in there, or another guy, what's gonna happen. I say, "Listen, I'm really new at this" and I start with my meek, apologizing attitude and she says, "Shut up and take off your clothes." I say, "Well, wait a minute. I'm really new at this. I really don't know how far I want to go. Maybe I'll just talk to you for the hour." "Just shut up and take off your clothes. I'm in charge here"—not her exact words, but real close. I try again. "Listen, I'm really new at this," I stuttered. "I don't know what I want to get into." "I'm in charge here. From now on, I'm Mistress Jennifer. You're the dog and I'm the mistress. And you don't even say a word without my permission." I tried again. "Really, I'm new at this. I don't know about this." "Just shut up and take off your clothes. When I come back, you scum, I want your clothes off." She took the money, $150 for the hour.

So she leaves the room, apparently to hide the money someplace. It's a well-lit room. And the only thing I'm thinking is there's a camera on me someplace and they're gonna use it in my divorce proceedings. She comes back in—"I told you to take off your clothes." "I'm sorry." "And I told you to call me Mistress Jennifer." "I'm sorry, Mistress Jennifer." I get into the bullshit. "I'll be back in two minutes. I want you naked."

I go down to my shorts. Now I'm nervous. Because once you take off your clothes—clothes give you a false sense of security—you get your clothes off, you are so vulnerable. It's something psychological.

She's back and starts yelling at me: "I told you to take off *all* your clothes!" I got into, "I'm sorry, mistress. I'm just so new at this."

"Get down on your hands and knees. And from now on, when you talk to me I'm Mistress Jennifer. Rub my feet"—something stupid like that, but not so degrading that I couldn't do it. Sometime along there I got her to commit to an act. "For $150, I've gotta get off." "All right, all right."

She turns around; she's facing the other way. I say to her, "Mistress Jennifer, I'm the police. You're under arrest." She doesn't turn around; she doesn't even look at me. She just says, "We'll get to that fantasy later."

Prostitutes are not like in the movies—beautiful, busty, miniskirted, exuding charm. Real streetwalkers are like creatures let out of the zoo. These ladies look like hell out there. Most of them are on dope—it burns them up and it ruins their looks. A lot of them are hooked up to violent guys who knock their teeth out. If I was a pimp, I'd think it was bad for customers.

It's very rare that you see a new girl who thinks she should look like a prostitute, maybe she puts on a miniskirt. It does your heart good to see a whore who looks like a whore is supposed to look.

One time, we saw a really good-looking girl on the street. She was wearing a garter belt. She looked like Apollonia with Prince. We turned the corner—she was gone. Someone must have grabbed her up and asked her to marry him. Another time, it was pouring rain and we saw a whore standing out there under an umbrella stark naked. We gave her an A for effort and let her pass.

Any man has at least a fifty-fifty chance of picking up a man on any stroll in Chicago right now. I think the ratio of gumps to female prostitutes is about sixty-forty. That's anywhere. When a female whore tells you that there's nothing but gumps in the area, that gives you a clue to what the ratio is. Especially in an area that used to be dominated by females at one time. And all the female whores tell us that all the time.

Gumps are also known as "he/she's." But actually, in their terminology, they're queens. And their code is "We're special girls." You go in a bar and ask a gump if he's a "special girl." They're queens. They're street people. They've found a way to make money off being queens.

How are you gonna successfully look like a woman if you've got a big Adam's apple? What a lot of gumps do is they have the Adam's apple surgically scraped.

They get their cheekbones raised. They get breast implants— that's real common. Only a few have the operation to have their organ cut off; I've only had one in eleven years who had it. You always have to ask them, when you're putting them in men's or women's lockup, "Have you had the operation?" They all say, "I'm in the stages of getting it. I'm just saving my money." They're all in the stages, but I've only known one who did it.

All queens carry on the façade all the time. Not only physically, but also mentally, that they are females. When we lock them up, they feel more comfortable being called "babe" or "honey" or "lady." "Okay, girls, come on." They love to call each *other* girls. "Tell that girl over there to come over here." They always call each other by their female names. We always treat the gumps like ladies. They love it.

Most gumps are black. Then you get Hispanic, then you get white, then you get everything else.

More often than not, the johns who pick up gumps *know* they're picking up a guy. I'll give you an example. My buddy's working Twenty-three, tac, and they see a gump standing on the corner flagging cars, working, okay? He's a black dressed as a female. Up pulls a big car—a Lincoln, a Cadillac—with a white guy in it. He calls the gump over; they drive away. The tac team's sitting watching all this; they're gonna see where the gump's taking this guy—he might be robbing him. They follow them to the lakefront. The guy parks. The tac guys wait a few minutes. Then they drive past *slowly*. And the *gump* is sitting up. The driver's gone. So now, their curiosity is aroused. They walk up to the car with flashlights out. The driver is orally copulating the gump. He *knew*. And he's paying the gump to give the gump a blow job. Figure *that* one out.

Whoever gumps might trick or trap impersonating a female, or even if the guy knows, they've got leverage on that guy because obviously the guy won't want to say anything. So the gump can rob him, take his wallet, do whatever he wants to do, and this guy isn't going to make a report. If they think they've got a real chump, they'll just take the guy's money out of his wallet and say, "What are you gonna do about it?" They'll beat him up if they have to. Remember, you're talking about a man.

*   *   *

Gumps are very dangerous. Fight? Boy, can those fuckers fight. They'll *disable* you. I had one gump once, I was fighting him. I screwed up—I lost my backup guys, I had to make the arrest by myself, and I shouldn't have. And I wound up in a battle with this drag queen in my car. And he was winning. He was winning the battle. He was wearing me out. Finally, a tac car came by and I yelled to the guys and they came to my rescue.

There's a new trend on the street now. Ex-cons who stand out on the corners waiting for these gay guys to pick them up. Then they get in the car with them and rob them blind. Who's gonna report this?

Besides the gumps, you've got gay street hustlers. They're not in drag. The gay hustlers you see now, most of them will be dead within a few years. AIDS. Hepatitis. These guys don't get beat up or cut up like the female prostitute, but they're exposed to gays or bi's who have a lot of sex; we've had guys tell us they have a thousand partners a year. They're not worried about AIDS. They're not worried about five years from now. They're just trying to get through tonight.

A lot of the young male street hustlers are runaways. They start out as runaways and they get hungry. You can do a lot of things when you're hungry. And most of them have it in their background that they were sexually molested by a man when they were a kid.

The young runaways are called chickens. The guys who look for them, like John Wayne Gacy did, are chicken hawks. The older ones are hustlers. And that's *all they do*. After a while, the competition knocks them out. The guys who are into this figure why go after a forty-year-old hustler I've had a million times when I can have an eighteen-year-old chicken? So they get into other life forms; they go into escort services if they're able, or maybe gainful employment. A lot become transients. You can't stay a chicken forever.

* * *

There are male prostitutes out there who carry on a different life during the day. They usually have nine-to-five jobs. They border on white collar rather than blue collar. A lot of them are in the medical field. They might advertise as masseurs, or cruise the bars at night, making new friends.

With these guys, for them to be arrested is very threatening. It's like their life is flashing before their eyes. They'll do anything to evade arrest. Fight? Kick? These guys fight like hell. They're all armed, anything from a straight razor to a butcher knife.

We get a lot of medical students. They moonlight as pimps and male prostitutes. We had one guy, he advertised as a masseur—"I'll get rid of all your kinks." He had a B+ average all through college. He was just about through with a degree in nuclear medicine. He could be your doctor someday.

I wish we had the statistics on how often whores are beat unconscious or threatened with a knife. I don't just mean street girls—all whores, call girls on down. No one ever tells you. No one ever says.

The life spans for the female whores are so very short. Their lives are over after their five years or so on the street. Many times, they are actually dead after five years. If they're not physically dead, they're dead to any real kind of life. As we know life, it's over.

It's drugs, sure, but more than drugs, it's just that life. You just can't last long in that life. Few have *ever* lasted longer than five years—whether they're on drugs, off drugs; they just don't last.

It's a hard life any way you cut it, but it's worse for the girls who have a pimp. In return for the services of the pimp, he requires absolute, total, complete obedience. That obedience generally drives you out into the streets. Eighteen, twenty, twenty-one hours a day—until the girls literally drop. And streetwalkers can't charge an awful lot, so they depend on volume. And a working girl can do it if she is attractive enough and on the good corner. It's nothing to turn twenty-five, thirty, thirty-five tricks a day, seven days a week. How long can you last at that rate?

Streetwalkers age real fast. An eighteen-year-old might look twenty-five. Some are out there who look forty years old and you find out they're only twenty. They look streetwise.

Male streetwalkers don't age as fast as female streetwalkers. They don't get hooked on drugs like the women do. You don't see a junkie guy turning tricks to support the habit like you do with the female. Only because, with the female, she has this pimp who guides her and tells her you gotta do this, this, and this. And of course he's an extreme opportunist who knows the only way to hold this person captive is to imprison her in a world of narcotics. With a guy, I don't think that's so. Almost none of the guys have a pimp; they're working for themselves. They're more practical; the females have more of a romantic dependency.

Plus the male prostitutes don't have the fear the females do. A street hustler, when he picks up a date, a john, the date is either gay or bisexual and these people tend not to be violent. So the hustler is not fearful of getting ripped off, cut up, slapped around, just to suck a cock. Whereas a female, when *she* picks up a date, this guy may be sadistic—who knows what may be in his mind? They've all been cut up and shot at. They get robbed constantly; they get beaten. So, of course, she's gotta put on a couple gray hairs every weekend, whereas the guy doesn't.

The white whores are more the junkies; all their money goes to dope. The black streetwalkers usually have kids; they use prostitution partially to support the kids. The ones with kids, black or white, a lot of times will have their kids go play in the park while they go out and work. The kids are watched by a girlfriend or boyfriend. When you arrest them, they say, "I have to tell my girlfriend. She's with my kid."

Sometimes they walk the street with their kids. The kid goes off and waits while Mom gets in the car or ducks into a gangway with some john.

If they've got babies, the babies go with them. I've arrested streetwalkers who had the baby next to them in the front seat of the car.

Chicago gets most of its streetwalkers from Wisconsin and Minnesota. Runaways. They come through the bus station and they just don't know where to go next. You know, I *got* to the bus station, what do I do now? Where do I go? I don't know.

So here's a guy who comes up and says, "Hello, how are you? Maybe I can be of some help to you. What do you need?" "Well, I just got here from St. Paul. I don't know where to stay." "Oh, *I* know where you can stay. In fact, you can stay with me. Don't worry, I won't bother you. I understand how you feel."

This guy, the potential pimp, approaches them, never as a pimp, but as a protector: "I will take care of you at a time when you need someone to take care of you. I will protect you. I will *be* the father or mother you left behind. And if you don't have a place to stay tonight, I will provide that place for you. If you are hungry, I will see to it that you eat." These are all immediate needs that have to be met. This is a kid who left home with thirteen bucks and doesn't want to go back and here is the answer.

They think someone has come to my rescue. And they end up walking the street.

Pimps always steer the girls into narcotics. Heroin. Heroin is the most likely drug. It's the most debilitating. It's the most immediately necessary drug. It's what keeps these girls in prostitution. Once they're into narcotics, then their lives are over.

You'd think pimps would be good-looking. But they're *sleazeballs*. They're ugly, ratty people. They smell. They wear old jeans. They look like they just lost their job.

Styling went out in the sixties. The broad-brimmed hats, the rhinestones in the teeth, gold chains, Cadillacs. Pimps found it brought too much heat. Judges think pimps still look like that—and judges should know better.

We got a pimp on Roosevelt Road. A real Skid Row guy. Just filthy. He's brought before the judge—"This man is no pimp. He's got no money. He has dirty clothes on. He can't be a pimp."

These guys know enough not to style in front of the judge; they don't even style on the street. Pimps all drive family station wagons now.

Pimps don't directly tell the girls to work the street; they don't force them; you'd have to put a gun to somebody's head to force them to work the street right away. The way they do it is they plant the seed. The pimp gives the girl drugs. This goes on for a while. Then, one day, she wants some drugs and the pimp says, "Honey, we need more money. If you want more drugs, why don't you go out and work the street a little bit. Just for today. See how you like it. Why not try it?" It's a very slow process of brainwashing. The next time the girl wants dope, the pimp says, "Babe, money don't grow on trees." By now, she *needs* the dope. Where do you think she goes?

We got one guy who was pimping for his wife over the phone. Two hundred bucks a shot. They were both medical students. He was taking time off from getting his medical degree in India; his wife was going to the University of Chicago Med School. We arrested her. He comes into the Eighteenth and he's crying all over the place—"Take me. Take me. It's my fault. I'm the one who set her up." They were hugging and kissing; he's confessing to everybody it's all his fault. We asked him why he was selling his wife over the phone. He says, "I owe money. I'm sixty thousand dollars behind on my medical school tuition." How many tricks is his wife going to have to turn to pay back his tuition? We said to him, "You better get out of this business. Stick to doctoring. You're not a good pimp." The bosses didn't believe us. They said, "No one admits to being a pimp. This couldn't have happened." The bosses are behind the desk too much; they lose contact with reality. It's like they watch reruns of "Police Story" to catch up.

*   *   *

Pimps are becoming passé. A lot of girls are becoming inde-
pendent now. Especially the black streetwalkers. Pimps are not
as necessary as they once were. The girls have learned to fend
for one another. If one girl should be arrested, it's not uncommon
that she would have made a pact with two to four other streetwalkers that one of them will post bond for her. You can com-
pare it to a union. It makes a lot more sense than getting beat up
every day.

It's more a question of are the girls psychologically able,
rather than physically able, to get away from the pimps. And
a doper will stay with her pimp because he's her connect.

Most pimps are bust-outs. They're dopers. Their lives get
worse and worse. They get into harder drugs. Their broads leave
them, they go off with someone else. Then they have nothing.
It's back to the basics.

Most pimps are old-time gang-bangers. They've come up in
the Disciples, the El Rukns, or some other gang. They find being
a gang-banger doesn't pay. They're always getting jumped;
they're always getting jailed. They're poor. Then it's like a
light bulb goes off over their heads. It's best to be a pimp!
You got somebody else working for you, you got regular money
coming in, and you don't go to jail. They never go to jail because
a woman will never testify against her pimp—they get beat up
all the time for nothing; they don't want to get killed.

Most prostitution clients are white suburban males, married,
with families. They like the excitement. They like the danger.
It's something strange. They've got the good wife at home—this
is a little excitement. It's like a challenge.

I've known some famous guys or real wealthy guys and
they're picking up street girls for twenty dollars. I ask them
why they don't go to a service. They say it takes too much
time—they have to call the service, be at a number where they

can be called back, and be somewhere where the girl can come to. With a street girl, she just gets in the car.

The ones you would swear would never do anything, they're the ones. They're the ones we see out with the streetwalkers.

Many prostitutes are lesbians. I've talked to many of these girls and they say these sex acts with guys are meaningless. After a night of prostitution, they go home with a girlfriend and have some serious sex.

The basic outfit of the streetwalker never changes. It never changes. As other styles come and go, they sort of incorporate a new style, but the basic streetwalker outfit is like your basic black dress and pearls.

It really changes very little in the winter. I've had girls tell me—you know those days we have every February, it gets down to 10, 15, 20 below—I have had them tell me they were glad that they were arrested. They still expect to get beat up for getting arrested, for being so careless as to get arrested, but the beating is not near as bad as the beating they would get for refusing to go at all. So they don't really object to being busted on those subzero nights.

I've arrested the same girl two days in a row. Now, they've probably got some fluid going in their veins the second day; they're either high on drugs or high on alcohol. One time, I arrested a girl, soliciting on a public way. She goes into lockup and what they do when they go to lockup, is they write on their hands with Magic Marker. Next day, I see her on the street, she just got out, she's still got the marker on her hand. I got her the second day.

One time I'm driving to work, I got my wife's car, and I try to pick up a girl, we make the deal, she comes to walk around to get in the car, she sees my police sticker on the window. "Ahh, you're a fucking copper." She walks away. We already had the deal down, but I wasn't gonna get out and rassle with her. So I go into the station, I go in, we have roll call, I put a jacket on, switch cars, hour later, I got the same girl. Got in the car.

It's funny. You'd be surprised what a pair of glasses or a hat or your sweatsuit hood pulled up can do.

I picked up a whore working the South Water Street Market one time; that's a big whore stroll, and she takes me back to the house. The problem was, it wasn't the house we were used to the whores using, across the alley from the market, but it was an apartment across from that one. I told my backup before I went in with her, but I couldn't be sure they'd know what apartment I was in.

We got in the place. I have no gun. Sitting on the couch is the pimp and a white whore who knew me, but she didn't say anything. I was lucky, that way. The whore and I go in a back room; she says it's fifteen dollars for the act. I say, "I'm the police. Just be cool. It's no big thing." She starts screaming, "Help me! Help me! Kill the motherfucker! Kill him!" The pimp comes in. I say, "Be cool." But she's instigating him—"Kill him! Kill him!" And my little heart starts palpitating—I'm in with no gun, I don't know where my backup is, and this pimp is gonna feel he's gotta be macho in front of his girls. He starts shoving me. She keeps yelling, "Kill him!" So I punch her in the face; I connected real good. She's out cold on the floor. "Okay, okay," the pimp goes, "You're the police."

I read a case report where here's a young kid on his way home, maybe he had too many beers, I don't know what the hell he was thinking about, but he stopped and picked up a girl at Madison and Western, and all he wanted was oral copulation and he was paying her twenty dollars. She took him to an alley. Her pimp and another girl followed them in. When they got done with him he had 180 stitches in his head and he was missing his $800 paycheck and his watch and jewelry. They left him in his car.

They found the girl, we charged her and the case is cleared, but the thing is, it isn't a victimless crime. Because you are going to have girls out there that say, "If he's got twenty dollars, he's got forty dollars. And if he's got forty dollars, he's got eighty dollars and what about that watch?" While you're laying back enjoying what they're doing to you, they're going to be going through your pockets trying to get your wallet.

So what are you going to go home and tell the wife? "Oh, gee, you know that Rolex watch you gave me, some whore took it off me at the Drake Hotel." And that's common. In reports from the Eighteenth District—girls will take rings, watches, briefcases—and what are these guys gonna do? A lot of these crimes go unreported. But, see, if we're not out there and we don't try to control it, nobody will be there and it will be running all over rampant.

There's no way you can call prostitution a victimless crime anymore. Not with AIDS. Female and male prostitutes pass it along. And then again the prostitutes, too, got the AIDS from someone, so they too are victims.

AIDS hasn't brought any change in the numbers when it comes to prostitution. We can only judge the amount of prostitution in the city by the amount of activity we have. We arrest all we can find. And our activity is just about on a par with the activity we've had for the past five years. There's been no change—no increase, no decrease.

We keep a file on those prostitutes that we know to have AIDS. And they are as busy and active as any of the others.

And they know they have AIDS; they've been notified. They simply don't care. They're out there every day. And they don't, as far as we know, use any form of protection.

It's really dangerous for a man to pick up a girl these days. And not just for them; they go back and have sex with their wives and girlfriends, who knows what they're passing on? They don't know what they're picking up; they're just spreading it.

How can they do it? How can they do it?

Last winter we arrested two street whores; they were sisters, the older one was pimping for the younger one. Both of them were covered with running sores. We could see the sores when we took their gloves off and when we put on the cuffs, we could hear them popping. This didn't look good.

They were yelling and screaming: "You can't arrest us. We got AIDS and we're gonna spit on you." That's the new threat on the street now. You can't shoot them. Spattering blood will infect you faster than if they spit. So you use reason. First off, I put on my sunglasses and turned up my collar. Then we calmed them down. "It'll be okay. We'll take the cuffs off." We took them off with gloves and when we got back to the station, we put them in scalding hot water.

I was just contacted by a little girl in Uptown. She's upset with her pimp; she wants me to do something about it. Anyway, she's fourteen. She has two sisters; she's the middle one. They grew up in Uptown. She says her parents deserted them when they were real young; the last time she saw her mother was when she was ten years old. All three of them became hookers. You gotta eat, right? The last time I saw her she weighed 140 pounds; she was a pretty little thing. Now she weighs 90 pounds—she freebases coke—and she looks horrible; she's skin and bones.

The best prostitution detective is the detective who has absolutely no feeling whatsoever. If you can divorce your personal feelings, it's one hundred times easier. I have known people who can do that. I can't do it myself.

What do you do when you pick up the girl who says, "I'm not really a prostitute. My two babies are hungry and I've got to get them something to eat." What really do you do? Do you arrest her? Do you give her five dollars to give the kids something to eat? Do you let them go hungry? Do you let her go back to work to do what she was doing?

I've done all of the above.

I absolutely believe that most prostitutes are self-destructive. They're masochists. Here's the proof: Prostitution in the state of Illinois is a minor misdemeanor. If there's a guilty finding, there's a sentence of two days, three days, five days. For a person accustomed to going to jail, it's never anything to write home about.

Now, in the past ten years or so, I have known and seen maybe a hundred prostitutes come close to committing suicide over this minor sentence. Most of them have the little razor tips under their fingernails for their own protection out on the street. I've seen them use those, inside a jail cell, to cut their own wrists. And, if they're not discovered in time, they will bleed to death. They know that, but they are hoping that someone will discover them in time to get them out of the cell and figure, this is too much to handle; let's take this minor prostitution charge off the books. I have to confess that there have been times that it's worked. That's the gamble that they take.

And they do this because they consider their lives valueless. Their lives are just not worth anything, even to themselves. I'm not trying to be a psychiatrist, but from what I've seen, they have no feeling of self-worth at all. Your worth doesn't extend beyond the moment, beyond the day. You go to jail, you try to get out of jail. And if you die trying, so what?

You can look at a lot of them and you give them six months. You know they either have six months to live, or six months to get on drugs, and for their lives to be over that way. It's like you look at them and you know what's left.

Mailbox Marilyn. Every copper who works prostitution knows her. She worked a long time in Twenty-three. She had a son that she put through military school. And the way she did it, she carried stamped envelopes with her address with her and after every trick, she'd stick the money in one of her envelopes, and drop it in the mailbox.

She did that. She put a son through school. Now you see her around Holy Name Cathedral. She stands on the corner and asks people for quarters.

In the Second District, along Forty-seventh Street, there's a stroll. The new, pretty girls will always go to Forty-seventh Street and Indiana, which is *well* lighted. After they've been out for a while and show the marks and scars of the occupation, they move to Forty-seventh and Prairie, which is less lighted. Then, from there, the last stop is *Forty-eighth* and Prairie, which has no street lights at all.

Prostitution:
Contributing Police Officers

OFFICER TOM BOHLING, Organized Crime Division, Vice Control Section. Bohling is one of the United States's foremost experts in pornography and obscene materials; in 1986, he testified before the Meese Commission. Bohling joined the CPD in 1968, was assigned to the Fourth District on patrol, served in Vietnam in the U.S. Navy, returned, and was assigned in 1973 to the Intelligence Section, Subversives Unit, for a year, and then went to the Fifth District on patrol. In 1975, Bohling was assigned to the Conspiracy Unit with the Vice Control Section, and has been with Prostitution/Obscenity for the past fifteen years. Bohling has a master's degree in criminal justice.

OFFICER JIM DILLON, Eighteenth District, Rush Street Detail. Dillon spent eleven and a half of his eighteen years on the force working Prostitution, longer than anyone in the unit. Dillon worked patrol for six months and tac for four years in the Sixteenth District before being assigned to Vice and has been assigned to the Eighteenth District since 1989.

SERGEANT TED FAULKNER, Vice Control. Faulkner was a supervising sergeant from 1977 to 1989, with twelve undercover officers working directly under his supervision. Faulkner joined the CPD in 1965, spent two years on patrol in the Second District, was then promoted to detective, spent five years in Area One Robbery and another five investigating professional thieves in the Central Investigations Unit. Faulkner retired from the force in 1989.

SERGEANT DAN FONTANETTA, Nineteenth District. Fontanetta has been with the CPD for twenty-four years and with Vice Control for eleven years. Fontanetta was first assigned to patrol in the old Nineteen (now Twenty-three), was promoted to detective in 1972 and worked in Area Five General Assignment before coming to the Prostitution Unit in 1979. Fontanetta was promoted to sergeant in 1990.

OFFICER JOE PABON, Vice Control. Pabon joined the force in 1977, spent his first two years on patrol in the Twelfth District, and was assigned to the Area Six Task Force and to Gang Crimes North for another year and a half before coming to Vice in 1983.

YOUTH OFFICER ROSE TORRES, Area Three Youth Division. Torres joined the force in 1982, worked patrol and tac in the Twenty-third District for three years, was detailed for one year to Women's Lockup, and was then assigned to the Prostitution Unit, where she worked until 1989. In 1990, Torres was promoted to Youth Officer and assigned to Area One Youth. In 1991, Torres was assigned to Area Three Youth.

DETECTIVE JOHN WEST, Vice Control. Detective West has been with the CPD for twenty-four years and with Vice for the past five. West was assigned to the Seventh District for two years after joining the CPD, then worked in the CTA Task Force, and the Seaport Security Force, which investigated Organized Crime cartage theft and narcotics operations on the waterfront. West spent the next nine years working undercover in the Gang Crimes Unit, investigating gangs, especially motorcycle gangs, and narcotics activity. West served in the citywide Narcotics Unit from 1980 to 1986, and was then assigned to Vice.

OFFICER JUDY ZYDOWSKY, Vice Control. Zydowsky joined the CPD in 1983, worked in the Twentieth District for four years as a tac officer, including work as a prostitution decoy in Operation Angel. Zydowsky has been in the Prostitution Unit since 1987.

CRIME SCENE INVESTIGATION

We used to have an assignment where we'd go and photograph all the unidentified dead, missing persons. We had one fellow that happened to be working with the Mobile Unit one time and he was at the morgue doing a routine case and he found his brother. This brother had been out of touch with the family, and the cop found him on a slab. After that, he just wouldn't have anything to do with the morgue. Here he goes to the morgue and he finds his own brother. The good thing was, he was able to identify him.

Lieutenant Jim Nemec
Crime Lab

People that have been burglarized like you to dust and throw powder all over. We don't really need to, but sometimes we do it . . . just for P.R. I get in there, throw dust all over everything, just splash it all over the place. They're *happy*. They're happy.

And you're screwing up all their furniture. . . . I tell

them, "Take some soap and water to it. I *think* that removes it, I don't really know. I never tested it."
CPD evidence technician

There's a homicide, a street gang shooting. I go to the scene of the crime with a guy I'm working with that evening. We're in an alley. He's feeling the garbage can, he's feeling the garage wall. I say, "What are you doing?" He says, "I'm getting a feel for the crime scene." So I say, "Just feel your way back to the squad car."
Gang crimes specialist

An evidence technician opens the trunk of his car: "I carry this radio with me to every scene. I've got it set on WLIT; you know that station? Easy listening. That's what I like. I listen to it as I process the scene—I'll be collecting blood samples, or dusting, or digging some bullets out of a wall, and it's just relaxing. Light. Easy listening.

"They issue each of us an evidence technician's case. You have your powders: white, black, black metallic. You have your powder brushes that are used for dusting. They're like makeup brushes, like a blush brush, only it's a little bit finer and the bristles are a little bit longer, because as you twirl it, it actually fans out. You have two of those. And with the black metallic powder, you have a little metal stick, it's about the size and length of a pencil, but it's magnetized, so that when you stick it in the top of the black metallic, it sticks to it. Then you have your various forms that are used. You have your camera; we generally use Canons, AE-1s. A potato masher—that's what we call the flash. Additional film. An extra lens. Black Magic Marker. Evidence bags, they're paper, about four inches by about two inches.

"I've got a lot of stuff in here. This is in addition to the stuff they issue us. I'm always picking stuff up and adding it to my equipment. Just in case. Baggies. A flashlight. A hammer. A chisel. Various screwdrivers. A measuring tape that's a hundred feet in length; maybe for accidents, I might want to measure the distance from something. Surgical gloves. Tweezers, scissors, wrenches . . . Here's a chisel. I got this hatchet for busting up walls. But if I'm not sure the wall has evidence, like a bullet, or I don't want to taint it, I'll send a piece of the wall, or the whole wall, down to the Crime Lab.

"Here's an extra shirt, surgical pants, a surgical mask, that's to keep the dust out of my nostrils—you've got fingerprint powders and dust flying all over in a lot of these scenes; you can get to be a real *mess*. This black cloth—I use it as a photo backdrop sometimes. A stopwatch. Someday I might need that. Toothbrushes. I've yet to use them, but you never know when a situation might pop up and you need them. Here's some bright yellow chalk. This is good for marking evidence on a dark night or to highlight an area where evidence is located so no one steps on it. You can also circle spent cartridges on the sidewalk with it. This police department ruler here—you put it next to a piece of evidence to show the size of it.

"See these little flags? I just made up these things; I took some toothpicks and some parts of wire coat hangers; then I cut out little paper flags and put numbers on them so I can number evidence on the ground as it's found.

"I get new stuff all the time. You never know what you might need something for. You never know."

Successful crime scene investigation can rest on the chemical composition of a hair, the thickness and dye content of a fiber, the minute scratches on a bullet, fingernail scrapings, bits of glass, a tool mark, a paint chip, a print. It represents the science and art of reading a scene: whether it's outside, inside, well planned, confused, frenzied.

Scene investigation takes off from what forensic scientists call the "transfer of material" premise: that whenever two entities come in contact with each other, material is transferred from one to the other. The entities might be two cars crashing, a pedestrian thrown onto the hood of a car, a burglar and a windowsill, a rapist and a mattress, a murderer and his victim. Crime scene processing entails recognizing and recovering all the bits and pieces that might show who did what to whom and why.

Who discovers, picks up, and transports evidence from the scene depends on the crime. In the CPD, evidence technicians assigned to individual districts process traffic accidents; property crimes, including auto theft, burglary, arson; and violent crimes—such as aggravated batteries, rapes, and robberies—where the victim is expected to live. Mobile Crime Unit technicians work citywide and handle the more serious crimes: homicide; suicide; unnatural or undetermined deaths; fatal traffic accidents; plane crashes; any police-involved shooting, whether death results or not; and crimes—like rape, hit-and-run, or battery—that may turn into homicides.

Crime scene processing is the province of the evidence technician, the Mobile Crime Unit technician, and the detective. The medical examiner joins forces with the detectives and crime scene technicians on homicides, suicides, or deaths in which the cause is unnatural, unknown, or undetermined, what investigators term "equivocal death."

Death investigations start with the willingness to consider all the possible scenarios that could have led to that particular end. As Will Beaton, chief special investigator for the Cook County Medical Examiner's Office puts it: "Somebody falls off a roof. So the question comes up: Did the guy jump off the roof, did he fall off, or did somebody take him up there and throw him? Somebody dies from a gunshot wound. Was he cleaning his gun, was he depressed and committed suicide, or did his neighbor shoot him? Was it suicide, accident, or murder?"

At any scene, the evidence technicians go after "real" evidence, physical evidence. The detectives go after what the scene reveals about the offender, what it reveals about the circumstances of the crime, and any other circumstantial evidence that interviews, canvasses, and background checks may unearth. "You're walking past a dead-end alley," says Captain Tom Cronin, an FBI-trained psychological profiler. "You see two people, one with a gun. The other's going 'No! No! No! No!' You walk on. Two seconds later, you hear 'Pow! Pow! Pow!' You go back. One guy's dead. Who killed him? Did you see the other guy kill him? That's circumstantial evidence." The best case blends circumstantial evidence with physical evidence: the print, the tool mark, the blood type, the bullet that can only have gotten these particular lands and grooves from this particular gun's chamber—each bit of physical and circumstantial evidence corroborating each other, nailing the bad guy.

Everything recovered as evidence at the scene, from accelerants found at arson scenes to the clothing of victims of hit-and-runs, is sent to the CPD Crime Lab (the country's first, founded in 1929 for the express purpose of solving the St. Valentine's Day Massacre) for analysis. "We've had doors in here. Garbage cans. Car bumpers and fenders for hit-and-runs. Mattresses, back seats of cars for rape scenes. Lamps, arrows, fans, clothes trees— we get them all in here; they're used as weapons," says Officer Jim Doran, head of the Criminalistics Sections of the Crime Lab. "We get everything in here you can kill a person with."

A mix of civilian and sworn personnel examine evidence in sections including Serology (the analysis of blood and semen relating to homicides and rapes),

Microscopy Trace (trace evidence, such as hair, fibers, soil, glass), Physical Chemistry (including arson, bomb, narcotics investigations), Ballistics (ballistics experts can identify with exactitude the weapon—not just the make but the weapon itself—from which a bullet was fired) and the Fingerprint Laser Unit. Fingerprint technicians themselves work out of the Identification Section of the Records Division.

The whole process rests on one hope: "Even the most skilled criminal may make a mistake," says Lieutenant Jim Nemec, commanding officer, Crime Scene Processing Unit. "He might get scared—he might leave his tools. We might find a flashlight left at the scene. Only a real dope would leave prints on the flashlight. But we'll go to the batteries inside. People don't think to wipe off the batteries. A tiny mistake. That's what we count on."

And it all starts with evidence technicians discovering and picking up minute bits of evidence at the scene. . . .

Usually when we go in, we just sort of put our hands in our pockets, and walk around and look at everything. Usually, there's somebody there that will tell you what happened, a detective or a police officer. They usually have . . . a story—whether it's the correct one or not—they'll tell you. Sometimes they're right, but they're not always right. Sometimes they're wrong.

My partner and I were called up to Area Six, that's where all the weird crimes are, Area Six, and they called us to a scene. We get up there—"What happened?" "Well, we have a mother and her two young children—one's a baby, less than a year, and the other is a toddler—they're at Edgewater Hospital. They're all in comas and they tell us at the hospital that this coma was induced by an overdose of insulin. The mother is a nurse." They all three later died.

Now, her husband and the father of these two children is a student nurse and he's at the scene, and naturally he's all shook up and stuff. And the detectives are focusing in on him as a suspect. Because, they say, if the mother did this crime, she would have had these babies *with* her. She would have had these babies in her bed with her. But each child was in its own respective bed and she was in her bed.

So the detectives think the husband may have done it. The commander of Area Six at that time said to me and my partner, "Come on, guys. Help us here."

We're looking, looking. If it's a suicide, where's the note? Looking, looking, looking. . . . Finally, my partner comes up with it. "I've got it!" There's this clipboard—on her desk, covered up with a bunch of other stuff, was this clipboard, and about three or four sheets down, is the suicide note. I've never seen them hide a suicide note before. She did it. She gave herself an overdose of insulin and the babies an overdose of insulin.

First thing at a scene, you get the overview. Then you focus in on smaller items of evidence. You record their location in your notes and with a camera. Then you collect them—you collect the evidence.

Firearms evidence is really good evidence. Every weapon has its own signature. We dig bullets out of walls, particularly wood. It's a lot of physical work.

We get a lot of jobs where we have to take hammers, chisels, and saws to take the fired bullets out of walls, floors, ceilings, what have you.

On one robbery we processed, the offenders came in and they wounded one of the store owners. They shot him and one of the bullets went astray, and it embedded in the wall. So I had to take my hammer and chisel because . . . that's *evidence*. That's evidence. And this is the best part, you get to destroy things while you work.

So I'm up on this guy's counter and I got my hammer and I'm *bang! bang! bang!* and I'm just hammering away, just having a good time destroying his wall, and what happened, I couldn't get the bullet, because once it embedded, it went into the wall, it struck some kind of poster board in the back, and then it went in about another two, three inches, and then it hit a *steel wall* and fell. The only way for me to get it out now was to tear up this whole wall. They didn't want me to do this.

But let's say if that wall had been solid wood, I could have recovered that round. Because it would only have gone in so far and stopped. But because the wood was only about a half-inch thick, then you had plaster board, and what stopped that bullet was that steel, and it just fell.

We're supposed to come to work dressed in civilian business attire, a nice suit or sportcoat, right? Because a lot of times, at a crime scene, the news media is there. Sometimes if we have to dig a bullet out of a ceiling, particularly, all this plaster stuff falls down on you and you get really dirty. And another thing—if you're dusting for prints. If you use white powder, that's not so bad. But sometimes you have to use black powder, and this black powder, it's lamp black, is what it is, it's soot—and it's real fine and floats through the air and it lands on you. And you get your clothes filthy sometimes.

Say an individual is raped. And they catch a suspect two blocks away. You work the victim's clothing up and examine the scene to find any foreign or trace material there. Then you also have the offender's clothing which you would take and look at. Fingernail scrapings, etc.; you don't overlook anything. You look for trace material that might have been transferred either way—it can go either way.

Many times, you don't have the offender. Now what you look for at the scene are fingerprints. If the offender left prints at the scene, he just left his signature.

Fingerprints are the premier piece of evidence. The fingerprint is the only real irrefutable piece of evidence where you can say this came from that person. Everything else, there's some degree of speculation. If the guy left his fingerprints, it's better than a confession. He can't deny . . . he may have a reason, or an alibi why the prints are there, but he can't deny that he was there.

You've got to print the deceased as soon as possible. See, what happens once rigor mortis sets in, the fingers just kind of *frwoop!*—they curl in. And trying to straighten them up to get the fingers straight for fingerprinting is difficult, very difficult.

There's a cliché that we have . . . "The right hand of a bartender is bad for prints." They're constantly washing glasses. Now if they start washing glasses by some other method, that print will restore itself.

Some people have the friction ridges that make up the fingerprints worn down. Housewives. Cleaning ladies whose hands are constantly in water.

Certain laborers that handle lyes, or bricklayers that handle rough surfaces, can get their fingerprints pitted from the lime and so on that's in the mortar. It will affect the recording of a fingerprint. But if they discontinue what they're doing, their skin will go right back to normal.

If you destroyed the friction skin itself covering the entire inside surface of the finger, then you would scar that area permanently. Example: Dillinger. John Dillinger put acid on his fingerprints, but he put it in the middle, figuring that if he destroyed the center portion of the finger, that they would not be able to identify him. But there's enough friction skin around the whole inside surface of the finger that they could still identify him.

Other people have tried to destroy their prints, usually by grafting new skin on. But once again, unless they go from nail to nail, there will be sufficient ridged skin there to identify them.

Whatever you touch, you're gonna transfer moisture. Especially if you're emotional in the commission of the crime.

Some people's hands are very dry. They're nonsecreters. If your hands are dry and you're not secreting the moisture, chances are you're not going to leave good prints. But this could change. Body conditions can change.

Your palm prints are as individual as your fingerprints. So are your sole prints. That's why they print babies' soles.

Standard question: How long does a fingerprint last? No one knows. It depends upon the amount of moisture transferred from the finger to start with, the surface upon which it's put—the rougher the surface, the less likely it is to last a long time—the humidity, the air temperature, the wind—all these factors come into play. There've been countless studies made on different types of surfaces in terms of how long a print would last. In some cases, it's been many years that the print could still be identified.

There are three different types of fingerprint powders: you've got a white, a black, and a black metallic. The black metallic can be used on cans, glass. White powder you might use on furniture, walls.

You test with the powders to see which one is gonna show up a print best. I'll go in, and if I see something I know I haven't dusted before, I'll look at the object first and make sure there are no prints on a certain location, and then I'll touch my scalp and put my own print on the surface. Or maybe two of them. And then I'll test it to see which one is gonna show up a print best. And that's the type of powder I'll continue to use to dust that particular surface.

Sometimes, a criminal momentarily will forget what he's doing. Wearing gloves throughout the commission of a crime—maybe burning into a safe—but then walking over to the water cooler to get a drink, removing the glove, taking a cup, filling it with water, taking a drink, and then putting the glove back on.

In some cases, burglars have found the need to urinate. Gone into a bathroom and lifted the toilet seat up, left their fingerprints underneath the toilet seat. Not thinking. We even found prints once on wads of toilet paper left in the toilet.

They've found fingerprints on matches, in the matchbook, where they've opened the matchbook and laid the thumb-print across the matches while they're striking it and left the matchbook at the scene. Carelessness.

I remember one case where the offender—and he was caught—he was observed trying to kick a car window in. And what sealed the case was, rather than breaking the window out with a hard object, a tire arm or something, he attempted to kick the window in. And when he attempted to kick the window in, he had gym shoes on. And he left a perfect foot imprint on the window. A photo was taken of it. And then the guy's gym shoe was inventoried as evidence.

No two gym shoe imprints will be the same. It's just like fingerprints, in a way, because people are gonna walk different-ly, okay? You're gonna have different size gym shoes, different brand names.

As you're walking with your gym shoes and glass gets embedded, first off, it's gonna cut that gym shoe in maybe a ridge. As you walk, pebbles might get embedded. You might lean on the inside, outside—the wear and tear on that gym shoe is gonna be different. It's much, much better than leather shoes. Gym shoes are a very good source.

In the Mobile Unit, they change us around; we don't work with the same partner all the time. Why? Because if you got to be a team, with the same two individuals *all* the time, when you go to a scene, you focus on that scene the same way. With different partners, you view it different; you view it from a different perspective. And that's what it's all about.

I've learned things from other guys a lot of times. One time, I got a new partner and we're called to a shooting in an Arab grocery store. Bullets had gone into a meat cooler. And I'm look-ing at this, and I'm getting out the hammer and the chisel, and I'm ready to dig this bullet out of the cooler, right? And Tim says, "What are you doing?" "I'm gonna get this bullet out." And he says, "Why don't you take a screwdriver and take these two screws out here and lift up that piece of metal trim—see if you can't see the bullet." Why didn't I see that? So we take the two screws out, lift up the trim, and there's the bullet laying down in there.

That's why they say they have us work with different people all the time.

You get scenes outside. You get scenes inside vehicles, on CTA buses, on el trains. The ones on el trains—if somebody gets killed by a train, they don't stop and wait for us there. They move this train to the end of the line, to the railyards where they park them, and here we are, we usually go with a CTA supervisor, walking across all these third rails, dozens of tracks, you're walking, you're scared, you think you're going to get electrocuted, but the CTA supervisor says don't worry about it. And then he'll show you the train and you get up under there and do your thing. Most of the el train deaths are suicides. But sometimes you get murders.

So much hinges on preserving the crime scene—if the crime scene is preserved and the people who come to the scene know the job, you are going to have a very, very high rate of solvability for violent crimes because the scene is where it's at.

This is true of all crime scenes. We had a guy murdered on the el. A guy was sticking passengers up; this guy said, "I don't believe that's a real gun" and the stickup guy shot him in cold blood.

What did the officers who responded to the scene do? Do you know what? They took the body off the train and let the train go. They said, "All right, go ahead." And there went the crime scene and all the witnesses. These two beat officers—they said their reason for doing this was, "Well, the conductor told us he had a schedule to meet."

We had a case where a guy drove his car off a bridge on Michigan Avenue over the Chicago River. We didn't know if it was an accident—did he lose control, or high-speed: did he go through the railing—or was it a suicide?

We got an automobile guy to reconstruct, to go over the car. It turned out to be a suicide. They were able to determine that he held the gas pedal down as he crashed through the railing and into the river; he had the gas pedal down and not the brake pedal. The brakes were not engaged. There were no skid marks. And he actually had his foot on the gas pedal.

Sometimes when we go to a scene—We went to a scene once, some guys were shot during a gang shoot-out. And street gangs now all have these semiautomatic weapons, or even fully automatic weapons, and there's usually a bunch of cartridge cases laying around.

They left an officer there to guard the crime scene, right? But some police officer before him had picked up about half of these things with his fingers and he had them in a small paper bag. And he says, "Here's your evidence," and he tries to give it to us in a paper bag like that. We refused. We said, "Well, we collect all our own evidence." Just picked the cartridges off the street. They do that sometimes.

Some detectives do some funny things. I've been teasing this detective about this. We had to investigate a murder in an abandoned garage. They had already removed the victim and he's at the hospital, dead. So we go to the garage and we're looking around and we're looking for any evidence, and all there is is blood: can't find any bullets, can't find any cartridge cases, can't find anything to fingerprint.

There are piles of crap. Sometimes in ghetto areas, people use abandoned garages to defecate in. So this one detective comes over to the scene and he tells us later, "We've got a real sicko on our hands." I says, "Why?" " 'Cause. They took this guy out to the garage and they shot him and then they took a crap right in the middle of his chest." I said, "I don't think so. The guy got shot in there and he rolled around in all that crap and it got on his chest. That's what happened." You know, when somebody gets shot, they don't always just drop down dead; sometimes they flop around, roll around. So we had to convince the detective that, no, we don't have a sicko on our hands, other than an ordinary murderer. Who's gonna shoot somebody and then stick around to do something like that?

I can remember being called to a scene, we get there, and about half a block down the street there's this big glob of blood and there's a trail of blood to the fellow's house and in the front room he's laying in a big pool of blood. The officers there said we called you guys because of all the blood. Maybe he was murdered.

We look. We don't see any wounds on him. He's hemorrhaged from the mouth. The cause of death was natural.

This happens sometimes with alcoholics. They drink so much, eventually the blood vessels in their necks get so weak, they burst. That's people that drink an awful lot.

A lot of times, the first police on the scene see a lot of blood, they think a crime's been committed. They call the detectives and us. Which is okay with us. We don't complain about it.

Outside crime scenes are generally easier than inside crime scenes. The outdoor crime scenes are pretty simple. There's virtually no evidence there except for a spent bullet or a cartridge case. If it's a street shooting, there's nothing to fingerprint, if the car drives by and somebody shoots . . . maybe if we find the car later . . . Usually, it's just a few pictures and maybe recovering some blood and some firearms evidence.

Don't take anything for granted. Don't take it for granted. You go to the scene of a street shooting, you walk up, why's that gun there?—"Well, we had to move it because there were too many people on the street." That's important, because when you go to take the photograph . . . But if you didn't ask, he might never have told you that.

If you have a shooting at a tavern, usually it's business as usual. The body is over there and people are drinking at the bar. . . .

The hardest ones are the inside ones. Usually you have to make fingerprint examinations, diagrams, and you might have to dig bullets out of walls and stuff. And it's cramped in there, with all kinds of policemen around.

It's a very difficult thing, with a big crime, or even a not so big crime, to contain everybody. Police officers are exuberant. Even some of the worst ones want to get in there and do something. And sometimes they lose sight of what they *should* do—what's the purpose of this thing—let's hold back and protect this thing.

One of the biggest offenders are the brass. They want to be . . . you know, "*I'm* walking in here and I'm taking charge. I want to know." Well—you want to know, sure, but you should first know that you don't mess with things.

Don't go to the bathroom. Don't use nothing. Don't flush the toilet, because . . . when things are dropped into a toilet, the way the water goes, it goes up underneath. They may have flushed the toilet after they dropped something in there. But toilets don't always work like they're supposed to do. So they flush it, they think that whatever they dropped is gone. It could actually just be . . . It may have floated on the top and then once the water settles, *now*—it slowly sinks to the bottom, but it might have slipped just beyond your eyeball look. So if you come in there and flush it, now you might flush it away.

You're called to the scene. You enter—the most common piece of evidence is blood. Be careful—choose your path to view the body. Because if an automatic weapon was used where the bullet or casing was expended, you could kick the casing—and the way the casing was expelled could give you some ideas as to where the guy stood when the shot was fired.

You come into a room in which there's carpeting. Carpeting, depending on the thickness of the pile, *hides* things. And a police officer wears these ridged boots and shoes and when they come in and they step on something, they pick things up.

You could pick up a live cartridge on the bottom of a ridged boot, never knowing you did it, and walk out of that house and that might be the only piece of evidence that might actually convict somebody and it's *gone*. It could be a live cartridge, it could be a spent cartridge, it could be a cartridge that comes from only one gun or certain make of gun and we may know who possesses this type of gun, but if that cartridge is picked up and it's taken away on the bottom of somebody's boot, okay?, evidence can walk out that way.

Evidence can walk out intentionally. A police officer may *know* something about what happened at a particular crime scene, get there, and because he's trying to protect somebody, will remove evidence. It could be a lot of things, but evidence has walked out with police intentionally picking things up.

The ones that always make you cringe when you get the assignment are the home invasions. The whole scene is ransacked, so you have a burglary on top of a homicide. Those are usually the worst ones.

Crime scenes used to be shot only in black and white, even when color was available. Eventually we did go to color. There was a lot of objection at first, especially with the violent crimes, that this depicted the thing too violently and would unduly influence the jurors. Now everything is in color. And of course it's so much truer in a way; it's easier for people to picture.

I can remember testifying in court and showing the jury a black-and-white photograph of some shell casings on the ground and the shell casings would appear as white objects in a black-and-white picture. And of course, along with the shell casings, there would invariably be a cigarette butt or something. Now you're faced with, which one is the butt and which one is the casing? Which was okay because nobody else knew, either, so you could say, "That's *it*. I *know* that's it." But you couldn't be sure it was the right one every time.

* * *

You get blood on your clothes. We try to wear these nice trench coats in the fall and spring. And sometimes, we'll have our nice coats on and we'll go in and there'll be a big puddle of blood. Most times, you want to take a sample of that blood, right? So you take out your vial, take your Q-tips, you bend over—sure enough, your coattail'll go right in the blood. And then you're standing there, cussing yourself for being so stupid.

Processing a burglary scene. It's harder to process a burglary than a murder. There are gonna be scenes that are so contaminated—the people come in and they're so distraught, because a burglar will leave a house in a disarray: table drawers open, desk drawers open, clothes everywhere—and, for the most part, the first thing the victims want to do is clean this mess up. The minute they clean it up, or they have their friends come by and clean it up, it's contaminated. Although the beat car when they first take the report, they generally tell them, "Don't touch nothing; leave everything as it is until the E.T. arrives."

But some people are very neat, tidy, they cannot stand to see . . . their house has been *violated,* and they don't want . . . they scrub, clean, put stuff away; they have friends come over. And they contaminate an area.

Most people, and especially women, when their homes are broken into, they feel violated. Almost to the degree like, "I was raped."

My garage was burglarized about a month ago and I had a lot of things taken out of it. And I can't even begin to tell you how nauseated it made me. The fact—just knowing that *somebody* other than me was *in my garage*. And they had to climb into it, because I've got a six-foot fence around my property, so they had to climb over the fence and down the fence to gain entry. You feel violated. Just knowing somebody was in here.

Some burglars will leave their calling card. In other words, they'll crap on the carpet. I've seen this. The guy actually took a dump on the woman's carpet. Was a nice blue carpet, she had just had the carpet installed, kind of like a powder blue, and he took a crap right in the middle of the floor, left his calling card. Now things like that, you don't inventory that, you say, "Lady, clean your rug." I'm not touching that shit.

A burglar picks a lock. But he picks that lock a certain way, using a certain tool, and he does this the same way every time.

When they jimmy a door open with whatever type of tool, they leave . . . marks. A burglar may have a certain way of prying a door, and he may leave a key feature, or maybe use the same type of tool. If you take pictures of it—and even send that lock down, that whole door down to the Crime Lab, they can determine what type of tool has been used. And if you get four, five burglaries that have these same key features, and let's say the sixth time he strikes, he's caught—Hey, wait a minute, we got five more cases the same identical way—you can pin those burglaries on him.

You do elimination prints. You print the owners because you're not sure if the prints you pick up are theirs or the offender's.

Some people refuse to be printed. "Why are you printing me?" They become defensive. That's because they're on warrants; they're wanted for something. And they don't know what you're going to do with them. And the only thing you're going to do with these prints is just for elimination. And that's the only thing you can use those prints for, but they don't know this. They're under the impression that when you get back to the station, you're gonna run those prints, now you're gonna find out who they really are.

One case, a guy was wanted on a murder warrant. The prints were run for elimination, but it came back—this guy was wanted for murder.

Crime scenes are only crime scenes for a couple hours. Then they're no longer crime scenes.

* * *

With evidence technicians and the Crime Lab, they're looking for the *what* of the crime. But homicide dicks—they're looking for the *who*.

In any kind of investigation the homicide detective looks at the obvious first. It's like baseball. You run to first first. In most cases, the obvious is what it is.

With domestic murders, there's always a history of violence. It's very rare that somebody just goes off. You just don't go to the dresser and get the handgun and shoot your husband through the Sunday *Tribune*. That just isn't done. There's usually a *long* history of violence. It's bullshit to think that somebody just pops.

You try to reenact the crime in your mind by figuring out what the offender did. Then you can retrace his route, or actions, and then look for evidence.

The body's gonna tell you things—whether you find bruisings, or impressions, or marks—it tells you more than just the person was shot: it tells you the type of weapon, the distance of the weapon, the angle of the weapon. If it's the angle of the weapon, the distance of the weapon—if the weapon was two feet away or more, then it's probably not a suicide, because the guy doesn't hold the gun way out *there* to shoot himself. You want to make sure you hit the target. Or if the guy's right-handed and the wound is at his left temple—it's kind of unusual for somebody to shoot himself that way.

There was a case we read about where the guy actually filmed his suicide. He was an engineer and he set up a videocamera, and it was a good thing that he did because it probably would have been considered a homicide, because he was shot twice in the head. This is in a textbook—we saw the film when we were training.

The videocamera, he turns the thing on and it shows him sitting there, he takes the gun and takes it up to his head and shoots himself in the head, falls over. And then he comes to; he's still alive. He picks it up again and shoots himself again.

He made the video for his wife; he was leaving it for her.

They used to say that men would shoot themselves in the head, whereas women would take pills. They always used to say that women don't do something that's gonna ruin their face or their appearance.

Doctors have commented to me that that's not necessarily true anymore. Women do the same brutal things to themselves that . . . We had a case where a woman took a saw, an electric saw, to cut her throat, cut her throat and to cut her head off, so . . . When I first started, they always said women didn't do things to their face or to their body, that they're more the poison, the carbon monoxide, and that men were more the guns and the knives. But I don't think that's true anymore.

The clothes will tell you things about what happened. Clothing can tell you the position that the person was in, or it might tell you how close the weapon was—if there's a lot of powder burns on the clothing, then the gun was real close; if there's stippling, little marks, then the gun was a little distance away, whereas if there's an impression in the clothing, then the gun was right against the clothing. If the victim's seated and he's shot, there could be a hole through the shirt in three different places. Someone will say, "Oh, gosh, he was shot three times," but it meant he was bent over when he got shot. Now, if you take off all his clothes, and you just see the body, you lose all that.

Wounds tell you a lot. Doctors can tell the difference, usually, between self-inflicted and defense wounds. If a person is being attacked, they try to defend themselves, they put their arm up and they get cut marks on it. Or you get cuts on the backs of your hands.

Now, they might have what they call hesitation marks, where a person is going to commit suicide and they're gonna cut their wrist and they do all these little cuts on the wrist and then finally they just *shoo-wit* . . . cut it. So it's like little, not deep, then finally you get up the nerve and you make the big cut.

Or stab wounds. With suicide, you have little ones and then they plunge in. Usually there's a difference between that and homicide, where the person is struggling, fighting—they may get stabbed several times, and some of them may be little stabs and some may be big stabs, but in a suicide you'll have the little stabs and then one big stab. In a suicide, you only have one or two big wounds, because after he's dead he's not going to keep stabbing himself. Obviously, if you've got after-death wounds, then it can't be a suicide. They can tell what wounds are inflicted after death—you're not breathing, so you're not going to be bleeding the same.

Postmortem lividity. The blood, after death, starts to settle in the body. It takes about two to four hours to develop. If a guy is facedown in a prone position and has this on his back—you know somebody's turned the body over.

With a hanging, the blood will settle in the lower portions of the limbs. If a guy's hung by his neck, the discoloration will appear in the side of the face opposite the rope.

At the scene, it appears to be one thing and it usually is—but not always.

We've had cases where—Was the woman hit with a blunt instrument or did she fall? They have what they call a "counter-coup" injury; that's when the brain actually moves after a fall and is bruised against the back of the skull or the front of the skull. When they do the autopsy and they take the brain out, they can see that the brain was thrown with a lot of force against the skull. That would indicate a fall, rather than a blunt instrument, which is just hitting somebody on the head.

We had a case where a woman was found by her friends and family at home, in bed; she appeared to be dead. They called the paramedics; the paramedics said, "Oh, she's dead"; they took her to the hospital, tried to revive her. She had all the symptoms of a heart attack. They signed out as a heart attack, natural death, and buried her.

Years later, a relative of hers came forward and said she didn't have a heart attack; she drowned. She was insured for a large amount of money and she was drowned and then the insurance money was collected. She was drowned, taken home, dried off, changed clothes, put in bed. And then they called the paramedics. She had a heart attack, so an autopsy wasn't done. So now, years later, she's exhumed and they find water in her lungs. She was drowned.

This particular woman had a cheap casket and it leaked. And she was buried in an area that used to be a swamp; water got in there, and during the winter, it froze. Now, normally, a cheap casket letting in water would actually make it decompose faster. But the fact that it was so bad that the water got in there and froze made it so that she was actually preserved, so the torso part of the body was preserved. When they did the autopsy, the lung, the heart, the liver, everything was preserved.

Her friends did it. Either they meant to kill her or she accidentally drowned. But they took advantage of the situation, covered up what really happened, and collected the insurance money.

The M.E. made this one a murder. This was an older lady; we did what the FBI calls a psychological autopsy on her.

We got a call. Nobody had seen this woman for days. This is a third-floor apartment on Astor Street, the Gold Coast. The front and back doors were both bolted. Nothing was missing from the apartment. We hear water running in the bathroom. We had to force the door open; steam had swollen the door. The woman's in the bathtub, nude and quite dead; she'd been there three to four days.

She had five puncture wounds right under the left breast. What happened, none of the five stabs penetrated the fatty tissue—she just sat in the tub and bled to death.

When the M.E. went to the scene later, he found some blood spots at the door—he figured she was stabbed and then ran into the bathroom.

This woman was divorced, older, getting fat. She was seeing a shrink and a medical doctor. He had just told her, "You're killing yourself. You've got to stop smoking and drinking."

There was nothing in the refrigerator. We found out from the neighbors she gave all her whiskey and food away—"I won't be needing this anymore."

The blood at the door? This was a big lady. After the wagonmen got the body out of the bathtub, they set her down on the floor before getting her on the stretcher.

The classic book on homicide: LeMoyne Snyder's *Homicide Investigation*. He reports a case of a farmer who was found shot to death lying in the garage, shot through the head. There was no *gun*. There was a little bit of dirt around this body, earth dirt. So one of the detectives got curious about it because immediately above was the roof of the garage; it had a ceiling, but there was a little hole in the ceiling right immediately above where the deceased lay. So this guy got a ladder and he crawled up and he looked inside. He found that there was a potted plant up there and what this guy had done was to get a piece of elastic on the order of the old inner tubes, opened it up, affixed it to a spot up in the rafters of the attic, took it down and stretched it, killed himself, and when he let go, the gun flew back up into the aperture, but on its way back, it hit this flowerpot and broke it. And that's where the dirt came from.

I've talked to other cops who have had people who have done the same thing, except stretching it through a little hole behind the wallboard.

We get these autoerotic deaths. These guys cut off their air passage and they get a high, they get a real good feeling. Now if you stop right there, that's fine. You have your orgasm, and you feel real good, and all this kind of stuff. But—if you pass out, and nobody comes and cuts you down in time, you die. Usually, they're either standing, or sitting, or kneeling, and they're leaning forward, and they get this real good feeling, and they fall asleep, and they suffocate. We've had cases where the husband has done that and the wife's known that he's been doing it for years. And there's people that do it all their life and never die, I guess.

This is a hanging, but it's not a suicide. They're not depressed; this is strictly a sexual thing that they do. It's an accident.

With autoerotic deaths, the family is very confused. They think the guy's been murdered. They'll call up and say, "Somebody came in and tied my son up and killed him."

And the beat officers will come and say, "Gee, we've got a murder on our hands." And they'll call the detectives and they'll call the Crime Lab and we'll get there and we'll put our heads together, and we'll find some clue that clues you in. The clue might be, he's wearing women's undergarments. There might be a mirror—he might be looking in a mirror and a woman's shoes might be nearby. Or erotic material might be where he can see it. They'll be tied up, have a rope around their neck or something. It's an accidental death; they just don't let go in time.

You talk about scene investigation. What if there is no scene? We don't find out about some homicides until days later, a week later. Now the scene is no longer there. What happens is, if the paramedics or the police think the person may still be alive, they rush them to the hospital. So now there's no scene.

In the case of a baby, they almost always rush the baby; even if they know he's dead, they'll rush the baby, because the pressure—the family is yelling, you know; they can't just leave the baby lying there. So most times, when you have a baby death, there is no scene. There is no scene. That's what makes these crib deaths, these SIDS deaths, so difficult, because there never is a scene. And in most child deaths, there is no scene. Once the body has been moved, or once the scene has been changed, you have a contaminated scene, and a contaminated scene isn't any good. So there's no scene investigation, which is a big part of the case.

There was a case where a two-year-old boy was found, supposedly by the grandmother, and the grandmother supposedly was the only one in the house—she found the baby unconscious in his room.

We were suspicious because when the baby was brought into the emergency room, there was a cord tied around the baby's waist. It was a cord from a girl's dress and it was just loosely around the baby's waist. And it just looked out of place. It didn't belong with the baby's clothing.

That got us suspicious. And we started talking to people. The grandmother had her daughter's children awarded to her by the state because the mother was unfit. Now, the older kids went off to school in the morning. So she was alone with the baby. And she finds the baby unconscious, she says, and tries to revive him. The paramedics come and rush him off to the hospital. They notice he was all wet, and he had this cord around his waist.

It turns out that one of the older kids didn't go to school that day and stayed home. The grandmother had told her to take care of the baby and the baby kept crying, so she put the baby up in the bed. The baby wouldn't stay in the bed, so she tied the baby. Then the baby started screaming and yelling, wouldn't keep quiet, so she tied him and put him in the closet. She tied him too much and too tight and the baby suffocated. There were rope marks around his wrists and ankles and a bruise on his head.

Then we found out that it wasn't the teenaged daughter who did this, it was the grandmother, and the grandmother had threatened the daughter not to tell. The baby kept getting out of bed and coming downstairs and then he kept crying and yelling. He was hungry; he wanted to eat. The baby had actually been hit and fell down the steps, and then put in the closet and tied up, the closet door closed, tied up tight, and suffocated. The grandmother got scared and tried to revive the baby. Called her brother and they poured cold water on him, trying to revive him.

It took a long time to put everything together. First the grandmother tried to have it not come out, then she tried to put it off on the girl. It was the grandmother who told the girl to get the baby in bed and make sure he stayed there, tie him into the bed. And the girl did it. But then when the baby kept crying and crying, the grandmother came up and moved him into the closet, tied him even tighter, apparently, and left him in there. And he was in there all day, from something like nine in the morning till the kids came home in the afternoon and found him.

I think they had him sort of like hog-tied. The rope was around his neck, to his feet and to his hands. He probably was pulling and struggling and yelling, kicking, and died in the closet.

The cord just probably slipped down and was hanging there loose. The paramedics just noted it, thought it was kind of unusual, brought it in with the body, so it was noted in the emergency room record, so then we looked for it, and we found it with the body too. And that's what cracked the case.

A former police officer got himself involved in narcotics. Maybe he was involved in narcotics even before he became a police officer. I don't know.

The police had occasion to come across an individual who was under investigation, perhaps for narcotics, who told them a story about he and a friend of his being involved with this narcotics operation that the ex-policeman was in. And for some reason, some deal probably went sour, the ex-policeman and his cohorts put this friend of his in the trunk of a car and shot him or stabbed him, whatever.

And then they disposed of the body somewhere. Now this survivor, who they let go for whatever reason, is telling the police this story. And he says they disposed of the body but he doesn't know where.

So they had the story about the commission of the crime and he told them who the victim was, a man named Anthony Masciano. And Anthony Masciano was a hoodlum; he had a pretty good arrest record. About a page and a half. And Anthony Masciano can't be found.

So they suspect, well, gee, maybe this guy's telling the truth, but there's nothing to corroborate his story and there's no body.

Three, four months later, they recover a badly decomposed body in the Des Plaines River. They fingerprint this . . . the remains, and we get the prints in. I look at the prints and, as an ident technician, this was one of my real interests, taking postmortem prints, bad prints, and trying to determine the classification so we could get into the proper place in the file.

They think this is Masciano. But the prints that were recorded are real poor. So I sent the technicians back to the morgue to take new prints . . . which they loved. So we ultimately got in a fairly decent set of prints. And I identified the print from the body as being identical with that of Anthony Masciano.

Now they've got some corroborating evidence. We had the informant. We had his word that it was Anthony. But we didn't have Anthony until he was found in the river. The case was successfully resolved. And the ex-policeman is now in the penitentiary.

And all this came from prints from a decomposed body, not from a crime scene.

It's always better to overdo with evidence. You always want to take the extra step. You never know what's going to happen. It's like Richard Speck. One fingerprint nailed him. You never know.

Speck was the most shocking crime I encountered. The thing that makes this such a distinct-type murder: He murdered eight girls within about four hours. It was during one of these periods that the survivor rolled underneath the bed, never to come out until she heard the alarm go off, and then she figured it would scare him away. Now this is the shocking thing: When she gets up, she doesn't know what has happened and then she goes through and she finds her friends had all been murdered.

He took all the girls into the back room and bound their hands behind them. Now the question becomes, why did they allow him to do this? Well, for one, he's got a knife and a gun. And second, like most sociopaths, this guy was a con man. He told the girls, "I mean you no harm." He told them he was a seaman. "The only thing I want is money so I can go to New Orleans and get a berth out." And then one by one, he takes them from the room. The survivor said she heard one of the girls say, "It hurts. It hurts." Of course. He sliced her throat.

I always tell people there were two things that got Richard Speck convicted: He left a fingerprint and he couldn't count. He meant to kill nine nurses and he stopped at eight. He left an eyewitness survivor.

*   *   *

I was in bed, six o'clock in the morning; my house was just two blocks away from where Speck had been murdering the nurses. My sergeant called me and he said, "My God! We've got eight murdered nurses." I said, "You're out of your mind, eight murdered nurses. It's probably carbon monoxide that killed them." Then he said, "Well, I'm on my way over there; I'll let you know." And I hang up and then I thought: Carbon monoxide—it's July. And then my sergeant called back and said, "Well the carbon monoxide theory just went out the window; you better get over here." And I went.

It was pretty grim, there was no question about that. There they were . . . one in the downstairs living room, one in the bathroom, three in the front bedroom, and three in the second bedroom. The girl on the couch in the living room—one of the first officers on the scene had dated her numerous times.

They found one print in the bedroom, eighteen inches off the floor. When you dust a door, you wouldn't expect to find a fingerprint eighteen inches from the ground. One of the Mobile Unit guys could piece together that Speck was raping girls on the lower bunk in the bedroom. At one point, he closed the door. That was the print.

I made the first identification of the fingerprints of Richard Speck. They processed part of the crime scene on the morning that the surviving girl hollered, "Everybody is dead!"

And from the bedroom where all of these nurses were tied up and kept, from the bedroom door, among other prints that were turned in to us, they recovered several prints.

I, along with Hugh Granahan, one of the sergeants of the Fingerprinting Unit, worked for many hours. I went out to the crime scene after they removed the bodies to look it over and so on. We were told that evening that they had a suspect—he happened to be Richard Speck—and that they were going to get fingerprints from Washington from the Coast Guard—he was a seaman—and that those prints would come into us later on that evening.

When they did come in, Sergeant Granahan and I had this
stack of latent prints from the crime scene and we concentrated
on the prints from the bedroom door, *one* of which was more
legible than the other.

It was a complete print. When I examined that print—I was
working prints at one desk and Hugh Granahan was across at
another desk—I said, "Huey, I think we've got him."

I gave them to him and he looked at them. And the latent print
was not as clear as you would like to have it. I said, "You take the
ink print and I'll call out the points from the latent print." Which
meant that I could see the points in the latent without looking
at the ink. When he saw that, he was convinced. But he said,
"It's not what you'd like to have." "Huey, it's all we've *got*. And
if we have to testify, I'm certain. I'm not gonna try to identify
something I'm not certain of." See, to a jury or the uneducated
person that latent print wouldn't be clear; to a fingerprint technician it was. And you always want to have the best visual evidence
possible.

I went home in the morning and came back in the afternoon.
By that time, they had gone back to the crime scene and they had
finished processing the door and they recovered another print
from the bedroom door which was down below the one that we
had made the ident on. And *that* was the one that we used in
court. That one was really nice, really nice.

I was called on to testify for the prosecution at Speck's trial.
I was up there about three hours. We provided the jury with
copies of the enlargements of the latent print and the ink print—
copy for the defense, copy for the judge—with the ridge char-
acteristics: these branchings and discontinuities, what we call
the minutiae—charted off on the ink print and the latent print.
And then the prosecutor would ask me, "What is characteristic
number one?" And I'd tell him. "What is characteristic number
two?" And I'd tell him. We went through all of the points; we
had charted seventeen points.

The cross-examiner, who was a former FBI agent, made
repeated attempts to convey to the jury that this loop impression
was identical with some of the victims'. There's arches, loops,
and whorls. Speck's was a loop pattern. One of the victims,

whose prints were on the door, also had loops. But if you and I have loops, and the overall pattern type is the same, the ridge structure that makes that pattern type is different. We may both have loops, but the minutiae that make up the loops will be different. The cross-examiner kept saying, "Because this is a loop and she had loops, they are the same, or *could* be the same." No, they can't. They can't be the same.

You have your prints from the fourth month in the womb until after death and decomposition. It's one of the last things to decompose, your hands. We've got pictures where there's no face left, it's the skull, and the prints are still there. Maybe it's because it's tougher, I don't know. Maybe it's because the Creator said, "This is your mark and I'm gonna leave it there as long as possible."

Homicide investigators see not only death—they see man's inhumanity to man. As a species, we are crueler to our own than probably any other species on earth. The mutilation and the destruction that we do to other bodies for whatever reason, for the reason that is known probably only to the killer—why this face had to be smashed open, why not just shoot him? But, no, we had to do this very personal attack. And that personalization is something. Violent Crimes dicks, they see this every day. You get a real perspective; you don't sweat the small stuff that much. You walk into a room that's ankle-deep in blood. . . . I'm happy every day I'm alive. Every day I wake up, it's a great day. I woke up. It beats not.

We had a guy who dismembered a young man's body, cut him up into eight sections, and put the pieces, in plastic garbage bags, in a garbage dumpster of the apartment building next to his.

The reason this guy got caught was he broke one of the first rules of urban living. There's like two major rules of urban living—number one: Don't park in somebody else's shoveled-out spot. And number two is: Don't throw your garbage in somebody else's garbage can. And he broke rule number two of urban living. He had taken his garbage and he had thrown it in somebody else's garbage can. The neighbors became incensed that somebody from this other building would throw his garbage in their building. And the janitor, early in the morning, was going to the garbage dumpster to check out what this guy had thrown in.

And he opened up the garbage and, lo and behold, what he found was the parts of this dismembered body. And he called the Chicago police.

The body parts were wrapped in two-tone plastic garbage bags; they were gray on the outside and black on the inside. We took the bags into the Crime Lab and Super-Glued them in the tank and developed both the inside and the outside of the bags. We found a lot of prints, but the one that was really interesting was the thumbprint on the *inside* of the bag that had I think the right thigh in it. Which means—how did that thumbprint get on the inside of that bag? Now, he said he went to the garbage can and touched stuff, which could account for his prints being on the outside, but this was *on the inside* of that bag. And the bag was tied and sealed.

They brought the body to the Crime Lab. We took it in the laser room and lased it for any latent fingerprints and for any type of trace material.

We went to the scene, too. We were looking for the victim's fingerprints. We figured since we had this Super-Glueing technique to lift prints and we'd tried it a couple of times on rooms . . . The chemical within Super Glue attaches to the water portion of a fingerprint (a fingerprint being composed of about 98 percent water) and sometimes it becomes visible, or it can become visible through use of a powder. We went to his house and we Super-Glued the whole bedroom, and we sealed everything up, around the doors and windows, with duct tape and masking tape, to keep as much of that vapor in as you can, and left it for twenty-four hours. We also did the same thing with the bathroom, same thing, sealed the whole thing up and put that Super Glue in the light bulb and everything—we used that light bulb; it's nothing more than a heating element that accelerates the Super Glue.

We left it there for twenty-four hours, came back, we purged the room—opened up the door, opened up the windows, got the Super Glue out—and then we went and powdered. We lifted the prints and brought them in. We found a hand print in the bedroom, but it didn't turn out to be anything. Same thing with the bathroom. We found some prints, but they weren't the victim's.

I'd say this case was an example of how insignificant things can become important. The big thing with this case was the poor kid, the dead guy, to connect him with the murderer. When we went to his apartment, he had cleaned up his apartment; he said, "Go ahead. You won't see any evidence."

Our people went in there—this was a rare instance where we took some of the people from the inner lab to the crime scene. They used a technique called Luminol, which when sprayed on an object, body fluids, blood, and some other elements do fluoresce. And all we had to do was go in there at night, black out all the windows, so there was no possibility of light coming in from the street, and then spray this material and it would fluoresce.

We were able to find minute specks of blood that couldn't be seen any other way on the walls and in the cracks of the tile and we saw some that were near the threshold of the bathroom door—we pulled up the threshold itself. He hadn't cleaned under there. And it was the victim's blood.

The whole premise of crime scene investigation is that anytime one person comes in contact with something else, they're going to leave some trace of themselves, or pick up a trace of the other material. There's always gonna be this transfer of material. That idea—that I can go into a crime scene and I know someone's been there because a crime has been committed—and there should be something there for me—it should be there. I've always liked that idea. It's like, you tell the dumbest policeman in the world: The offender is on that street corner, in that crowd of thirty people. You just have to look. Same thing with crime scenes. You just have to look in that crime scene.

*   *   *

One of my main things is going into a hardware store. Especially the old ones, that have the little wooden boxes filled with things. You walk into the hardware store and you pick something up—what do they use this thing for?—and there *is* something, it's used for something very important—gee, I never saw it before. You go over and you look at something else—I wonder what they use this thing for? And there's a logical answer for it. It's good to ask questions. It's good to wonder.

Crime Scene Investigation: Contributing Police Officers

SERGEANT ED ADORJAN, Area Six Violent Crimes. Adorjan worked Homicide for twenty-four years, as a supervising sergeant in Area Six Violent Crimes eleven years and before that, as a homicide detective in the old Homicide Unit. Adorjan joined the CPD in 1959, worked Vice and Gambling in Eighteen, was assigned to the CPD's first tactical unit in 1963, and became a homicide detective in 1967. Adorjan retired in 1991.

CAPTAIN THOMAS J. CRONIN, Fifteenth District. Cronin was selected by the CPD in 1985 to be trained in investigative profiling by the FBI's National Center for the Analysis of Violent Crime. Cronin joined the force in 1969, worked patrol in the Thirteenth District until 1971, when he became a crime analyst. In 1973, Cronin was promoted to detective and worked Robbery in Area Two for two years and Robbery in Area Five for two years. In 1977, Cronin made sergeant, in 1985, was promoted to lieutenant, and was promoted to captain in 1990. Cronin, who has a master's degree in social justice, is one of only twenty-seven FBI-trained police investigative profilers in the world.

OFFICER SIDNEY DAVIS, evidence technician, Eleventh District. Davis joined the CPD in 1983, and was assigned to the Seventh District, where he worked as a patrol officer for three years, and then as a patrol specialist, before joining the tac team. In 1990, Davis was assigned to the Eleventh District, where he serves on patrol and as an evidence technician.

OFFICER JIM DORAN, commanding officer, Criminalistics Sections, CPD Crime Lab. Doran, who has a bachelor's degree in biochemistry and a master's in social justice, started in the Crime Lab in 1969 as a civilian in the Microanalysis Section. In 1973, Doran became a police officer and was assigned to patrol in the Fourteenth District until 1979, when he returned to the Crime Lab. In 1982, Doran was assigned to a new Crime Lab unit, Laser Latent Fingerprint Development Section. In 1986, Doran became commanding officer of the Criminalistics Sections, including Serology, Microscopy Trace, Controlled Substance, Physical Chemistry, and Laser. In 1990, Doran took over the administration of the federal grant for the Illinois Criminal Justice Information Authority.

DETECTIVE BOB ELMORE, Area Six Violent Crimes. Elmore joined the CPD in 1977, worked patrol in Fourteen and Twenty-three for one and a half years, made detective in 1979 and was assigned to Area Six Robbery, and has been a Violent Crimes detective since 1981.

COMMANDER FRANK J. FLANAGAN, retired. Commander of Homicide, 1961–1970, Director of Chicago Crime Lab, 1970–1977, Chief Investigator, Medical Examiner's Office, 1977–1985. Capt. Flanagan headed Homicide longer than any commanding officer in the history of the CPD. His thirty-year career encompassed investigative work in the old Hit and Run Unit from 1947 to 1951, training in the Army Criminal Investigations Division, and working as a homicide detective from 1951 through 1961.

COMMANDER EMIL GIESE, retired. Giese served as commanding officer of the CPD's Fingerprint Unit from 1966 through July 1973, and has been a past chairman of the Fingerprint Subcommittee of the International Association for Identification. Giese's thirty-seven-year career in the police began with the old Park District Police in 1949 (which merged with the Police Department in 1959). In 1959, Giese was assigned as a fingerprint technician in the Bureau of Identification. In 1960,

Giese was promoted to sergeant; in 1961, Giese was promoted to lieutenant. Giese, as sergeant and lieutenant, was assigned to the Fingerprint Identification Section. After he served as commanding officer of the Fingerprint Unit from 1966 to 1973, Giese was watch commander in the Twentieth and Twenty-third Districts. In 1979, Giese became district commander of Twenty-three, where he served till his retirement in 1986.

DETECTIVE JIM GILDEA, Area Six Violent Crimes.
Gildea has been a robbery and homicide detective for the past thirteen years. Before that, Gildea spent eight and a half years working Special Operations and a year and a half on patrol. Gildea joined the police in 1966 as a cadet and went on patrol in 1969.

DETECTIVE SCOTT KEENAN, Area Six Violent Crimes. Keenan became a police officer in 1971, worked eight years on patrol in Twenty-three, spent one year in the Preventive Programs Divisions, became a detective in 1978, and was assigned to Area Five Burglary. In 1980, Keenan joined the Sex Crimes Unit. Keenan worked Area Six Violent Crimes from 1981 till 1989, when he was detailed to Detective Division Headquarters. In 1990, Keenan returned to Violent Crimes.

LIEUTENANT JIM NEMEC, commanding officer, Crime Scene Processing Unit, CPD Crime Lab. Nemec, who joined the CPD in 1965, has been with the Crime Lab since 1968, where he was an evidence technician for two years, worked with the Mobile Unit for eight years, and served as Crime Lab watch commander till 1985. Nemec has headed the Crime Scene Processing Unit since 1985.

SERGEANT TED O'CONNOR, Twenty-third District.
O'Connor was promoted to detective and assigned to Homicide three years after joining the force in 1967. O'Connor and Adorjan were partners in the old Homicide Unit, under Captain Flanagan, from 1973 to 1978. In 1978, O'Connor went undercover in an operation targeting Outfit-controlled

businesses, then joined the DEA Narcotics Task Force for five years. O'Connor then served as the Sex Crimes analyst for the CPD and as administrative aide to the Deputy Chief of Detectives. O'Connor was part of the Joint FBI/CPD Task Force investigating unsolved Mob hits from 1988 until his promotion to sergeant in 1990.

DETECTIVE CAREY ORR, Area Six Violent Crimes. Orr came on the CPD in 1978, was a patrol officer in Fifteen until 1980, when he was promoted to detective and assigned to Area Six Violent Crimes.

LIEUTENANT CINDY PONTORIERO, field lieutenant, Twenty-first District. Pontoriero, the first woman detective in the CPD, was assigned to Area Five Homicide in 1972, to Sex Crimes North in 1980, and to Area Five Violent Crimes in 1981. Pontoriero has twenty-three years on the force and seventeen years' experience as a Violent Crimes detective. After being promoted to sergeant, Pontoriero served as Area Six Sex Crimes Coordinator from 1985 through 1988. In January 1989, she was assigned to Detective Division Headquarters. Pontoriero joined the force as a policewoman in 1967. In 1990, she was promoted to lieutenant.

OFFICER THOMAS A. REYNOLDS, Crime Lab Mobile Unit technician. Reynolds joined the CPD in 1966 and was assigned to patrol in the Second District, where he served till 1970. In 1970, Reynolds became an evidence technician in the Task Force, which became part of the Criminalistics Division in 1975. In 1979, Reynolds became a Mobile Unit Technician.

SERGEANT TOM REYNOLDS, Gang Mission Team sergeant, Nineteenth District. Before being assigned to Nineteen in 1990, Reynolds served six years, from 1984 to 1990, as a sergeant in the Major Accident Investigation Unit. Reynolds was a detective for fourteen years prior to his promotion to sergeant in 1984: ten years as a robbery and burglary detective in

Areas Four, Five, and Six and four years (from 1980 to 1984) as a detective in the Office of Municipal Investigations. Reynolds joined the force in 1965.

DETECTIVE DAVE RYAN, Area Six Violent Crimes.
Ryan joined the CPD in 1977 and worked patrol in the Eighteenth District for three years. Ryan was promoted to detective in 1980, and worked in Area Two Property Crimes till 1982, when he was assigned to Area Six Violent Crimes.

DETECTIVE JAMES SPENCER, Area Six Violent
Crimes. Spencer has been on the force since 1971; he worked as a patrol officer in the Fifteenth District till 1973, and then was assigned to Special Operations in Areas Five and Six for seven years. Spencer has been in Area Six Violent Crimes since 1980.

DETECTIVE LAWRENCE THEZAN, Area Six Violent
Crimes. Thezan joined the force in 1973, worked patrol and tac in Twenty till 1975, then worked tac in Twenty-three and Twenty until he was promoted to detective and assigned to Violent Crimes in 1981.

DETECTIVE TONY VILLARDITA, Area Six Violent
Crimes. Villardita came on the force in 1978, worked in patrol in Twenty-three till he was promoted to Robbery detective in 1980, and has been with Area Six Violent Crimes since 1981.

MAJOR ACCIDENTS

An upright adult, a pedestrian, gets hit by a car. Often, they get knocked right out of their shoes. Literally. It's the whip effect. They're pulled so fast, that the body goes out of the shoes and the shoes stay right where they were on the pavement.

That's not just loafers; that's with laces. Even shoes with laces stay on the pavement. Even laced-up gym shoes. I've seen them where they're knocked out of their socks, too.

You go to the scene and you see their shoes and socks standing there. It can be a pretty accurate way of determining the point of impact.
CPD traffic specialist

You don't want to see us," says an accident reconstructionist in the CPD's Major Accident Investigation Section. "You don't want to see us. Because if you see us, you know you've had it. We're like the Grim Reaper."

They come to the scenes of all fatal accidents and to all SPIs (serious personal injuries) that have the probability of becoming fatals, and to the scene of all hit-and-runs: teams of traffic specialists and accident reconstructionists. They each bring their own tools: a Canon A-1 35mm, a couple of rolls of film, a good flash, a Polaroid camera, a hundred-foot fiberglass tape, a twenty-five-foot steel tape, and a "Measure Master," a device that can gauge distances up to a thousand feet. They bring an evidence kit for storing evidence that they pick up by hand: bits of debris, pieces of plastic, fibers, paint chips, grease gobs—the flotsam of vehicle wrecks and pedestrian accidents.

They've all been trained, with accident reconstructionists going on for more intensive study, in at-scene accident investigation, vehicle dynamics, cause analysis, the laws of conservation of energy and momentum, and the use of mathematical formulas to determine speed, point of impact, angle of impact—everything science can do to determine responsibility and guilt.

"What we use in accident investigation and reconstruction," says a CPD accident reconstructionist, "are the basic laws of physics, the basic laws of motion and conservation of energy. It's just simple laws of motion—if you hit something this way, it's gonna fall that way—we use it with vehicles, that's all. It's just black and white."

The science of accident investigation was developed in the thirties by an engineer, J. Stannard Baker. Baker wrote the classic in the field, the *Traffic Accident Investigation Manual*, and taught accident investigation and reconstruction for years at Northwestern University's Traffic Institute, the first and still the foremost center of traffic studies in the U.S., drawing police from all over the country and the world. "It's the Harvard of traffic schools," says one traffic specialist. Major Accident's traffic specialists and supervisors have all trained in Baker's accident investigation techniques, some of them in-house in the CPD Traffic Division, many of them at the Traffic Institute.

Major Accident cops usually work in teams of two, one traffic specialist watching out for the other, because they often process crime scenes with emergency vehicles cutting through, regular traffic streaming past, and pedestrians trying to get close to the area.

Samples from the scene, ranging from microscopic trace elements to hoods and grilles of cars, along with all of the victims' outer clothes, recovered from the hospital or the morgue, are sent to the Crime Lab for analysis. In some cases, Crime Lab evidence technicians assist at the scene. In all cases, photographs are taken, diagrams and measurements made, samples collected, witnesses interviewed, just as in a homicide investigation.

"Every fatal accident scene *should* be treated as a crime scene," says Lieutenant James Carroll, former commanding officer of Major Accident. For example, what appears to be an accident actually may be premeditated murder, with the driver wielding the vehicle as murder instrument. "It happens more often than people think," says one accident reconstructionist. Or it may be a case of reckless homicide, in which the driver's behavior before the accident leads directly to someone else's death. Or it may be a hit-and-run, the driver taking off, leaving the surviving family of the person killed to wonder if that person *might* have been saved if the driver hadn't panicked: "If somebody hits a child, and takes off," says a Crime Lab technician, "that person may have been the only one who could have *saved* that child's life by stopping and rendering first aid or calling for a paramedic. If they leave them there, and nobody notices, at night or on a deserted road or something, that kid could die before anybody even knows. That life could have been saved if the driver had stopped. That's about as close to murder as you can get as far as I'm concerned."

Whether or not the hit-and-run driver is discovered and successfully prosecuted, whether or not the charge of reckless homicide sticks, depends upon the tenacity and eye for detail of the Major Accident officers and Crime Lab techs, all of whom know that an entire case may hang upon a shard of glass, a paint chip, a single hair. . . .

When people say to me, "What type of accidents do you handle?" I say, "We handle people that are dead or wish they were."

I mean that in two ways: Either the person is grievously injured, or dying, so badly hurt they wish they were dead—or the person has just struck and killed a child, say, and wishes he was dead.

We end up with dual victims in a lot of these things. We've had ones where you see the driver of the car, he's in the hospital, and he finds out the eight-year-old kid he hit is dead and he just completely falls apart.

*   *   *

It's kind of a cold question that we ask a doctor before we send our people out to a scene. We don't respond to every accident, just the ones with the probability of death.

Say it's four o'clock on a Friday afternoon. And the beat guys call us up; they make the notification from the hospital and they say, hey, there's a guy in the hospital that got injured in an automobile accident.

So first of all, you're talking to a police officer. Police are beyond a doubt the worst medical authority you could ever have. Because it's always—worse. If they could make them deader than they already are, they would.

So the beat car notifies us from the hospital. That's when we get down to the cold question. We get the doctor, the nurse on the phone: "Doc, does this person stand a fifty percent or better chance of buying the farm as a result of this accident?" And if they say yes, we saddle the troops.

It's a chaotic scene. The ambulance, the fire department, tow trucks. When we respond, the district units are so glad to see us because we arrive on a scene that's in total chaos and we can say, "All right, we're gonna do this. We're gonna photograph these cars right now. We're gonna take these measurements. I want those officers to interview those witnesses over there. I want the Crime Lab notified." Bam bam bam bam bam—they know what they have to do.

We take a scene that's in utter chaos and we straighten it all out. We have to take charge. That's why we can't cry. We can't cry. Because when we get there, everybody looks to us, what should we do. You put all your emotions aside and go right in and do the work that has to be done.

I was a detective for fourteen years. I worked in the Robbery Section; I worked on a number of robbery-homicides.

I've seen a lot of bodies—I've seen a lot of people who've been shot, and stabbed, and murdered in a myriad of ways. But I'll tell you something. It's nothing compared to people when they're involved in automobile accidents. It's undoubtedly the goriest form of death. It really is. The most gruesome thing that can happen to someone happens to them in auto accidents. Or if they're pedestrian accidents—if they're struck with enough force, bodies break apart, they split in half—limbs fly off.

People that are shot—they're shot, what do you generally have? You have a gunshot wound and a lot of blood. A lot of shootings and killings are neatly packaged. Homicides, you don't get that many that are in pieces.

But take a look at what happens to people that are killed inside automobiles. Some of these people look like they come out of a goddamn Veg-O-Matic.

Motorcycles—we call them donorcycles. That's where the organ donors come from. I'll tell you—it's true. If you were to go out and talk to the harvest teams—harvest teams are the teams of doctors and nurses that fly into hospitals and harvest organs for people needing transplants—you know what they'd tell you? Motorcycles keep them in business. They are *donor*cycles.

Motorcyclists die, more often than not, from massive head trauma. Everything else—A-OK.

Whereas in a car, you get a lot of blunt internal trauma: the steering wheel will rupture the aorta, you'll have punctured lungs, torn left ventricle to the heart. . . . You sustain a tremendous amount of internal trauma in a car accident because you're bouncing around in it. You're in a motorcycle, you get launched, you come down, head first, case closed, you're dead, and the rest of you is pretty good.

There's no safety on a motorcycle. Without a helmet. *With* a helmet. But cyclists think the helmet gives them an immunity.

Would you wear a helmet, climb up to the fourth floor of a building, jump out, and land on your head with a helmet? Would you do that? It's about the same effect you would have driving down a street at fifty miles an hour and you hit the back of a car and . . . you get launched. And if you're going sixty-five miles an hour on the expressway, I don't care if you've got a body helmet, it's all over.

What a motorcycle does, it turns the human body into a projectile. It's like a slingshot. If the bike is traveling sixty miles an hour, you're traveling sixty miles an hour. If the bike stops, you go.

I think we see more children . . . and we see more innocent people killed than homicide dicks do. You know, in Homicide, you see a lot of people that are street people, dope dealers, pimps, whores—the proverbial term "dirt bag people"—as the victims of the crime. In Major Accident we see more . . . just the average Joe—children, wives, people's mothers—these are the people who are the victims of the auto accidents.

Children particularly. You see a lot of children as the victims, on their bicycles, crossing the street, dart-outs. A lot of people don't realize that the leading cause of deaths of children are accidents. Auto accidents.

It seems the innocent people are the ones who get killed. Every police officer I know feels this way and I'm one of them: The drunk driver who causes the accident always walks away. Now, nationwide statistics don't bear this out, but they're taking into account every single accident, country roads, deserted roads. . . .

One of the most serious accidents that I've seen was the Dan Ryan case, where five members of a family burned to death on a Sunday morning when they were rear-ended by a drunk driver. The person charged in that case, a guy by the name of Timothy something, not a scratch. Not a scratch on old Timmy.

You might go to a scene and find the drivers in both cars are dead. Or the cars have been towed away. And you have no eyeball witnesses. You *still* want to know, How did this happen?

Or you've got a car crash and that guy is dead, and this guy's alive. The guy who made it is not gonna say, "Yeah, it's all my fault." He's gonna say, "This guy ran the red light and struck me." People lie. A lot. You're gonna go back to him and say, "If you had the green light, why did you leave thirty feet of skid marks before you entered the intersection?"

*   *   *

A very poor, a *very* poor source of information is witnesses. In accidents—or any crime.

Very few people ever see an auto accident. They don't witness the accident. Say you have a person crossing the street. It's highly unlikely that anyone is watching that person cross the street—everybody's going about their business. That person gets hit by a car. With so-called eyewitnesses, the first thing they're gonna hear is the skidding of tires, the screeching of brakes—or somebody screams, or they hear a crash, or a thud, and they turn around and look.

If the striking vehicle is continuing on, the *next* vehicle coming down the street may appear to be the one that hit the victim. And the witness is gonna say, "That's the car that hit him."

Or with a two-car collision, when you ask them, "Did you see the accident?" "Oh, yes. I saw the whole thing." They didn't see *anything*. An accident begins and stabilizes within a matter of seconds. So they saw what they saw after they turned around.

The hardest part about that is, in collisions with automobiles, more often than not—the classic example is a head-on accident—the vehicles turn around and end up pointing in the opposite direction from where they came; it's the laws of motion, unless it's a perfectly centered hit, which you very rarely see. But in most head-ons, the vehicles are hit, and they'll spin around so someone will hear that crash, they'll turn around and they'll look, and they'll see one car going west and one car going east and say, "Oh, yeah. I saw them. That car was going east"—and the direct opposite happened.

Even with what you think would be reliable witnesses, what you see and what you think you see are two different things. With an accident, your attention has to be attracted by something—rarely do you *watch* an accident occur. It's extremely rare to get a witness who was looking at the street and saw the whole accident developing.

You never discount a witness, though. It might be the one time you find that little old lady sitting in a window watching the street. This is what homicide dicks are fond of talking about—you know the old thing, "Go knock on doors. Find somebody that was watching the street"—we had one Homicide commander famous for that. Boy, did he believe in little old ladies. Those little old ladies are getting harder to find.

With a pedestrian hit-and-run, the victim never sees the guy who runs him over. If you've got a car coming at you, you're not gonna be looking to see who's driving; you're gonna be looking at that front bumper, thinking how do I get out of the way. And it usually happens so fast that the victim, if they survive, can't even tell you the color of the car.

This might sound bizarre, but I think if you have ten people that've witnessed an incident, it's my theory that it's one in ten, a ten percent chance, you're gonna deal with a 24-carat kook that's gonna tell you something that's so off-the-wall, doesn't make any sense at all, but what it does—it screws you up. Sometimes those kooks can be very convincing and they can tell you some shit that's just totally believable and it'll take you four hours before you finally realize and . . . "Get him or her *out* of here." You know, they were five blocks away, but they come up, "I saw the whole thing and the man was in a blue Chevrolet and I can give you his description. . . ."

I'm serious. One out of ten people you talk to is nuts. We see it in accidents all the time.

Often we get people who say, "I saw the car. It was a blue Chevy and here's the license plate number." But we can't arrest a car. We have to be able to positively identify who was driving the vehicle. So it's often frustrating for the public—"What do you mean? I gave you the color and make. I gave you the license number—What?" We can't arrest the car. We have to identify the driver.

It'd be the same thing with an armed robbery in a bank. Somebody sees the getaway car. But unless we can prove he's the guy who pulled the trigger, we've got to find other ways.

You need some evidence that can't be refuted. If the fire department pulls somebody out with chest injuries, and the steering wheel's collapsed, we'll say, yeah, he must have been driving because he couldn't get those injuries any other way.

You don't have to have even one witness saying, "I saw that driver." All you need is physical evidence.

Physical evidence is where it's at. The classic line is: "Physical evidence speaks for itself."

We had a case—fellow was married, had a girlfriend, left his wife, was living with the girlfriend, was fooling around on the girlfriend with another girlfriend. Girlfriend number one is following him around; he's going out to girlfriend number two's house.

She's waiting there; he comes out. She gets out of her car and confronts him, calls him all kinds of names. He claims that during the course of the argument with her, the car bumped into gear and he rolled over and accidentally hit her, killing her.

It was written up as an automobile accident. Two of our officers were able to work the case up, show that what he said did not coincide with the physical evidence of how the tires were turned, how the blood spattered up underneath the wheel, and they were able to establish that this guy actually ran over her.

We can take facts from the road that will absolutely eliminate or disprove any story the offender might tell. The laws of physics are absolute.

We did a reconstruction on an accident where the car left a hundred and ten feet of skid marks before it slid through a stop sign, striking another vehicle, killing the other driver. Now, the skid marks were laid down on the wrong side of the street. From the length of the skid mark, it was not possible that he was traveling at less than forty-five miles an hour. He was in a forty-mile-per-hour zone. Realistically, he was probably doing fifty-five.

Armed with that, we go to the state's attorney and we say, "From the skid mark, we know he was driving on the wrong side of the road, he ran the stop sign, and he was going too fast."

Now we have the elements for reckless homicide. From a skid mark.

There's an equivalent to fingerprints in accident investigation and that's damage to the vehicle—point of impact, angle of impact—and marks in the road, meaning tire marks in the road.

I can go to the scene of an accident, and see things that other people can't see. Just the street can tell you things. I might see the point of maximum engagement of the vehicles by gouge marks in the road—when two vehicles hit and the impact just forces them down into the pavement, the underparts of the vehicles hit the ground and they'll actually dig out part of the asphalt.

Say it's a question of who was on the right side of the road. I say I was on my side of the road and you say you were on your side. Well, if the gouge marks are on your side of the road, that's where the accident happened. You can bring in a thousand witnesses and they all say, "No, no, it was on the other side" and all I have to do is say here's the photograph, here's the measurement, it's on that side of the road. It speaks for itself.

You can also determine the point of impact by looking for scrub marks in the road, what we call a collision scrub. The car is moving forward or sliding forward in a skid, or whatever—when it is hit, and knocked in a sideways direction, you get that real heavy black mark. That shows us where that wheel was at the point of impact. It can show you where the car was, exactly, at impact, because that locates the tires for you.

You can look at skid marks, when the tire is just sliding, and determine speed. The weight of a vehicle has no effect on its slide-to-stop distance. If a Volkswagen and a Greyhound bus were traveling side by side, let's say at forty-five miles an hour, and if both drivers jammed on their brakes, the Greyhound bus and the Volkswagen would both slide to a stop at the same distance.

You can look at yaw marks, these are marks where the tires were both sliding and rolling and you know, say, that the guy was going down the street at sixty miles an hour and made a hard left without hitting the brakes—the car's gonna veer off. Yaw marks show the guy was exceeding the critical speed of the curve.

You can look at a pile of dirt in the road and determine the point of impact. If you have a head-on, the dirt and filth and rust on the underside of the car will fall off at the point of impact.

Damage to the vehicle can tell a great deal about the accident, either with another vehicle or with a pedestrian.

With any rider, you're gonna have damage to the car interior. Especially in a head-on—you get hit head-on, you're going forty-five and they're going forty-five, it's like you're hitting a wall at ninety miles an hour. Collapsed wheel, smashed dashboard, broken windshield.

You can tell the movements of the driver or the occupants in the collision phase. In a head-on, for example, anytime the head goes into the windshield, the chest goes into the steering wheel and the wheel can sever the aorta. I've seen steering wheels bent in half by the force of going into someone's chest.

The importance of knowing what injuries are caused in what position in the vehicle is if there's some dispute about who was driving. If you have one passenger who says he wasn't driving, but there's severe contact damage to the interior of the windshield behind the steering wheel, and he's got a very bad head injury and the other person doesn't, you can place the injured person as the driver.

If it's an upright adult pedestrian hit by a car, you look for damage to the top of the grille, the front of the hood, the top of the hood, and the windshield, because they get thrown over the car. With trucks and vehicles like trucks, it's under.

With cars, it's up and over. You will land on the hood and hit the windshield. You go under the car if you're a child, usually, or if you're falling. It's like tackling in football, it depends on your center of mass.

You fit this with the injuries to the pedestrian, too. An upright adult will invariably have a broken hip, ribs, shoulder, and a skull fracture, or a terrible laceration to the skull area.

* * *

What's amazing is the amount of damage that a human body can cause to a vehicle. I've always found it amazing that hitting a human being, with our soft skin, causes so much damage to a car. A tremendous amount of damage. The front of the car will be crinkled. The windshield will be cracked. Broken headlights. Plus contact damage where the steel part of the vehicle will actually be pushed in.

We handled a reckless homicide where a bicyclist got struck in the rear and he was thrown back onto the hood of the car and then his head hit the roof of the car and put a two-foot deep U-shaped dent in the roof where the roof line meets the windshield line. Knocked it right in just from his head.

You take a two-hundred-pound bag of sand, throw it over a car going forty miles an hour, see what happens.

Physical evidence shows you what happened. And *lack* of physical evidence also shows you what happened—no skid marks, no debris can also indicate something—like *not* trying to stop.

Let me put it this way. If I'm mad at you and I want to kill you, and I run you over with a car and stop—it's pretty difficult to prove that I murdered you. You have to show motive and everything else. Every accident scene should be approached as a potential homicide scene.

A lot of the hit-and-runs now involve dope dealers. You get two dope dealers having a conversation; one's standing at the window, talking to the guy in the car. He walks away from the car, walks down the street; the guy parked down the street starts the car and takes off, hits the guy and keeps on going. And it's no accident.

A woman's body was found in an alley, underneath a fire escape. This was an alley behind a retirement home.

Area Six handled it as a death investigation originally. The body went to the Medical Examiner's Office and a doctor there came to the conclusion that this was in fact an automobile accident. And he came to this conclusion due to the fact that he classified the fractures to her lower legs as "bumper fractures" caused, naturally, by the bumper of the vehicle.

The guy I do quite a lot of work with and I took quite an interest in this and together we started an investigation.

We picked up the building manager of this retirement home to identify the body at the morgue. When we went to the morgue, the manager identified the body and then we looked at the body. And the fractures, so-called bumper fractures, were about three inches above the ankle bone. So I looked at my partner and my partner looked at me and I said, "Bumper fractures?" I said. "How many Indy race cars or Lamborghinis were going through that alley?"

So now we're certain that this was not an automobile accident. She had to jump. When you . . . splat . . . you know, it's different if you take a pancake and you flip it in the air and it hits, or if you take the pancake and *slide* it—again, it's the laws of physics.

Now we ask for the Crime Lab pictures when the dicks did their investigation before the body was removed. And her pants legs, the old-style, wide-bottom pants, they were pushed up, which wouldn't be consistent with a car accident. You have to think what caused those pants to pull up.

So we picked up the manager of the retirement home again so she could let us in this woman's apartment. Nothing was disturbed. We're talking to the building manager—because we're thinking suicide, suicide, suicide—and she's saying, "Oh no, she was very happy. There was no reason why . . ."

So we continued on in the investigation. Her only living relatives were a sister-in-law and niece. We go out there and tell the sister-in-law we're doing the follow-up investigation. "Yeah, it's a shame. I heard she got hit by a car." The sister-in-law's daughter comes out and asks, "Why are you here?" "Well we're here on so-and-so." "Oh yeah, well, she finally did it." And I said, "She finally did what?" "Well, she finally did it." I said, "What do you mean, she has a history of . . . ?" "History?! She tried to hang herself, she swallowed poison. . . . What else did she try, Mom?" And obviously, this girl's mother did not want us knowing all this.

Well now, you talk about lights and sirens going off. So, armed with all this information, we again went back to the Medical Examiner and he stood by his claim. Because naturally doctors know everything. Just like policemen.

You know, when I first went into Traffic twenty years ago, an old-timer told me, he said, "You're gonna be handling a lot of accidents. Get out and look at these cars. For a long time, you won't even know what you're looking at. But after a while, with experience, piecing everything together, things are going to start fitting together."

At first, you just don't know what it is. And this doctor, not having the experience or whatever, didn't know what he was looking at. But when we looked at the body and the photos, I said, "This isn't an accident." It just wasn't consistent with everything else that I've seen for twenty years. The way this one ended up, the homicide dicks reclassified it as a suicide.

The big problem we have is—we want to preserve the scene. And people want to clean it up for us, especially if it's grisly and horrible.

An accident scene, to a novice, it appears like—whoa—we better sweep the street, or wash it down. The fire department will come out, and if there's oil or gas on the street, they'll wash it down. They've just washed away evidence. The attitude that this is an accident, not a crime, prevails.

Look at it this way. If you came upon the scene of an ax murder, where somebody chopped somebody up, the Detective Division that handles a homicide would go crazy if somebody came and washed the scene down and put the body parts in a bag or something.

If there's a clear and apparent danger to the safety of people around, if there's gasoline leaking from a ruptured gasoline tank—of course. The safety of the general public and the people that are around takes precedence. I agree. But I mean, I've had them where there's like a drip of gasoline, they call for a wash-down. They call for a wash-down; what they forget is there's a lot of evidence goes right down that city sewer.

When we get back from the scene, sometimes we do what they call a "thrust diagram." It's done rarely. Most of the time, you know what happened. By the combination of all the evidence: physical evidence, witnesses. The thrust diagram is for when you *don't* know, when it's still a mystery.

Say you've got two vehicles in a right-of-way accident—in these the position of the two vehicles is very important—but let's say you can't tell the position from any marks in the roadway, or the vehicles have spun off from each other, so the scene can't tell you what happened. And maybe both drivers are dead, and you can't tell from the scene, or from witnesses, how it happened.

The thrust diagram will show the position these vehicles were in at the time they struck, at maximum engagement, they call it, when they were stuck together the fullest. That will tell you where they were in location to one another.

You take the photographs from the scene and draw little shapes for the vehicles, like rectangles, and jagged lines on the rectangles indicating the damaged portions. You match them—you put them side by side on the diagram, or you can cut them out. Let's say you've got two cars, one has damage on the front end, the other has damage on the right side. You don't have to be a physics major to realize that if one of the vehicles has damage on the right side, then the thrust must have come probably from the other direction, from the car with the damage on the front end.

You've got either centered thrust or eccentric thrust in a collision. Centered thrust is easy, and rare, even in a head-on. A perfect head-on collision is rare. If that is the case, one vehicle just pushes the other one straight back; neither one of them rotates.

Eccentric thrust gives you problems. It just means off-center. That's when you get rotation of vehicles; they rotate around the center of mass. So the vehicles end up spinning off and facing in opposite directions from where they came. To the layman, it would look like the struck car was the striking car—and they'd have the guilty person as the victim and the victim as the offender.

Many times, when you have an accident, one of the greatest things is if you have a fracture match. In other words, you have a piece of chrome here and another piece of chrome here—one was left at the scene—you find the car and you put it together with what was left at the scene and it's a perfect fracture match. We've had that with paint too. Paint chip here, paint chip there, you put it together and you have a fracture match.

That's very important. What it means is, the law of probability for any two pieces of material fracturing at that precise angle is astronomical. So what you're talking about is two pieces that at one time were one and the same piece. One was found at the scene and one was found on the car. And that's especially important for solving hit-and-runs.

Once you've gone out to the scene and taken those figures and measurements and collected the evidence, talked to any witnesses, then the next day—or a year from now—you can reconstruct that accident.

We had one going back five years. A beat car arrested a guy for urinating in the alley. While he was in police custody, he said, "Listen. I got something I gotta tell you. I was a passenger in a car and this guy hit a little girl five or six years ago." The driver was drag racing—this little girl, nine or ten years old, she was with either her grandma or her aunt, stepped off the curb, and was struck by this car and killed.

Here are these two beat officers—this guy and his statement could have been totally overlooked, but they took it upon themselves to pay attention. So many super-major crimes have been solved by some little, insignificant detail that beat cops paid attention to. Routine police work. So here's this wino taking a piss in the alley and he starts talking—gee, maybe we oughta see if this is legit. And they did, they called us, and brought him down.

We still had the reconstruction from five years before. A piece of grille had been found at the scene.

We went and arrested the guy who was driving; he worked in a factory. What was amazing—he couldn't even remember the name of the street where he killed the girl. Didn't even know where he was.

And what was kind of unbelievable, this guy still had the car, never repaired the car—the car still had the damage on it from all the years before, from striking the pedestrian. It's amazing. People kill people every day in the city of Chicago and they get away with it. And you arrest them one or two years later, and they still have the gun, or the car, that did it.

In this case, we had a piece of grille that we had inventoried at the scene and it matched up with the car that the offender still had—it was a perfect fracture match.

So we had the guy, we had the evidence—a perfect fracture match—and we had the perfect eyewitness: the guy who was sitting in the front seat of the car at the time of the accident, knew the guy who did it, and was willing to testify. That makes for a pretty good case.

The only thing we didn't have was a timely arrest. The statute of limitations had run on that case. It's three years for reckless homicide. And the state's attorney tried like hell to get around it: he took the position that a reckless homicide fell under the homicide statute and there should be no statute of limitations.

He tried it. He gave it one hell of a shot, I'll give him that. But the court disagreed. He took it up on appeal and the appeals court upheld the lower court.

Subsequently, the guy beat the case. And he beat it by the statute of limitations. This guy fled the scene of a fatal once and he walked away again after he was finally caught.

Most accidents that we see are just that, accidents. Nobody leaves their house with the idea in their mind that they're going to commit a traffic accident and kill someone. It's a motiveless crime. And I think that enhances the tragedy because it leaves a lot of people standing there saying, "Why? Why did this happen?"

And it's awful hard to try to explain to the victims' families that, in the majority of cases, that's all it is. It's an accident.

And in a lot of cases, the person who caused the accident—the wrong-doer—feels just as bad as the victim's family.

The one that I remember was—one sergeant, an old-timer, after he heard about this, he said, "You know, I've been on this job a long time and you think you get hardened to these things but . . ."

It was on Mother's Day. And there was a flower-garden shop out on Pulaski and Southwest Highway. So the father takes his kids out to buy a plant for Mother's Day. They're walking through the lot, and the youngest boy wants to carry the plant; you know, "Let me carry Mommy's plant." So here they go walking through the parking lot.

Now, there's a guy in a parked car, ready to back out of his parking space. So he's looking in his rearview mirror and he sees the father walk by, and the other kids, one or two or whatever, because they're tall enough to be seen. But now, here comes the littlest one carrying the plant. Well, he doesn't see him. Puts the car in reverse and runs right over him and kills him.

The driver of the car is crying, the father's crying; I mean, I'm almost crying. The father's blaming himself, the driver's blaming himself. Like we say, they're either dead or wish they were. It works both ways.

I was driving down the Kennedy in my own car one time, going home. I was in the first lane, that's the lane all the way to the right. And I saw this young man, standing on the shoulder of the road. I've seen people standing on the shoulder before, but you usually also see a vehicle on the shoulder that they're having trouble with—it's a flat tire, or it's out of gas, or something.

As I passed him, I noticed that there was no car. I looked in the rearview mirror; I couldn't see a car back or front. So I drove past, and I thought, "This is very strange."

And about two or three hundred feet behind me was a big truck. So I looked in the rearview mirror—and I saw him leap—from—the shoulder of the road right in front of the truck.

The truck pulled over. I pulled over. And I waited for the
police to arrive and I gave them a verbal statement. I wanted
them to know that this wasn't the truck driver's fault. Later on,
it was learned that the young man had just killed his mother.
So he committed suicide.

And you know what scared me? This poor truck driver was so
distraught, the accident was not his fault, no way, but still he had
to become involved in it, to live with that all of his life.

This man was so distraught. He said, "Please, I didn't do it. I
didn't mean to do it." This poor truck driver was crying. I just
felt angry about it. I felt, Why did he have to do this? Now this
trucker's gonna have to live with this. This poor truck driver was
just crying.

Not too long ago, we handled a case, a little boy run over by a
school bus. This young boy was being dropped off by the school
bus.

What happened was, every day, this kid would get off the bus
and he would walk down the south side of the street. The reason
being was that he went to the baby-sitter's house because his ma
worked.

This particular day, the mother didn't go to work. So he was
gonna go home, on the other side of the street. The driver
dropped the kid off and just didn't see him because that kid
never goes in front of the bus; he always goes over—and he
pulled away. He struck this young boy and killed him; the
wheels ran over his head. The mother witnessed the whole
thing. She was standing there. She knew what time the bus
dropped the kid off, so she was standing on the front porch.
She saw the whole thing.

It was just a gruesome sight, a gruesome thing. In fact, of all
the jobs that I've handled where you see brain matter, this, in
the street, was ninety-five percent of his brain. The way the tires
went over his head it just squished out his brain. And the mother
saw this whole thing.

But the thing about it, what amazed me—the mother, I guess
you could call it the mother love for her child—she insisted on
being with that kid in the hospital. She was sitting in the room,

holding the child's hand. And, not trying to be real gruesome, but that kid's head was as flat as a knife.

I sat with her. And I was having a hard time accepting—being a parent myself, I think to myself, I don't think I'd want to see my child like that. But obviously she had another way of viewing it—that she was going to be with him because she was his mother.

There are accidents that get to your heart. There'll be something that will bother you. You'll see that one face—and I don't know what it is, but something goes right to your heart. I've seen police officers cry. I think all of us cry at one time or another. A lot of policemen cry. There's nothing wrong with that. We don't want to become hardened.

But—when we go to these scenes—there's so much destruction and so much chaos, and everybody looks to us to kind of take control of it. But if we cry, how can we do that? So maybe we cry inside.

Kids are the worst. The saddest part is, life has just started for them and now it's over. Usually because of impatience—somebody has to get from point A to point B in a hurry.

I don't know how you cope with it. I go home and look at the kids and thank God for every day I got them. Because I know I don't have the right to think that they're all gonna be there tomorrow. It's happened to other people. It can happen to me.

Policemen have a notorious reputation for being callous. I think a lot of that is Acting 101. They put on the mantle of this callous attitude so that they don't fall apart.

Probably the biggest escape mechanism that policemen have emotionally is humor. Gallows humor.

I can't remember all the facts, but we were at a hospital once and the victim was unusually tall. Well, stretchers aren't made for tall victims. And he was dead, and as they were carrying him out, I mean, he's like—his head is hanging off one end and his feet are hanging off the other end. When they set him down, his head hits the pavement and stuff like that.

The policemen there were making any type of joke that you could imagine about a tall person on a stretcher. Some people who were there, I guess, friends or acquaintances of the victim, they weren't too thrilled with it. I forget who made the comment but it was true. We said, "Listen, if we weren't laughing about it, we might be crying about it." And that's true.

We had a fatal once that was sort of tragicomic. We got a call of an SPI [Serious Personal Injury] at Cook County Hospital. We go to the trauma unit, located on the third floor.

So we walk inside the door, ask who's there.

In this case, there's a crowd. They're all sad. They're all crowded around this one table. Tony's gurgling his last.

Story we got is he was hit, as a pedestrian. We go back to the scene; we're out in the middle of the street measuring. We start looking around for witnesses.

There's one old woman standing in the doorway. I go over, start talking to her, "See it?" She said, "I was sitting in my window. Poor Tony. They were always picking on him." "What happened?" She says, "They made him lay down in the street."

We went at it the next day and it took quite a bit to sort out what happened, but in a nutshell: Tony and his buddies were out on Grand Avenue when this TV station's Minicam pulled up, parked their van, and went over to the hot dog stand on the corner.

These guys all got the idea—"Tony, you lay down in the street, play dead; we'll get the Minicam to take your picture."

They went over to where the Minicam operators were in the hot dog joint and Tony laid down in the street. The Minicam guys kind of shook off Tony's buddies.

In the meantime, here comes Louis tooling down the street. Never saw Tony. It was a real misty night, anyway, and Tony's just laying on the ground in the eastbound lanes. Snags him, scoops him up, Tony's on the undercarriage of the car, the guy thinks he's hooked a piece of card-board—that's what he told us, he thought he was dragging a cardboard box.

So Louis's car drags Tony down the street and around the corner.

Tony's buddies run after Louis and get him to stop. And by this time the guy realized he had something under there he wasn't going to shake off, so he was gonna stop anyway. Tony's buddies start trying to jack up the car to get Tony out.

Now the Minicam has a newsworthy event. They come out and start to set up their lights. Tony's pals are pissed; now they *don't* want Tony on TV—out come the tire arms, they start busting up the Minicam. Started out as a prank, trying to get the Minicam to take their picture, and it ended up for real.

I think the hardest part of the job is when you have to go up and ring that doorbell.

They're taken by surprise—most of the victims, almost all of the victims, were coming home from work, going to the store. . . . They just said goodbye to them and now they'll never see them again. It's always hard to lose someone, but I think it's extra hard to lose someone so suddenly.

And there's very little we can do or say. Except just be there. Offer them help, drive them somewhere, call someone, call a priest, call a family member.

They want to know how it happened. "Tell me how it happened. Tell me." Mostly that. "Tell me how it happened."

Everybody talks about what causes an accident. Like there's one single cause of an accident. Well, that isn't true, with the exception of a very small minority of accidents. There's a multiple factor of things that cause an accident.

In other words, if going through a red light caused an accident, then anybody who went through a red light would cause an accident. Going through the red doesn't cause the accident. It's going through the red coupled with a lot of other things. That's what's kind of bad with accident reporting—cause of accident: red light. The real cause may have been the person wasn't paying attention—he went through the red light, the car that struck him was going over the speed limit—I mean, there's just multiple factors.

* * *

You know the expression, "There goes an accident waiting to happen"? It's true. You'll be behind somebody going home, you'll see he's drunk, he's all over the road, you say, "There goes an accident . . ." So if he does get involved in an accident, you saw him maybe twenty miles prior. The accident was, in fact, beginning to happen long before he ever got to the accident site.

Again, talking about cause analysis people—they might say the accident happened when he was in the bar drinking and consciously made up his mind that "I know I'm drunk but I'm gonna drive anyway."

A lot of people think that an accident happens when both vehicles touch one other. An accident happens long before that.

I mean, I have a green light; I see you start to go through the red light. Now the accident is happening. I have to decide what am I going to do? You may not know you're going through a red light, so now all of a sudden you see me—now what are you going to do? So the accident starts long before the vehicles actually meet.

There are some cause analysis people who say an accident starts to happen the moment you leave your house.

The most serious reckless homicide case I ever handled was a case-in-point of—When does an accident start happening? It ended up with two people struck and killed in their car, a nurse and an attorney, they had just started dating, and they're killed in their car when this woman comes at them like a bat out of hell.

When did the accident begin? According to witnesses, a husband and wife were arguing in a bar. This woman and her husband owned an import-export business on the Gold Coast. They left work and went across the street to a restaurant and they were in the bar. They were arguing.

Then they both went to the nearby garage to pick up the car. The husband was behind the wheel and, I guess, they were arguing—"You had too much to drink," "You're drunk"—the wife pushed him over; she got behind the wheel. She floored the gas and just took off. She killed two people: a nurse, she was the head of the cardiac recovery unit at Grant Hospital, and a lawyer, he had his own firm. They were traveling in a Toyota, northbound on State. The offender was driving a Nissan west on Chestnut. The Nissan struck the Toyota on the right side, causing it to flip over onto its roof; it ended up facing in an easterly direction—it started on fire and became totally engulfed in flames. It lay under a canopy of a high-rise apartment building; in fact the canopy sustained fire damage from the Toyota. The offender and her husband were treated and released for minor injuries—the woman stayed in the hospital two days.

We've noticed this time and again. The people who are in the striking vehicle always seem to fare better than the people who are struck. The poor jamoke who is going down the street doing thirty miles an hour and gets broadsided by the guy that's doing seventy-five—the guy that's doing seventy-five tends to walk away more than the guy doing thirty.

I was the supervisor at the scene. We closed State Street, closed it from Pearson to Walton. It wasn't a weekend, it was like a Wednesday or a Thursday. Traffic specialists are out there climbing all over the cars—they're taking photographs, they're taking measurements, gathering evidence—this turned out to be one of the biggest reckless homicide trials we've had.

I got a lieutenant from Eighteen; he looks at me, he walks up—"Are you the Major Accident sergeant?" "Well, yes I am." He says, "You've got *State Street* closed here—how long are you gonna keep it closed?" "Until my men are through doing their investigation." Five minutes go by, he's back at me again, when am I gonna . . . ? Finally, I told him. I said, "Lieutenant, for years, we've closed State Street about twenty times a year for every goddamn parade you could ever think of. What's the problem?" And you know, when you finally tell them like that, once in a while it sinks in. This was a crime scene.

We charged her with reckless homicide. Now, this was a tragic car accident. No one said that she did this intentionally, but in reckless homicide, intent does not enter in. The charge of reckless homicide is pretty cut-and-dried. All it states is you operated your vehicle in a manner that was likely to cause death or great bodily harm. And she did.

So we know *how* the accident happened. We know that. Now we're into *why* it happened. The drinking, the argument—they weren't thinking clearly, she was gonna *show* him.

This woman's defense was sudden acceleration and faulty brakes. We concluded it was pedal misapplication—she stepped on the gas instead of the brake. None of the witnesses who observed that car traveling at a high rate of speed saw brake lights go on on that car when her car was approaching the one with the victims. However, when we examined the offender's car immediately after the accident, the brake lights worked just fine. That leads me to believe she never touched the brakes. But that was her defense. It was a totally bogus defense.

She knows it's bogus, because she was the one who came up with it. *We* know it's bogus. And now the National Highway Safety Council has come out with a study that *shows* that that defense is bogus—their study says there is no vehicle sold in the U.S. whose braking system cannot override its acceleration system. You can try it—if you press the brake at the same time you're on the gas pedal, the brakes are going to override the gas.

There were just too many red flags in that defense. How come this only happens when someone is dead? Why aren't there a whole group of people saying, "Gee, I backed into another car, I caused seventy-five dollars damage," or "I hit a shopping cart, it must have been sudden acceleration syndrome." You get it in reckless homicide cases because they realize the degree they screwed up and that they better come up with a good story for it.

She had a bench trial presided over by one of the few judges people in Cook County voted not to retain. She was found not guilty. We could sit here all day and try to figure out what the reasoning was behind this decision. There's a classic line that kind of says it all: "Nobody ever said you should base legal precedent on Cook County court decisions."

We had four people killed on account of an unsigned Valentine. This truck driver and his girlfriend went out on a date for

Valentine's Day. She had parked her car, and she was with him in his truck, which was a semitractor, it didn't have the trailer on it. He evidently gave her a Valentine's Day card and she got all upset that he hadn't signed it.

So she got out of the truck and jumped into a taxicab. The cabdriver said the trucker started chasing them down the street, and when he saw him coming, he pulled the cab over to the right. This guy then went right through the light with his truck. And he struck a car broadside, killing the people inside the vehicle.

They were two couples, three teenagers and a twenty-five-year-old, out on a Valentine's Day date. These people were just driving, they had the right-of-way, they had the green light, and this guy was just so involved in his emotion over really nothing that he killed them—it was willful and wanton disregard for human life.

He abandoned the truck at the scene. We knew he'd come back; those trucks are very expensive, so we had a beat car waiting for him. The next morning, about eight in the morning, he came back to the scene and the beat officers grabbed him.

We charged him with four counts of reckless homicide, drunken driving, running a red light, and driving too fast for conditions. He was pursuing somebody down the street with a sixteen-thousand-pound semi, he ran a red, and killed four people—I'd call that reckless homicide.

There's something the cause analysis people call "the first harmful effect." That's the first thing that ultimately leads to the accident. In other words, if you're going down the street and you hit a hole and you lose control of your car and get in an accident, the first harmful effect was your hitting that hole. With this trucker, the first harmful effect was his anger.

Ninety-five percent *plus* of accidents are caused by human error. I would even go as far as to say ninety-nine percent, but ninety-five percent is the accepted statistic. Vehicle defect as the cause of accidents is like the old example of convoluted thinking that wet streets cause rain. It's like going to an accident and saying, "Look at how damaged this car is. You know, every time I see a car damaged like this, it's in an accident. I'll bet that's what's causing it!" It's convoluted thinking. But common sense and logic have to enter into this scenario somewhere along the line.

When you talk about how ninety-five percent of accidents are caused by human error, people say, "No, no, no. It's been established and there have been cases . . ." That's a lot of shit. What it is is, there's been a lot of people filing lawsuits and they try to present a case for mechanical error. When in doubt, sue the manufacturer.

Human error—driver attitude—is *the* leading cause of accidents. It's not mechanical failure—oh, no—mechanical failure accounts for less than five percent of accidents. That fact is mentioned very rarely by defense attorneys.

Like, for example, an unprotected intersection is an intersection where there are no signs or signals regulating traffic. So at that intersection, the vehicle on the right has the right-of-way.

Now, what I used to tell people when we got those—I'd ask them, "Can I speak freely?" Because each one would be blaming the other one. I'd say, "It takes two . . . mopes to have an accident at an unprotected intersection. One mope doesn't do it. Because one mope, not paying attention, is gonna go, speed right through, and I'm gonna see him and stop. Or vice versa. It takes *two* mopes. It takes this guy saying I don't care, I'm not slowing down, and this guy, I don't care, I'm not slowing down, to crash into one another. It's not a one-mope accident. It's a two-mope."

A lot of times little kids—we call them dart-out accidents—they just dart out between parked cars, and the parents—I mean, there may be some negligence on their part and they realize it. So they turn their anger on the person who's driving down the street, basically minding his own business. If you're driving along, twenty, twenty-five miles an hour, some little kid runs out from between two parked cars, there's really nothing you can do.

*   *   *

Accident analysts talk about the point of perception, the point of possible perception, and the point of no escape. And very often, the point of no escape happens *before* the point of possible perception. In other words, there's no hope. Many times, before you even perceive that the accident is going to happen, there is no escape.

Everyone thinks you're gonna get a warning. Everyone thinks all right, I'm gonna see the car and I'll take evasive action. I'm gonna be able to avoid this. I'm gonna be . . . Mario Andretti and I'm gonna drive around whatever comes up. It doesn't work like that.

Like the little kid darting out between parked cars. If you're going forty miles an hour, that kid darts out in front of you—at forty, you're traveling sixty feet per second, there's no way you can avoid hitting that kid.

Or take Lake Shore Drive—we call it "Death Shore Drive"— we get crossover head-ons there all the time. The speed limit's forty-five; say the car crossing over is doing sixty and even if the person in the opposite lane, traveling in the opposite direction, is doing forty-five, with forty-five this way and sixty that way, you've got a closing speed of over a hundred miles an hour. So the person that's in his lane, minding his own business, has no chance to take any evasive action, because he's got a car coming at him going sixty miles an hour while he's doing forty-five.

Some accidents are totally unavoidable.

There was a young guy who dropped his girlfriend off at her job in the shopping center. He's got an early seventies Buick, kind of souped-up, pin-striped; it's got a bumper sticker on it that says EAT SHIT AND DIE.

So he's going to impress his girl on the nice ride that he has. So he drops her off heading toward Fifty-first Street and he figures, "Well, I'm gonna really show this"—here comes a semitractor trailer—"Well, I'm gonna peel out. I'm gonna cut right in front of this guy. She will really be impressed."

He had calculated everything into the equation of speed as far as he was concerned. But what he didn't calculate in was what the reaction might be of the driver of the semitractor trailer who, upon seeing this kamikaze coming towards his truck, hit the brakes. And what the kid in the Buick succeeded in doing was hitting the exact center of the trailer, right between the wheels. And he sheared off the complete top of the car he was driving and about ninety percent of his head. And came out on the *other* side of the semitractor trailer and broadsided a car going in the other direction.

So now, my partner and I are at the scene and the truck driver returns to the scene. He explains to us what happened, where the truck was, because we needed pictures. So I said, "Was that trailer loaded or unloaded?" "Oh, it was loaded." "What was on it?" He said, "Forty thousand pounds of soap." So naturally this victim became "Mr. Clean."

There was an interesting case—the Chickenhawk and the Chicken. Nineteen eighty-five or '86. Halloween night. At the corner of Hubbard and Clark.

Here was a young guy—you'd refer to him as a male prostitute. We refer to him as a fruit hustler. So what he does, he gets out there and he tries to find himself an avowed homosexual who's prowling the neighborhood in his car looking for one of these male prostitutes.

So he succeeded in getting the attention of one particular individual cruising past—it was, you know—"Watch what I can do! I'm wonderful! Watch this—"

There was a semi driving down the street very slowly. What this guy decided to do was, he was gonna do a barrel roll between the front tandem and the rear tandem of this semi. This is a forty-foot trailer.

So the fruit hustler is going for the thrill factor—to heighten their emotional response to each other. He rolled underneath the truck as it was rolling down the street. And the guy in the car is watching—"Oh, so good!" And the fruit hustler goes, "Now I'll do it going back!"

He dove—going back. Only thing was that he failed to calculate that the speed of the truck had increased and he was run over by the rear wheels of it.

This was a truckload of potatoes. So naturally the victim was henceforth referred to as "Mr. Potato Head."

Kind of a sad note to the whole thing—the kid was from Wisconsin. I called his family and said, "Listen, Junior was the victim of a very serious accident." Father said, "So what? I wrote him out of my life a long time ago. I'm surprised it took *this* long."

People's cars become almost like a vehicle for their emotions; they take it out on the road, on every other driver.

It's like an extension of their psyches—it's unbelievable—it's like an extension of themselves. You are what you drive. You can get in a whole psychological . . . It's like they say in Southern California—you don't own your car, you *are* your car.

People get a sense of power behind the wheel. They feel indestructible. They don't realize how dangerous this power is, how tragic it can be.

Ad campaigns for car manufacturers have a lot to answer for. Everybody knows about planned obsolescence. Along with that now, a new thing is, whether it's Detroit or Tokyo, they've come to the realization that there's a tremendous profit to be made in auto parts. They all talk a good "We're trying to make safer cars" and "Buckle up" but, all right, dammit, if you're trying to build a safe car—why are you showing what you show in commercials—what do they show you? Speed, driveability on some damn road where they're doing eighty, ninety an hour, hairpin turns, cars airborne . . . Who's buying these cars? The guy in Bloomfield, Iowa? Hell, no. The guy on Lake Shore Drive, and where's he driving it?—he's driving it down Lake Shore Drive.

There's a big market for these replacement parts and they don't want to admit it, but accidents provide it.

If you want to build a safe car, if you want to protect lives and save lives, and ease all this pain and suffering out there, then goddammit, don't advertise your car like you'll become Fittipaldi for the weekend when you get behind the wheel.

* * *

There isn't enough data yet, but wait and see how many accidents are caused by car phones. You got this power guy, he's driving his BMW down the street, he's conducting his business—time is money—"Can you afford to lose out if your customers can't reach you?"—this guy's on the street, he's on the expressway, he's talking high finance—and he's talking to his secretary and she says, "I just want to let you know. Joe Blow just turned around and is canceling his contract. . . ."

It's the mental thing. You are conducting maybe some high-level business thing and you've got some heavy chips on the table here—"Am I gonna get this ten million dollar contract? This phone call's really important"—and the last thing in the world you're thinking about is this car that's coming up next to you driven by Marvin Mope. And suddenly, it's all over.

How'd you like to be talking to your stockbroker when you're riding down the expressway doing sixty miles an hour and he's just told you you just lost $75,000 because the market just went down twenty-four points? Do you think you're really going to be concentrating on what's going on?

You know what it does? It makes driving almost a secondary activity. And you know what else? It brings a lot of pressure right into the car with you. I mean, you get a call from your wife, something's wrong at home. Your girlfriend calls and tells you the rabbit's dead. Whatever it is, it brings it right into the front seat with you where you least need it.

I think what's happening, they're turning automobiles into offices, concert halls, and living rooms. They put everything in the damn car to make it an extension of your office, an extension of your home—add a sound system; people are encouraging you to buy tapes so you can learn a foreign language. . . . Do all these things while you're driving—How're you supposed to be concentrating on what you're doing, which is driving that car?

The attention span of the average driver is not that great to begin with, now he's mucking around with his car phone, his CD player, the makeup mirror—you want stage light? I'm serious.

Everybody's lost sight of the fact that what you're supposed to be doing is sitting behind the wheel driving the car and not only that, you gotta be a defensive driver. You gotta watch out for all the other lunatics that are out.

There's a West German safety film. A seat belt experiment. They took prisoners and gave them pardons if they'd be in test crashes with seat belts. It was like "Get Out of Jail Free." They were having head-ons at sixty. You watch this, see them smashing into trees, the rear ends of trucks. You see the impact, the damage, and the person walking away from all of it.

Here's this guy. Fifty miles an hour, he's gonna hit a tree. The camera's in the car with him. My question is—What did he *do*? I think I'd take my chance in jail before I'd drive a car into a tree.

But I'll tell you one thing, that film really makes a believer out of you. So does this job.

We have automated our case reports to where we keep a data base on our records. And what really got to me is one day when I indexed on the age of the victims. And you start looking at the ages with the names. And all the kids under fifteen in the last three years. And when you think about it . . . each one is a child who's died, who's left a mother and father and brothers and sisters and aunts and uncles and friends and relatives . . . and you think of how the tragedy gets compounded day after day.

And how it really doesn't get the recognition it should get on the severity of the crime. Even with reckless homicide, what do they get on it? What kind of time if they get convicted on it? Five years maximum. And they're committing, as far as I'm concerned, murder. It's kind of hard to justify to the family.

Hit-and-run is a Class A misdemeanor. It carries up to a year, up to a thousand-dollar fine, or both. That's maximum. If someone dies—even if ten people die.

If you kill someone in an accident, it's a traffic violation until you take off. Then it's hit-and-run. It upgrades the offense. But unless reckless homicide can be proven, it's a traffic violation.

It's sometimes a problem for people, especially with accidents involving small children. You know, how do you tell the parent well, this is a traffic ticket. We had an incident where a woman went to a school to pick up her kids and she lost control of the car, went through the fence, into the schoolyard, and killed several kids on the school steps. Well, she had no intention of doing this. It was a driver error. She wasn't on alcohol or drugs. She had her own kids there at school; it could have been one of her own kids. It wasn't reckless homicide, she's not going to do time, but she's gonna have to live with this for the rest of her life.

Speeding alone is not considered reckless homicide. If you're under the influence of alcohol or drugs, or drag racing, *that's* reckless homicide. But if you're speeding and you're sober, you're not on drugs, you're not drag racing, you're not necessarily acting recklessly.

Speeding alone is a traffic violation, unless it's part of willful and wanton disregard for human life. Example: If it's three in the morning, there's no traffic and you're driving light-to-light fifty miles per hour, they're not gonna get you for reckless driving; they'd get you for speeding. But if it's three in the afternoon and it's a school zone and there are small children on the street and you're going down the street, cutting in and out of cars, you may be doing forty in a twenty zone—what would a reasonable person assume their actions might cause? Reckless homicide goes according to—a rational person would think you shouldn't be doing this, you should have known there's a good possibility that somebody's going to be seriously injured.

With DUIs—all you gotta do is go over to Traffic Court, and see on the last one thousand DUIs how many convictions were there, and how many people actually served time? It's a joke.

This is DUI where there *isn't* a fatality. But everybody who's charged with DUI should realize he's damn lucky he *didn't* end up killing somebody.

We handled a case of a seven-year-old girl killed while sitting on her family's front porch. There was a guy who came out of a party drunk, drove a couple doors down the street, lost control of the car. He went between two parked vehicles, up on the sidewalk, right up on the porch, killed this little girl. Severed the body on the steps. Her mother came out. Found her daughter cut in half from a drunk driver coming out of a party down the street. The little girl sitting on the porch. I mean, how safe can a kid be? What do you do? Lock the kids in the house so they can't go outside?

Reckless homicide is one of the most difficult things to prove in court.

They all get jury trials and you get twelve people that all drive and the defense harps away on it: "We've all been driving down the street and we've all made U-turns, we've all exceeded the speed limit, haven't we? You're driving down the street, two pedestrians walk out in front of you, what are you gonna do?" The old "This could have happened to anybody."

When we talk about criminal trials, and reckless homicide is what we deal with basically, you're not talking super top-of-the-line attorneys. You're talking low-end-of-the-spectrum state's attorneys and low-end-of-the-spectrum defense attorneys.

When you're talking DUI, again, it's money. The ones that can afford it are gonna go with the jury. Drunken driving is a crime that the whole population can relate to. Who the hell hasn't been drunk and driven a car? And the DUI offender sure *will* get a jury of his peers, because, unless you're in a town of Quakers in Pennsylvania, at one time or another, every one of them has driven a car drunk. So the defense attorney's gonna harp on the fact that we all drink—this guy had a few beers, he's not a bad guy, he's a family man. And the jury feels sorry for him: "Gee, it could happen to me; it could happen to my husband."

Juries have a tendency—it's human nature—to believe the witness, the eyewitness. They put more credence in what the eyewitness tells them than in the physical evidence.

Even attorneys do that. Even state's attorneys. When we calculate a speed from skid marks, the state's attorney will say, "Yeah, but this witness says he was going eighty." We say, "The physical evidence doesn't show that." "Well, yeah, but . . ."

The average person on a jury is suspicious of science; they're afraid of technical testimony—they want the eyewitness.

We're all victims of decades of being led down the primrose path of the *eye*witness. We've read books, we've seen TV shows, we've seen plays written, classics written—you know, the eye-witness points the accusing finger at the perpetrator. So every-body puts so much stock in the eyewitness. And nine times out of ten, the eyewitness didn't even *see* it, if it's an accident. "Did you actually see the cars collide?" "*Welllll,* no. I heard a crash and I turned around."

That type of thing that is subjective, this is what the attorney's going to go after. He's gonna try and avoid the real, physical evidence. He steers clear of this. He tries to steer clear of expert testimony.

In my opinion, a hit-and-run fatal accident is *the* most difficult crime to solve. It's far more difficult to solve than a homicide. Homicides—you usually don't kill someone unless you have some sort of motive or monetary reward; you know, "I'll give you $5000 if you kill that guy." There's a connection. You can tie things in.

But I could fly to California tomorrow, rent a car, go to a party, have too much to drink and run somebody down and kill them, and turn the car in to the rental agency and fly home. And that's it. There's no motive; I'm not even from that area. It's a tough thing to work on. That's why it's so satisfying when all the pieces come together.

With homicides, probably eight percent of the time, the vic-tim knows the offender. With accidents, you're dealing with total strangers. It's highly unlikely they even live in the same neighborhood.

With most accident cases, with most *any* case, if you don't solve a thing in the first forty-eight hours, your chances of solving it start really getting less and less and less. It's true of all cases, but especially of hit-and-runs.

* * *

Very seldom does a hit-and-run driver ever come forward. It's a misconception on the part of a lot of people that these people are laying awake at night, staring at the ceiling, thinking about that image of that little child in front of their cars before they hit them. . . . That is *not* the case. I think that's a Tinsel Town version. It's very seldom that these people ever come forward once this thing is no longer fresh.

We try to use the media to intensify whatever guilt this guy might be feeling while it *is* still fresh. We're hoping that this guy's gonna be reading in the paper, oh, these kids were wonderful kids and it's gonna pull him in the door.

Most hit-and-run drivers are good persons. It could happen to anyone. It's one of those unintentional crimes. The only thing that makes it a crime is when they take off. Half are under the influence of alcohol or drugs. Then you get the ones who are driving without a license, or on a suspended license. Or kids who've borrowed the family car and are afraid of being found out.

Some hit-and-runs don't even know they *were* involved in an accident. It's true. You know, an eighteen-wheeler turning the corner goes up on the curb and hits somebody, he's got no idea he hit him. Buses and trucks, that's very common. A guy gets off the back of a bus, bus driver sees him get off—he slips, slides, slides right underneath the back wheel, the bus driver keeps right on going. Never even feels him.

With hit-and-runs, when you find the striking car—you work according to the scientific premise of "transfer of material." You're trying to prove that it was this car that was at that crash site at that time. In the Crime Lab, we work under the premise that anytime there's any type of crime where there's contact between two objects, two persons, an object and a person—there's a transfer of material from one to the other. Trace evidence—you try to match a known to an unknown. In everything. Say you're a burglar and you crawl through a window and you've got paint from the windowsill on your clothing—it's submitted to the Crime Lab. The techs can say, "Oh, yeah, we got a gray color of paint and it's not an automobile paint; it's a house paint." Not only that, but you cut yourself going in. So you've got blood on the window or on the floor.

Virtually anything can be transferred. We look at glass, paint, metal, transfer of fibers from the clothing to the car; blood is the big one, and of course any greases or oils. The Major Accident people go looking for the car: when they find the car, they'll look for fibers on the car, they'll look for any type of trace material, blood on the car. . . . We work together in getting the match.

We handle clothing from the victims—there's a lot of blood, sometimes there's skin and such things on it, and there could be brain material on it, depending upon how serious that accident is. This could all be on it.

Some people are squeamish about it at first, but they get over it very quickly. You don't get emotionally involved; if you do, it's gonna tear you apart. It becomes a job to you.

We handle the person's entire exterior clothes for accidents. We're interested in the blood on the clothing because we're interested in finding *that* blood on the vehicle that struck the person. And we're not interested in the fibers on the clothes per se; we're interested in the transfer of the fibers onto the vehicle that struck the person.

The thing of it is, when you get a little kid's clothing—a little, tiny sweater, little jeans and stuff like that. And you look at it and—here's a person that's not gonna go . . . I mean, that's it. That's as far as they're gonna go in life. That's it. It's over. Three, four, five years old. That does something to you. I don't care what type of person it is did this—here's a little kid that got hit by a car and the car never even stopped to give first aid or call for assistance.

We had a reckless homicide hit-and-run that came down to the fragments of a sideview mirror. Two teenagers were crossing the street and were struck and killed; one of their bodies hit the mirror as it was flung through the air, breaking it.

The night that it happened, these two kids were crossing Damen Avenue from the east to the west. The boy was fourteen; the girl was fifteen. I guess they had just sort of started almost like a date-type thing; they were holding hands—a case of puppy love. They were crossing the street. It was about eight o'clock at night.

What made the whole thing such a bizarre accident was that there's a viaduct, about a hundred and fifty feet long, and it's divided, with concrete pillars in the middle. So these kids, they're crossing the street about a hundred feet north of the viaduct—when they stepped off the curb, they looked to the south, and they saw that there was nothing coming. So they walked out to the center of the street and now they look to the north.

What had happened was, underneath the viaduct, a driver became impatient because the traffic was slow. He swung over into the southbound lanes and drove his car north in the southbound lanes under the viaduct.

These kids are in the center of the street. They look to the north, here comes our guy on the wrong side of the viaduct, driving at a high rate of speed. The car was occupied by two men and a woman. All three were Cook County employees: one was a deputy sheriff; the other two were clerks of the court, Traffic Court. The driver never saw the kids. The kids never saw the car.

They hit both the girl and the boy. It would be my guess—and they were both pronounced dead at Children's Memorial—but from the amount of blood that we saw at the scene, and some of the brain tissue and what have you, these kids were killed instantly. I mean, they were just smacked.

The Fourteenth District got the whole thing blocked off; they preserved the scene. We called for an evidence technician to come and assist us. It was as dark as you could imagine; the E.T., Foley, very methodically and systematically picked up all the pieces of plastic there—we didn't really know what it was at that time, but we figured it was part of the striking vehicle. The E.T. picked up and bagged all these parts.

What we were hoping was that those parts would lead us to a make of the vehicle, because we were getting conflicting stories.

The problem was, when this guy came under the viaduct, people saw cars that were driving the right side of the street, in the proper lanes, but then people on the other side of the street saw the striking vehicle. So people on the east side of the street were telling us it was a brown Oldsmobile or a Buick, and then you had the people on the other side of the street telling us, "No, it's a dark blue Toyota or a Mazda or something." And then there were people telling us two cars were racing. You find that so much with witnesses. You get such discrepancies it's unbelievable.

We had a little sitdown, a case meeting in the conference room. One of our traffic specialists had gone down to the Crime Lab that day and picked up all the parts. The Crime Lab had already processed them to see if there was any hair or skin on them. And we wanted to have the pieces available in case we ever found the car.

We're sitting in the conference room, saying, Okay, what has to be done? What's next to do? Picking each other's brains—Who have we interviewed? Who has to be interviewed? We're just sitting there trying to think of what avenues to follow. And the guy who'd gotten all the pieces back from the Crime Lab just takes the plastic bag and says, "Let me see if I can put this together." He went out and he got the tape dispenser and he opens the plastic bag and just starts taking all these pieces of black plastic. . . . It was a virtual jigsaw puzzle, that's about the best way to describe it; there were about forty pieces.

What it turned out to be was the plastic frame for the driver's sideview mirror. And, just to give you an idea of the tenacity of that E.T. who gathered these pieces up at the scene, our guy reassembled that casing and he used Scotch tape to hold it together and I was watching him, I couldn't believe it, he put the whole thing together, and he had it all together—that E.T. had gotten *every* piece off the pavement. There was not one piece missing from that mirror; there was not even a little sliver missing. The goddamn tenacity of that guy, that evidence technician, picking up these tiny pieces, pitch dark, with his flashlight, broke the case. And if even one of those pieces had been missing, it could have been the key one; we would have been through.

People tell you that's luck. Bullshit. That's not luck. That's just goddamn good work. That's a guy who didn't go about it haphazardly and think, "Well, I'll get that; I'll get this—to hell with it, they're not gonna figure this out anyway."

So our guy, Larry Clark, pieces all these tiny pieces together; he says, "Well, now we're on to something." And there were very small Japanese markings on the bottom of the back of the casing.

We started hitting import dealers. The second one we went to, a Honda place, we walk up to the parts guy and he goes, "That's off a Honda Civic." In fact, the guy even told us it was a four-door because the sideview mirror on a two-door has a little different shape. Then we knew it was a Honda.

Then we approached trying to identify the driver. We went about it in two separate ways. We started doing what they call an off-line search with the secretary of state's office. Armed with the description of the driver we had—we knew he was a white Hispanic, and that there was a woman with him, on that the eyewitnesses were unanimous—we took the areas geographically that had the highest population of Hispanics living in the city. And we requested the registration on all Honda Civics in the city and checked them for Hispanic names. When we got the information back from the secretary of state's office, we were gonna turn around then and run title searches on Honda Civics because then we could get color information—we knew it was blue.

What the offender did was, he reported his car stolen after the accident, about one-fifteen in the morning. He told the policeman that responded that he had parked his car in front of his home about five-thirty at night. And that's the last he ever saw of it. He said he got up in the middle of the night because he had to get medicine for his sick kid; he said his wife was sending him for medicine, he looked out the window, you know, and the car was gone. So this covers the car at the time of the accident—even though he's reporting it after the accident, he says the last he saw it was five-thirty.

The car was recovered the next afternoon. A beat officer found it in the alley where the sheriff and the clerk dumped it the night before. So the beat guy files a report; there are boxes on the "Recovered Vehicle Supplementary Report" where you mark damage, if any, on the car when you're recovering it.

"Front end damage" was marked. "Cracked windshield" was marked. And then, God bless that Sixteenth District police officer, he wrote on the report, "Missing left sideview mirror."

The car was found in the same condition as after the accident. If he had fixed it, we wouldn't have had as good a case. Also, a single hair from one of the victims was found in the trim along the window where the windshield meets the roof.

So the owner was notified that his car had been recovered and he picked it up over there. And we were being notified of all recovered steals.

A week after the accident, we went to his house and there was the car parked right in front. There really wasn't much doubt in anybody's mind.

He came down out of his house, we asked him if this was his car, he said yes. We told him that we thought the car was involved in a fatal hit-and-run accident. He said, "Nah, that couldn't have been my car." By this time, we decided we were gonna question him and we advised him of his rights. He's still denying it. "No, no, I got nothing to do with it. My car wasn't involved in no hit-and-run accident."

We asked him if he'd come with us to our office, we wanted to ask him some questions relative to how he found the car and how he reported the car stolen and what have you.   '

He rode in with the lieutenant. And on the way in to our office, he asked the lieutenant: "What happens to people that kill people in accidents?"

The lieutenant told him what can happen, what does happen, and what doesn't happen and he said, "I think I got something I gotta say," and the lieutenant says, "Well, listen, you've got the right to remain silent," and the guy says, "No. I want to get it off my chest. I was driving the car."

We were back in the office. The lieutenant walked up, grabbed me, and said, "Guess what? He just confessed. He admitted everything." He flipped. You know that expression? Flipped? He gave himself up.

And then he told us who was in the car with him. And he told us what they did. After they struck the children, the boy and the girl, they drove around for a while and he parked the car. He was absolutely panic-stricken. He got out from behind the wheel; the girl got behind it. And they drove up to a body shop on the North Side, an alley mechanic that she knew. Wanted to know could they get the car fixed. He said yeah and he'd tell them later how much it'd cost.

They then drove back to his home. They all went up to his home—there are four people now, the owner of the car, the female Traffic Court clerk, the deputy sheriff, and the guy's wife—sat there and tried to figure out what the hell kind of a story were they going to come up with. They had their own brainstorming session. So they watched the news and they heard that the two kids were in fact dead. And they came up with the great idea, well, what we'll do is we'll report the car stolen.

Then they left the offender at home. The clerk of the court along with the deputy sheriff got in the offender's car and drove it round the corner from her house, parked it in the alley, and left it. She didn't want to walk too far. And then she drove the sheriff home.

He was charged that night with reckless homicide. Two counts. The state's attorney chose not to charge the other clerk of the court and the sheriff because they were cooperating; he was very happy with their statements. We wanted to get them before the grand jury to lock them into their statements so down the road, when this thing comes up for trial, they don't say, "I didn't say that." Then they're staring right at the perjury.

The attitude of these two people was—I mean, they were very callous. The driver of the car, the guy that actually killed the two kids, he was very remorseful; he was broken up, he felt terrible, he was crying. But these other two—they just sat there like, big deal. The sheriff asked me in the office, he said, "How long am I gonna be here?" with a real attitude. "Oh, probably about three to five."

They got before the grand jury and promptly took the Fifth. We knew then that they had no intentions of cooperating. Members of our unit placed them under arrest as they left the County Building, put them in protective custody, and we received the approval from the state's attorney to charge them with compounding a felony. They were both arrested and charged and they were both going to go to trial.

So that was the end result of a lot of hard work. It's a textbook example of every single cop doing his job, from the district cops to the evidence technician on his hands and knees picking up pieces of plastic to guys in our unit knocking on doors, looking for the one key witness.

It looked like we had an absolute mystery on our hands. No eyewitnesses who could positively identify the car. It was strictly physical evidence that was taken from the scene, preserved properly. . . . It wound up, the accident happened on the fourth, and they were arrested on the twelfth.

While we were working on this, I talked to the boy's father every day. These were dirt-poor people. I'll tell you something, the father really loved that kid. They fished together, they camped together—when I say camping, I mean they took an old tent out someplace. They sure didn't have much.

I told him that night in the hospital; I said, "Listen, you know . . ."—that's one of the toughest things we have to do in this job, tell a parent his kid is dead—so I said to him, like we say to all of them, "Here's my card. We're gonna try to find out who did this. Call me day or night."

He called me every day. "Did you hear anything?" "No, we're working on it." And he used to always apologize—"I don't want to be a pest, sergeant." "You're not a pest, Mr. White." All he wanted to do was talk to somebody. Get a little reassurance that. . . .

One of the good feelings I got was, the night we charged the driver, I called the father at home. He had told me before that he couldn't sleep. He said, "You know, I haven't been able to sleep. I nod off for a while; I can't sleep. I get maybe an hour, two hours sleep," it was bothering him so much.

I called him on the phone that night and I told him, I said, "We cleared the case. The man's in custody, charged with reckless homicide." The man cried like a baby when I told him. And all he said was, "Thank God I can rest. Now I can rest."

This kind of erases the theory that a lot of poor people have that they're not going to get any service from the police. A lot of poor people, black and white, "What are the police gonna do for me? They don't care for me." Well—we do.

The whole thing hinged on one broken mirror, multiple pieces of glass that were meticulously picked up by the evidence technician and actually put back together with Scotch tape.

You know, those pieces of mirror were the result of one of those kids' bodies breaking it. It was like that kid's last living act was to say, "Get the guy that did this to me."

So many policemen have the attitude, and I've heard it since I've been on the job . . . there's this expression coppers use: "All traffic is bullshit." You're not doing police work; you're not a real policeman if you're doing traffic or accident investigation.

Tactical officers especially—they have the mindset of "I'm on the street. I'm the real police. You're not."

So the example that I use when I teach at-scene accident investigation is that—Let's say there's an accident, it happens at a big intersection. And at the very same time, Al's Beef Stand on the corner gets broken into. The guy steals the cash register. So the original beat man gets the call to Al's Beef Stand, sees that we have a big crime, someone's broke the window, crawled in, and taken the cash register.

Same time, at the middle of the intersection, two cars have collided, each car is worth about five thousand dollars. One driver is drunk and the other driver has her kids in the car. The drunk kills one of the kids. He paralyzes the woman for life.

Now, the car that gets this call—"Well, you're handling an accident." The other car is handling a *real* crime. The other car is handling police work. "We're doing police work; you're doing bullshit. That's just a traffic accident."

Primary function of the police officer is the protection of life and property. There are more lives lost, more property damage caused by traffic accidents than *any* other crime. Period. It's unbelievable the amount.

So now the lieutenant comes and he pulls up and he sees the two cars out in the middle of the street; maybe there's a lot of physical evidence there that a traffic specialist might be able to use—"Get these cars over to the side!" because this is traffic, this isn't police work, this isn't crime. And let's concentrate on Al's Beef Stand that got his cash register stolen—he's got a total of let's say a thousand dollars. Both of the cars are totaled, ten thousand dollars, there's a loss of life, the woman is paralyzed, her hospital bills are gonna be $500,000 plus—but to the police mindset, that's bullshit.

You hear all these stories, if you don't have phobias now, you never will. Where are you gonna be safe? Hide in the basement? We had one, there was a garden apartment, half above and half below street level, a car went out of control and it just went right through the brick and the front end of it drops down on the bed where a little kid is sleeping. It killed him. You're not safe in the basement—hide in the attic.

You have to live two lives. You think to yourself on the way home—"Okay, now it's time to shut that life off. Now I have to go home and be a good mother." No matter what you saw that day, you get in the house, you say things are fine. You shut everything else off—"Okay, what school activities are on for tonight?"

Even as adults—my kids are grown now—they'll say, "Mom, were you involved with that accident?" You weren't going to tell them anything about it. They saw it on TV. "Was it bad, Mom?" You say, "Oh no, it wasn't as bad as TV makes it look"—when you know it was horrible.

When I go to these scenes and I look at these people, I know that could be me. That could be a member of my family. Any one of us who walk out of our home at any time, day or night, could be involved in something like this. Whereas—I can't imagine myself being a victim of a homicide. But the odds of being a traffic accident victim are so much greater.

A guy in our unit got killed on his motorcycle a couple of years ago. You'd think he'd know better, wouldn't you? A brilliant accident reconstructionist—he taught the course.

I was with him when he bought the motorcycle. And again, police humor, I said, "You gonna reserve your fatal number now?" We have numbers assigned to fatal accidents. And he said, "No. When I kill myself, I'll do it on the expressway. That way, the state'll have to handle it." And he did. He was on the feeder ramp going up to the Kennedy when he was killed.

He was one of our best officers. One of the very best. Killed in a motorcycle accident. It happened on the midnight watch.

He was just excellent. He had a wonderful mind for mathematics. He'd go to a scene and tell you exactly what happened and how it happened. And he was in the process of writing a training program for in-service officers in our unit when he was killed.

One of our own. It's ironic, isn't it? And there's nothing more eerie. . . . We make file folders on all the accidents we do. And we have the victim's name on the front of the file folder and a number, it's called the fatal number. It's just the most eerie feeling in the world to look at that file folder and to see the name of somebody in your unit. And to think . . . someday that could be me.

Major Accidents:
Contributing Police Officers

LIEUTENANT JAMES CARROLL, Sixteenth District; former commanding officer, Major Accident. Carroll's twenty-six-year career has included work as a beat officer, tac officer, and vice officer in the Fifteenth District; eight years as a burglary detective; assignments as a field and tac sergeant and a field and tac lieutenant; and service as the head of Major Accident, which includes the Hit-and-Run Unit and the Public Vehicle Unit, from 1984 to 1990.

OFFICER JIM DORAN, commanding officer, Criminalistics Sections, CPD Crime Lab. Doran, who has a B.S. in Biochemistry and a master's in Social Justice, started in the Crime Lab in 1969 as a civilian in the Microanalysis Section, which deals with substances such as blood, hair, fibers, glass, paint, and soil. In '73, Doran decided to join the force—he went on the street as a patrol officer in the Fourteenth District until 1979, when he returned to the Crime Lab. In 1982, Doran was assigned to a new Crime Lab unit, the Laser Latent Fingerprint Development Section. In 1986, Doran became commanding officer of the Criminalistics Sections of the Crime Lab, including Serology, Microcoscopy Trace, Controlled Substance, Physical Chemistry, and Laser.

SERGEANT ROSEANN FITZGERALD, Thirteenth District. Fitzgerald served in Major Accident from 1984 to 1990. Fitzgerald joined the CPD in 1974 as a "policewoman," during the time when the distinction was still made between "policemen" and "policewomen," and served in the Youth Division. In 1976, Fitzgerald became a police officer and was assigned to patrol in Nineteen. From 1978 to 1981, Fitzgerald taught courses in case reporting, report writing, and CPR at the Police Academy. In 1981, Fitzgerald was promoted to detective and assigned to Area Five Violent Crimes. Fitzgerald made sergeant in 1982 and was assigned to the Traffic Enforcement Section which, at that time, patrolled all the expressways. In 1984, Fitzgerald came to Major Accident. Fitzgerald has a master's degree in English and American Literature.

TRAFFIC SPECIALIST BOB KULOVITZ, accident reconstructionist.

Kulovitz served in Major Accident for eleven years. Kulovitz joined the CPD in 1966, was a patrol officer in the Grand Crossing District till 1969, worked with Customs and Immigration as boarding officer in the Port Security Section from 1969 to 1973, then went to the Ninth District on patrol till 1979, when he joined Major Accident. Kulovitz has taught the At-Scene Accident Investigation course for the Traffic Division at the Police Academy, refresher courses within Major Accident and, with Traffic Specialist Tom McKenna, has designed a course in accident investigation so that supervisors and traffic specialists in the Traffic Division may be trained in-house. Kulovitz and McKenna also have structured a condensed version of Accident Investigation for the Chicago Fire Department. Kulovitz retired in 1990.

SERGEANT KAY LOUIS, Major Accident Investigation Unit.

Louis joined the force in 1966 and worked as a youth officer in the Youth Division for nine years, with a concentration in missing persons and runaways. From 1975 to 1977, Louis was a patrol sergeant in the Twentieth District. In 1977, Louis was assigned to the Homicide Unit and Rape Unit in Area Six as a detective. Louis joined the Labor Unit in 1980, where she worked on the air controllers' strike and firefighters' strike, among others, as part of the CPD's peacekeeping force in union conflicts. From 1985 to 1986, Louis was a patrol sergeant in Twenty-five. Louis joined Major Accident in 1986.

TRAFFIC SPECIALIST TOM McKENNA, accident reconstructionist.

McKenna has been in Traffic for all of

his twenty-three years on the force. McKenna came to the Major Accident Investigation Section in 1983. McKenna is now one of thirteen accident reconstructionists in Major Accident. McKenna has also taught classes in at-scene accident investigation at the Police Academy and codesigned an at-scene investigation course for the Chicago Fire Department.

SERGEANT TOM REYNOLDS, Gang Mission Team

sergeant, Nineteenth District. Before being assigned to Nineteen in 1990, Reynolds served six years, from 1984 to 1990, as a sergeant in the Major Accident Investigation Unit. Reynolds was a detective for fourteen years prior to his promotion to sergeant in 1984: ten years as a robbery and burglary detective in Areas Four, Five, and Six, and four years (from 1980 to 1984) as a detective in the Office of Municipal Investigations. Reynolds joined the force in 1965.

HOSTAGE / BARRICADE INCIDENTS

A good male hostage negotiator can talk the pants off a nun. And a good female negotiator could be caught in bed with another man by her husband and the next moment would be standing up, putting her clothes on, acting like it was a big joke, convincing the husband that nothing happened. And after a while, maybe he wouldn't believe it, he's not stupid, but it would put some doubts in his head. . . .
CPD hostage negotiator

What we mostly do doesn't get on TV. People's only conception of what we do is from what they see on TV. They might see a brief news flash of a highly stylized assault, because that's what makes news. They wouldn't see the policeman laying for eight hours on his stomach, just watching, because that's not high video.
CPD containment officer

The problem with hostage-takers is they've seen too many old movies. Visions of Jimmy Cagney and Al Pacino dance in their heads.

And if the cops who respond to the reports of someone holding hostages or waving at passersby with a gun have seen the same old movies and the same TV dramas, and believe that's the way it's played, the script will probably end in death.

"We call it the 'Father Mulcahy Syndrome,'" says Lieutenant John Kennedy, who originated and designed the CPD's Hostage/Barricaded/Terrorist Unit in the late seventies and who now coordinates all hostage negotiations and containment operations. "A lot of what police used to do was based on old Jimmy Cagney/Barry Fitzgerald movies. Before there was HBT training, how did police know what to do in a hostage situation? You could go through your whole career without getting one. So all of a sudden, you get a call, and there's a hostage situation. How did the police know what to do? *Hollywood* told them what to do.

"Somebody would make a movie and make things up and police would go see the movie and at some point be confronted with a hostage situation and think, 'What do I do?' And what the police officer had seen before in the movies would click in. 'Oh, yeah, I remember—

Get a priest. Get the mother. Get the father. Put them all on the phone. Leave my gun outside. Go in. Exchange myself for the kid.' All these things, which are the *worst* things in the world to do in a hostage situation, the things that got people killed, are what, traditionally, police would do."

The whole point of an HBT Program, says Kennedy, is to get away from the script, get away from the stereotypes that, if played out, might end up looking and sounding great on the nightly news: the crackling of sniper fire, police scuttling for cover, the bodies being carried out in shiny black plastic bags.

Since the first official HBT incident in July 1980, when a man went barricade in his backyard and talked to hostage negotiators over the back fence while he whittled on his arm with a hunting knife, Chicago's HBT Program has chalked up more than two hundred incidents with no killings of hostage-takers, hostages, or barricaded persons.

There *have* been deaths and serious injuries—some who went barricade ended the situation by killing themselves; private citizens and responding police officers have been shot and killed before the HBT force arrived; HBT officers have been seriously wounded at the scene—but no hostage situation has ended in deadly assault.

The true drama of the hostage situation is one that can't be seen on the screen. If the negotiation works, it won't be heard of at all. The times that hostage negotiators succeed in talking a shotgun barrel out of someone's mouth, the times that containment officers wear a homicidal subject down by ringing his doorbell or fooling around with the heat or air conditioning, don't get reported. And if they do, all the subtle psychological and physical maneuverings involved don't get reported for lack of space, air time, or knowledge of what really goes on in a hostage/barricade situation. Old movies and TV shows blind everyone except the people specially trained to cut through all the stagey, deadly stereotypes.

The CPD's Hostage/Barricaded/Terrorist Unit is made up of seventy hostage negotiators, trained in talking people out of desperate acts, and one hundred containment officers, skilled in military tactics to keep the hostage-taker or barricaded person confined, and, if necessary, to run in and subdue the offender or "take him out"—kill him. Containment officers in other cities are called SWAT teams or snipers, but the CPD terminology plays up restraint, as in the "antisniper" guns that are trained on Chicago hostage-takers.

The "Terrorist" component of HBT basically means that if a terrorist creates a hostage/barricade situation, he or she will be treated to the HBT Program, with the addition of the FBI's Chicago Terrorist Task Force and the Bomb Squad, if necessary.

HBT is called up when a domestic dispute, a man-with-a-gun call, or a crime gone sour crosses over from what the first officers on the scene can settle, as they often do, into a dangerous standoff. The hostage-taker poses an obvious threat. But the person gone barricade, the guy holed up inside with a gun and overwhelming despair, is just as dangerous—he can turn his resentment on anyone who gets near him, he can take hostages, and may have a hostage or hostages with him no one knows about.

An HBT incident is like a talk show ringed round by men carrying rifles. The negotiators divide themselves up into three-person teams, with an intelligence-gatherer (who finds out everything possible about the person inside—what to say, what might spark violence), a relayer of information, and a primary negotiator (the cop on the bullhorn or phone who keeps the person on the other end talking until the impulse to kill passes). All the while, containment officers carrying "antisniper" rifles surround the hostage-taker or barricaded person, mapping out a quasimilitary terrain: the inner perimeter, the inner ring of police keeping the bad guy in; the outer perimeter, the farther reaches of the scene; and the Kill Zone, which is as far as the offender can shoot. They practice probes, diversions, assaults; waiting it out, but ready to go in as soon as things turn critical.

None of the negotiators or containment officers works HBT full-time; they're pulled together for the incidents from their various divisions. The vast majority of hostage negotiators are detectives, since detectives are skilled in getting people to talk. The majority of containment officers come from the three Gang Crimes units. All these officers receive special training in the best ways to convince the desperate, the criminal, and the psychotic to give it up.

Both hostage negotiators and containment officers are skilled in playing on the subject's common sense and nerves until he gives the hostages or himself up, alive. "Time is on our side," says one long-time hostage negotiator. "We've got nothing but time. We might have 50 police officers at a scene. There are 11,500 Chicago coppers altogether. We can always send this 50 home and get another 50, endlessly. The instinct of most police is 'Let's kick the fucking door down and get it over with'—in HBT, we don't want to unless it's necessary. But we're not afraid to." So HBT plays a waiting game, negotiating, stalling, manipulating the guy's heat, his air conditioning, his door bells, his whole environment, wearing the guy inside out.

"Before HBT," says Kennedy, "some nut would grab a kid or a stickup guy would grab a liquor store clerk if the robbery went sour; shots might be fired, the guy barricades himself in the house or goes in the back room of the liquor store and the police arrive. The supervising officer would show up and everybody would look at him expectantly and he'd say, 'Follow me, men,' and they'd go into the back room and get killed. Now, they have an option."

Every hostage situation is a homicide-in-progress. That's exactly what it is. You've got somebody threatening to commit a homicide.

Even when there are no hostages—in a barricade situation, where the guy doesn't have to keep an eye on the hostages and is free to roam around, the threat of homicide is still there. The police are in great danger. *And,* with a barricade, you never know for sure if the guy has a hostage in there with him or not—you can't take a neighbor's word that he doesn't, and you sure can't take his word. So the threat is there.

All HBT situations are dangerous. Every single one of them. It's always an act of great desperation.

We get a lot of suicidal people. They're extremely dangerous, because suicide and homicide are two sides of the same coin. If they think life sucks, they might want to put whoever else is with them out of their agony too. And if they're willing to take their own life, it doesn't usually matter to them who else takes the trip with them.

Most hostage-takers have a hidden agenda. The death of this person they're holding hostage is not their primary goal.

The goal of the hostage negotiator is to find out what the hidden agenda is, what the true goal is.

For example, a husband might be in a rage at his wife. He could take her hostage to scare her, to terrorize her, to seek vengeance. But if he takes their *child* hostage—he's not doing it to terrorize or seek vengeance on the child. He's after the wife.

Ninety percent of the people we see are drunk, wiped out on drugs, or nuts. They may have been nuts for years, and something sets them off, or they may just go off, just get that one final frustration that puts them over. It could be anybody.

A lot of people go off because their wife or girlfriend leaves them—that's a big one. Or they get evicted. Or they lose their job. Those are the Big Three.

*   *   *

There's something we've seen so much in these things that finally we gave a name to it—the "Double Whammy." We've been to a lot of hostage/barricade scenes where the guy inside, by all accounts, is just a regular Joe. And this regular Joe encountered what we call the Double Whammy.

That's when somebody, usually it's a guy, loses the job, and loses the wife and family within about two weeks.

It seems like somebody can lose their job, but if they've got the family, and they go home and they get the solace and the compassion, then they can get it together. They economize for a couple of weeks and they go out and find another job.

Or a guy loses his family. Guy comes home from work and finds a "Dear John" letter and she and the kids and the money are all gone—he's got eight-hours-a-day, forty-hours-a-week, he's got his buddies from work, he can cry in his beers after work, he can beef and moan about her and he's got a focus for his life—he has to get to work. And he'll get over it.

But—the boss says, "You're fired" and he goes home and finds the "Dear John" letter. He's just been double-whammied.

They end up holding the child, wanting the wife. The great threat is that if the wife is brought on scene, he'll kill the child to show the wife, to hurt the wife, and then try to go for the wife and kill himself. He wants her to pay. He'll try to make her be the homicide audience and the suicide audience.

Suicide is a constant threat in any hostage/barricade scene. You get manic-depressives. You get people who have gone off. They want an audience. If they didn't want an audience, they would have just *done* it.

But they want to go out in a different way. They want somebody to know *why* they're killing themselves.

If somebody's intent on committing suicide, you can't stop them. You might get them to defer their decision, but if they're determined, they'll do it. There have been cases of people ripping out their own throats in jail when every conceivable suicide weapon had been taken from them.

One case—somebody saw an old guy in a window with a gun. Whether he threatened anybody before we got there is vague. He never threatened us. He never threatened to take his own life *to* us.

It only took about an hour and a half to get him out. He gave up his guns. He agreed to come out. But then he came to his front door and couldn't find the inside key to let himself out. He's shouting through the door at us, but it's all muffled— "I can't find the key! I'll come out the back door." We yell, "Wait! Wait! Don't do that!" Because we've got the surrender procedure established; the police are all in their positions. So now we've got to run around and change all our positions. I tell him, "Start at one hundred and count back to one. And then come out the side door." "Do I gotta do that?" "Yeah." "Can I count from one to one hundred?" "Well, okay."

So he starts counting. We run around the side; everybody gets organized there. And he comes out with all these pictures of him and the late Mayor Daley. This guy had been a neighborhood politician. He had to bring all this stuff out with him. He had to show us the pictures, that he had been friends with Mayor Daley.

So we go through all this elaborate putting the stuff down on the stairs, turn around, you have him wriggle his fingers, palms up, palms down, make sure he's got nothing concealed; you can have a knife in your sleeve, under your wristwatch. So we go through all this. He surrenders. We take him off to the mental health center, he gets out in a week, and ten days later, kills himself.

There's a case of "Why do you do what you do?" and we did it and it didn't do any good anyway.

Suicide by cop. Somebody's suicidal—maybe he's just found out he has brain cancer—but he doesn't have the balls to commit suicide himself. So he tries to do it by pointing an unloaded gun at a cop. That's what's really going on with a lot of our barricaded depressed subjects. They want to commit suicide by cop. This is common. It's a big thing.

* * *

When you're on the phone with a suicidal subject, you know they're gonna go, they're gonna do it, when the voice goes absolutely flat. Suddenly, it's dead. No emotion. And that comes just before suicide. It's like they're already gone.

Paranoid schizophrenics are the great hostage-takers. It's hard to figure out where they're coming from. But they've got their agenda; they've got their perceived or real problem, you know, and the FBI and the CIA and the moon men are after them and everything.

The big problem these people have is nobody ever listens to them because they're loony. So we *will* listen to them. Just listen. And after a while, they get tired, their attention is diverted from the hostages, the hostages start to escape, or they decide to give it up because you've given them some alternative, and they surrender.

The religious fanatic is the most dangerous of all hostage-takers. He's listening to messages from God. How do you compete with God? Why would a religious fanatic even consider that you could help him?

With these people, it seems like hostage scenes really go bad. And they kill people atrociously. They scare me.

Criminals are the easiest of all the hostage-takers to deal with. This idea of the desperate criminal is all wrong. Criminals are very logical people. They're logical. They're businessmen. They're out there sticking up; they're making money. They've invested their $35 for a pistol and they're gonna go out and make a 5000 percent profit. But it turns sour. The police have come; they've been frustrated in their escape, so they take this hostage so the police won't get them.

Criminals always go through two stages in these things: First come the demands for escape and then come the demands for survival.

You just let enough time go by where all of a sudden the light goes off over their heads—"Hey, they're not letting me out of here. They're gonna kill me." And then, if you can assure him he won't be hurt, he'll surrender.

By far, most of what we see are barricaded men. Women are the reason men barricade. Nine times out of ten, if you have a barricaded man, it's a woman who's put him there.

Mostly, it's a romantic thing. The big thing with barricaded men is they ask us to bring the wife or the girlfriend on scene. You might get them to get information, but you don't put them near the barricaded man because, if he sees the wife or girlfriend, his plan might be to kill himself in front of them or to kill *them*.

Sometimes they want us to bring both the wife *and* the girl-friend. I've thought, "Maybe this guy should not be the one who's upset here."

We have a lot of jobs on Sunday nights. There's a great rush of domestic disturbances on Sunday nights and a lot of hostage/bar-ricade situations grow out of domestics. A guy gets his paycheck on Friday and shows up on Sunday night with no money. He's drunk, she gives him a hard time, they get in a shouting match, she gives him a push, he fires a shot, and he grabs the kid and runs up to the attic.

We get a lot of people when the weather first turns nice. Springtime's the great suicide time. One of the great myths is it's Christmastime. That's not true. What will happen is, everybody's depressed in February. How can you be in this city in February without getting depressed? It's just a miserable, rotten month. End of March comes around, beginning of April, the birds, the flowers—everybody feels good.

Except this guy. He's been blaming his despair on the weather because everybody's been in despair. It's just so damn rotten. Now everybody gets happy, but he's still in despair. And that's where there's no light at the end of the tunnel.

You'll find that the person of average or middle education and intelligence is easy to talk to, easy to control, whatever you have to do. The average, everyday working guy that is pissed off at his father-in-law is going to take his kids hostage or something, he's gonna threaten their lives for hours and hours and hours because he hates the father-in-law; once you get him off of the father-in-law, however temporarily, the problem is solved.

The person of low education and intelligence is more difficult to deal with. You can't get to him. I'm not saying you're smarter, but you don't know where they're going sometimes; they disappear on you. But he'll often control himself. In other words, he'll go off, and then all of a sudden, lose why he's gone off, he'll lose his train of thought and help control himself.

But the superintelligent people are *real* hard to deal with. They're suspicious of everything you say to them. They analyze things.

For about the first twenty minutes after you've been taken hostage, you have absolutely no control over anything. The only thing you *can* control is your breathing. It's a terrible and traumatic thing to be taken hostage. You're under threat of imminent death. Somebody has control over you like you haven't experienced since you were two months old, whether you get a drink of water or not, whether you stand up, sit down, go to the bathroom. The gun is on you. It's brutally terrifying—even if nothing else happens, *this* is terrifying.

People have developed all kinds of defense mechanisms to cope with this situation. They'll tune out. They'll go to sleep for twenty hours. They'll knit.

If you're taken hostage, what you *don't* want to do is isolate yourself away from the hostage-taker. You want to interact with this person. Because it's easy to kill a stranger, but it's harder to kill somebody you know.

But at the same time, you don't want to push it. So you don't violate the hostage-taker's body space. You don't stare into his eyes. You do what you're told.

You want to be responsive, that you understand their situation, that maybe they're right and the police are wrong, and what can you do to help him.

What will normally happen, even without you intending it, is you *will* become responsive, you *will* identify with the hostage-taker, you *will* swing over to him—"What's wrong with the authorities? This guy says do this or he's gonna kill me and they're not doing what he wants. What's *wrong* with these people? This guy—this guy did have a couple good points in what he was saying. And he's not that bad a guy." That's all a coping mechanism. It's the basis of the Stockholm Syndrome. That term comes from that bank robbery in Stockholm, Sweden, where the bank robber took three women into a vault and demanded that police bring his buddy, who was in jail, to him in the bank. The police did. So the two buddies held the three women hostage in the bank vault for six days. Then they surrendered. None of the women would testify against the hostage-takers. Two of the women got engaged to the two offenders. Now we call it "Stockholming," when the hostage identifies with the hostage-taker.

What usually happens, they get compatible with the offender and that in turn causes the offender to look at them as human beings and makes it difficult to hurt them. It works in our favor. It may be just enough to buy us enough time and enough hesitation on the part of the bad guy that if we do have to enter, he won't kill anyone.

Sometimes a negotiator gets all hung up on the guy. He's Stockholming. This is a bad thing; it's very dangerous. The problem comes when you start caring about the bad guy. Then you might say something like, "Listen, at six—they're coming in. You better get your act together and come out now" or, "I have to know in fifteen minutes." You're inadvertently telling the bad guy there's fifteen minutes till the assault. You're tipping him off. That's a highly dangerous thing to do.

We try never to mention the hostages to the hostage-taker. We've talked to them on the phone sometimes; they've gotten on the phone, but we don't like to. We've got to focus on the hostage-taker. We don't bring up the hostages to him—we don't want his attention on them. And we try to make him realize that *he* is of most concern to us. It's not that the hostages aren't our greatest concern; they are. But we try to put him in the main focus, convince him that he's the most important one. We play down the hostages in our conversations with him because the last thing you want him to do is go, "You don't give a shit about me. All you care about is these people in here. You don't want me to kill them." "I don't want you to kill anybody—yourself, them, me—I don't want anybody to die."—you get back to *him*— "That's why I'm talking to you. *You're* the one I care about. *You're* the one I'm talking to."

The way we get on to these things—usually it's a neighbor who calls the district police and then these officers call us if it seems out-of-control. A guy fires a shot out the door or neighbors see a guy with a gun inside or he's outside and threatens somebody with a knife and runs back inside. It's rare that the person holding a hostage or going barricade calls the police himself.

A lot of these things start out, but they get resolved instantly by the beat officers or the district police. Maybe the fellow hasn't set up properly to where he feels he can defend himself against the police. Or the hostage gets away. Or the guy suddenly realizes he's in trouble and he better just stop it before it gets going.

Or, most important, the right policeman, or policemen, gets to the scene and handles it the way it should be handled and takes care of it before it gets started.

When you get the call, you listen in on the air to get a sense of where this is, if the approach might be difficult, if you could get hit going up.

At the scene, you meet people you don't see that often, except at these things. There's one guy always comes up to me, he's a containment guy who stood next to me in a hallway with his shotgun one time while I shouted down the hallway at this barricaded man. It took hours. The containment guy always comes up to me. "I hate your voice," he says. "I hate your voice."

* * *

When you get there, it's a mess. It's a circus. People are standing around. Kids are running all over. Everybody wants to get involved. People keep coming up to you—"But I know him. But I know him." You say, "Tell me about it." You write it down. It might be important. At the least, it makes them feel important and they go away.

The first thing you do is, you've got to contain the guy so he doesn't come running out. You've got to secure the scene. You can't let it get out of hand or get any bigger than it is. And then you condense it down. If he has the run of the whole floor in a hotel, you want to get him into one wing, one set of rooms, one room. If he's in a house, you get him to one floor. You close him down.

Containment officers try to get as close to the guy as we can without blowing our cover. We're right in the building with the guy, we're in the house, we're in his apartment. Many times, we're right outside the apartment door. That's a very likely spot.

You *can* hide on a guy. It can be done. For example, if you get into a house and you stay three, four feet back from a window, the window can be open, and as long as you don't have a light behind you to silhouette you, you cannot be seen behind that window. All the guy will see is a black hole.

There's a lot of ways you can do it. You don't put yourself in an obvious position. If the guy looks at an open window across the street—it's winter; every other window is closed, there's one window cracked a few inches—you don't want to be hiding behind that crack in that window. He's gonna say, *"That's* where the guy is."

We get in some really uncomfortable positions. You'll be in a cramped hallway for hours. Or in an alley, behind garbage cans, with rats running all over. Some of the places we're in, they smell, they're filthy, they've got roaches, rats.

*   *   *

I was in combat in Korea. It was so cold, you would spend ninety percent of your time surviving the weather, not the enemy. It's just the same as a combat zone when you do an HBT: you're stuck outside in an alley or a gangway; it's the same as sitting out in the middle of nowhere. And it's *cold* if you do this in a Chicago winter. It's hard to keep your concentration, your body functioning; it's almost impossible. So maybe you give up your alertness just to survive the cold. It raises the danger factor.

The guy you're watching is nice and warm inside. He can run outside and he's functional for say five minutes, because he's all pumped up. He can be on top of you, just with a T-shirt on; he's not feeling that cold. He's got the jump on you.

As far as knowing the containment is out there, we don't like them to see containment officers because if they see them and they're armed, they might shoot. But we certainly want them to know that containment is there. So, a lot of times, a fellow will say, "I see those guys. I don't want to see them." Or, "You've got police out there." We tell them, "Of course there are police, do they bother you? We'll tell them to stay back." And then we tell the police, "Just try to keep down, guys."

What we do when we first get involved in these things, if the person inside doesn't have a phone, we throw them a field phone. Many times, we have people who have torn the phone out of the wall in a rage, or they're in a place that doesn't have a phone, like a garage.

So we've got what we call a "throw phone," a military phone. It's this thing in a canvas bag—it's military—with a big zipper across the top. And you open it up and you get down to this black, heavy-duty plastic combat phone. You pick it up—it's got a crank on the side. You go *crank-crank-crank-crank-crank-crank-crank*. And you then talk over this thing and you feel like Lee Marvin in an old war movie.

So finally we decided—here we're trying to have empathy with the guy and say stuff like "I'm your buddy" and "Let's talk this over"—and we're throwing in a combat phone. So we changed. What we have now is a baby blue Princess phone. Now, instead of going *crank-crank-crank* on the old military phone, the guy has a little Princess. We tried to get a pink one, because that's supposed to be the best color. But our Vice Control Section got this baby blue one on a gambling raid, so we went with that. We put a SMILE—HAVE A NICE DAY sticker on it.

The two most dangerous times in any hostage situation are the initial confrontation and the surrender. In the initial confrontation—shots may be fired, things are all confused, stress levels hit the ceiling.

The offender's inside, looking around—he's hearing the sirens, he's hearing the police radios squawking, he's hearing the police officers yelling back and forth, he's hearing them running back and forth.

The guy's in a panic. He thinks Rambo and three SWAT teams are about to come swinging through the window. That's when he's gonna make a mistake—he's gonna start firing shots out the window, he's gonna shoot a hostage, he's gonna do something desperate.

The phone rings. He picks it up. Here's a voice that represents that entity out there. And it's a calm voice. He starts calming down. Just by getting one of our guys to call the bad guy on the phone solves half our problems.

The police are in a panic too. They're running around. They don't know what the hell's going on. And all of a sudden the word comes over the radio that somebody's got the bad guy on the phone and they've started talking to him. Right away, the police are gonna calm down too.

What we try to do, right from the start, is reduce the threat level of the new environment. The situation will start off—the offender has all three hostages on the ground and he's telling them, "Move and I'll shoot you in the head." And he means it.

Now the phone rings, a calm voice on the other end; lo and behold nobody has crashed through the doors and windows on him, he gets familiar with the sounds of the place, the smell of the place, the lighting, nothing happens to him—he relaxes control.

Now one hostage is in the john, the other one's sitting on the couch, the other one's looking out the window. What happens is hostages begin to escape. Because as time goes on, the offender's control becomes looser and looser because he becomes complacent. Escaping hostages is a common resolution of hostage situations.

We avoid using bullhorns as much as possible. It's hard to sound compassionate over a bullhorn. It's electronic and it's loud and here you're trying to be empathetic. How can you be empathetic over a bullhorn? You end up sounding like Broderick Crawford. So we use bullhorns to get them to pick up the telephone.

There's a big difference between what you can say on the phone and what you can shout through a door or across a roof with a bullhorn. They tell you, when you're being trained how to handle suicides, you should always say to the person, right up front, "Are you going to commit suicide?" Try shouting that across a rooftop—"ARE YOU GOING TO COMMIT SUICIDE?" It sounds like you want them to hurry it up.

The way I do it, when I get the guy on the phone, I say, "I'm Mike Hogan. I'm with the Chicago Police. And I'm here to help. Hey, listen, I'm here to help you."

I don't give my rank. In the old days, coppers always said, "I'm Sergeant So-and-so" because "Sergeant" gives you a certain authority, but not absolute. You don't want to say you're the highest authority, because then you couldn't stall the guy on checking with the bosses on whether you can do certain things. I leave it vague. I say, "I'm with the police and I'm here to help you."

The guy might say, "I don't need your help."

"Well, somebody needs some help because, well, we got five hundred policemen out here and we got you in there, so, you know . . ."

"Oh, you're one of those negotiators, right, that are trained to tell me this and get me to do that. I know what you're up to."

"Hey, listen. Look, yeah, we have a program. Of course we do. You know. But I'm here to help you. I'm here to talk to you. That's why we have the program. Because sometimes people get in situations that, one, they don't want to be in and, two, they never *thought* they'd be in. We're here to help."

"I know all your tricks. I know you're supposed to get me to give in. I know you're gonna shut my heat off. I know that you're gonna make me cold . . ."

"Well, you're very knowledgeable, but let me tell you something. As long as you know all those things, I want you to know that I really want you to get out of this thing alive and I don't want anybody to be hurt. And if I had to bring my mom down here to talk to you to do that, I'd do it. And if I had to bring *anybody* down here to get you out, I'd do it. What kind of job do you have?"

"I'm a welder. So big deal."

"I look at you welding, I know that you didn't just start out welding. Of course you didn't; you were trained. But they didn't train you to be a nice person or a person who wants to keep life rather than take it away. *That* you did on your own. That's why I'm here. I'm trained to be a negotiator but I also want to keep you alive, me alive, and everybody else alive."

You gotta be honest with these people. Actually, I like it when a guy starts telling me what my job is, because that gives me something else to talk about. So I might go on something like: "What do you know about my job? Tell me what you know about negotiations."

"Anhh, I saw so-and-so do it in such and such a movie. This is what they did. Blah blah blah blah."

"No kidding. What happened?"

"Well, the guy came out, the cop put handcuffs on him and they both jumped off a roof."

"Hey, pal, I'm not gonna put a handcuff on you and jump off a roof with you."

You gotta be a good listener. That's the key. They want to talk. They're the ones with the problem. You look for any kind of hook that'll get them going. You play with that. That's all you've got to begin with. Keep them going.

* * *

Once they agree to talk, then you play off what they tell you and all you have to do is adjust to what they say.

"What's your name?"

"Tony."

"Tony, is it. You're not Italian?"

You phrase it like that instead of saying, "Are you Italian?" or "That's Italian." And why? Because if he *is* Italian and he likes it, "Yes I am." If he's *not* Italian and he hates Italians, you've already said he's not Italian. So he's not mad at you. So you give him an out immediately from the statement you've made.

"You're not Italian, are you?"

"What's wrong with Italians?"

"Oh, I *like* Italians."

Or it could go: "I hate Italians."

"Yeah. I do too. I didn't think you were Italian."

You play off what he says. But if you use the wrong word, if you say, "That's Italian, isn't it?" and what set him off was his great-grandfather in Italy wrote him out of the will and his wife here took off with all his money and she went back to Italy and you don't know that, because it's the first ten minutes that you've been there, you might have lost before you even started. You've gotta guard what you say, I guess. You're riding the fence, you're always riding the fence, you've gotta go one way or the other depending on what the response is.

A nut can be sitting there and say, "Get these goddamn green bugs off of my wall." Now you don't start saying, "Yeah, I got green bugs on my wall too, buddy. I know what you mean." "No you don't. You don't have green bugs on your wall. You think I'm nuts. You're making fun of me." You don't get into his world. "Are you saying you see these green bugs? Where do these green bugs come from?" "Hey, man. If I knew where they came from, I could get rid of them."

You find out what's wrong with this guy by finding out if he's been in a hospital, by getting a hold of his psychiatrist or analyst and he's going to tell you, "Bill should be taking medication. When he doesn't, he becomes a schizoid; he starts seeing bugs on his wall—and don't mention his mom because this thing all started when his mom died five years ago."

You talk about anything to make it more human, less police, less criminal. You talk about the weather, you talk about sports, you talk about the wall. You're trying to establish a rapport with him. You're trying to gain his confidence. You want him to trust you—"You're in this awful situation, but I want to help you"— you're his anchor—it's sort of like, "Through me, you'll live."

You don't insult the guy's manhood. You don't set deadlines. You don't go face-to-face with the bad guy. Nobody ever walks up to the bad guy and hands him something. If you have to give him something, this can be done with ropes and fishing lines and buckets and satchels. Nobody walks up and hands the guy a pizza.

The people the hostage-taker has are in great danger because of his decision. If we allow somebody to go in, they're in great danger because of *our* decision. No citizens are allowed to go in. No policeman goes in face-to-face with these people. No exchange of hostages. All that is Hollywood.

We've got one real hard and fast rule. You don't bring in the wife, the girlfriend, the priest, the rabbi, the minister, and let them talk to the offender. We might bring them in and get information from them. But if you check it out, the reason *why* they've gone off is probably because of the wife, the priest, the relative, whoever they want you to bring there. And they want to commit the final act in front of them. They're the suicide audience.

There was a guy that had problems. He shot his wife in the head. Killed her. Her head is gone.

She's on the landing, at the bottom of the back stairway. Sitting on the top of the stairs is the guy. There are eight stairs; I counted them because I wanted to know how many leaps I'd have to take if I had to come after him.

When I got there, here's the wife's body, no head, and standing next to it is a Catholic priest. Bad thing to do. Priests give you the last rites, priests give you absolution, priests are associated with weddings, christenings, and the end. So he's symbolizing the end. The district cops brought the priest.

I get there, I don't know what's going on, but somebody tells me there's a priest up there talking to this guy and the priest's not saying the right shit.

Now ordinarily, I would never have gone face-to-face with this guy. There was a doorway to the right of the guy, the upstairs kitchen doorway. I would have talked to him from the doorway because—first—looking down the stairs at the priest, the guy's looking at his wife's body. He's looking at the blood. And he's got the high ground. I don't *like* to be on the low ground. I don't want to go face-to-face with a man with a shotgun. Shotguns scare me. Guns and knives don't scare me. Shotguns scare me.

I would have gone to the kitchen doorway, but the priest is there. So I stand next to the priest. I start talking to the guy; he spoke good English, that's fortunate. He's Cuban. Carlos Carbello. The priest was smart enough to keep his mouth shut. I changed places with the priest. I get to a position on the second stair, leaning on the railing. That's my comfort zone. I take position there, knowing that I can just take a header down the stairs if I have to.

I'm hoping the priest will say something like, "I've got to go to the bathroom" and go away. If the priest goes away, I'm gonna go away. Somebody else can go upstairs and start talking to him.

The priest won't leave. I threw my sportcoat over the body so the guy wouldn't focus on it. Pissed me off. And I made the guy believe it was *me* that was bothered by the body. That took a while to try to figure out how to do that. I wanted him to quit looking at the body. So my sportcoat goes on the body, I'm talking to this guy, we only talked for about an hour and fifteen minutes.

The guy is standing there with the shotgun in his mouth and his big toe on the trigger. I'm debating where to go. I figured I could make two leaps and have a shot at the shotgun. Then I figured, Aw, that's not the way to do this.

You could see his toe on the trigger move and relax. He's tense. He's relaxed. He's tense. He's relaxed. He'd take the shotgun out of his mouth and talk. Sometimes he'd lay it on his shoulder and not have his hands on it. He'd have his toe off the trigger.

After a while, you could orchestrate it. If I wanted his toe on the trigger, I'd say something to get him tense. You play with bringing the guy up and down so that you can control the situation.

You get it down to a science—If I say this, he's not gonna get *too* excited, but he'll put the shotgun in his mouth. "You don't like Castro, do you?" *Boomp*—the shotgun goes in his mouth. And then we started to talk baseball; he liked baseball, I played baseball, I was a center fielder and first baseman, he didn't like first base. So we didn't talk about playing first base anymore. We talked about playing center field. He played shortstop. He complained about the throws from center field and how some players didn't know the right throws. And then we talked about, and actually had a disagreement over, the proper cutoff man. Think things about baseball, you know?

And then all of a sudden he'd start to go off. He'd disappear into a tangent. He'd start to look at the body. He'd start to look at me. I says, well, then it's time for him to put the shotgun in his mouth again.

"Castro played baseball, didn't he?" *Boomp!* Shotgun's back in his mouth.

Then I started learning how to make him cry. Without talking about the dead wife. We talked about his home, and his family, and let's see what happens when he gets a little bit upset. When he'd get upset, he'd cry and what I noticed was that when he started to cry, he would relax totally. The gun would be on his shoulder, he'd have his hands together, and his toe was off the trigger. His most relaxed position that I had seen was when he was crying.

So after a while, you'd get him to cry a little, cry a little more— you didn't want him to go off, but you'd let him cry. One time I thought, "Let's get him to cry a little longer and see what happens." Unfortunately, we were running out of things to talk about after only an hour. So I let him cry for about forty seconds. That's the longest time that I went without saying something to him.

The priest thought something's wrong. He thought I ran out of things to say. So the priest says, and I quote, "Carlos, it's okay to cry. Men cry sometimes, Carlos. Get it all out. Get it over with."

The next sound you heard was a roar. The next thing I felt were various parts of Carlos from above Carlos's neck. On me. Because when the priest said the words, "Get it over with," Carlos took that four-word remark totally out of context and did what he had intended to do all along. It wasn't my fault; it wasn't the priest's fault. Later, they found a note. He was gonna kill his wife; he had asked his kid to come over; he was gonna kill him, too, and then commit suicide, because his wife was gonna leave him. He was dead before we even got there.

My next words, exactly, were to the priest: "What the fuck did you say that for?" The most terrible thing you could say to somebody who thinks it's his fault.

This old man ran down the stairs and down the alley, ran all the way back to his parish.

Now, I went home, changed my shirt, the sergeant poured me about a quart of Scotch in a glass, and then we had to go off to court, because we had a surrender on a murder with a gun. So we took care of that, I got back, and the next thing you know the First Deputy's Office calls. The First Deputy's Office says, "Would you take a ride over to the rectory"—he gives the address—"a priest wants to talk to you."

So I go and it's another priest, this young guy, who wants to see me. He says, "Can you do me a favor?" "What?" "Can you talk to Father So-and-so? This poor man, he's suicidal. He thinks this is all his fault." It turned out this second priest was at the scene the whole time, listening. "I heard the whole thing," he says. "I believe you're the only one who can talk to him." "He's not doing it, is he?" "No, he's just in the parlor and he's staring into a teacup."

So I went in there and talked to him, just talked to him about the situation. He asked me about the program and asked about everything and he got to a point where he leaned forward, touched me on the wrist and said, "How do *you* feel, son?" Soon as he said that, I knew he was cured. Soon as he was looking to take care of me, I knew it was time to get out of there.

* * *

I have two simple rules. Never make a promise that you can't keep, and if you do, make it a promise that the guy will *understand* you can't keep.

I violated my own rules one time. And to this day, I second-guess myself on this one.

A guy stabbed the shit out of his father-in-law, thirty, forty times. Now here's what happened. He's fighting with his wife, who's pregnant, he's got two kids; they're not his kids, they're her kids. She's pregnant with his baby.

He's fighting with her a lot. He's an abuser, a beater. They live with her father. The father, who knows that there's a problem on this particular day, trying to protect the daughter from further abuse at this particular moment—he's not banning the guy from the house; he's not throwing him out; he's trying to defuse this moment—he locks him out of the house.

The son-in-law crashes a window. He tries to climb in through the window. The father-in-law therefore hits him with a baseball bat. The son-in-law gets a knife, a genuine, a real butcher knife—a real one!—a real butcher knife, stabs the father-in-law, I think, in the thirties, the high thirties.

He knows he screwed up. He grabs the two children, goes down the basement stairs, and holds them at knifepoint. The father-in-law had already called the police, the police are coming, the father-in-law is dead when they get there.

Two policemen from the Twentieth District arrive. They had known the son-in-law from domestic disturbances before. So now they're standing there, at the doorway, looking down into the basement. And they're standing there talking to this guy who's got this butcher knife and he's got both of these little children, four and five years old, I think. And the one copper was good talking to him and the other copper was good talking to him with one problem: One partner could bring him up, get him hyper, and the other partner could bring him down. And you use those techniques to control the guy, to manipulate his mind. But they didn't *know* they were doing that. The one cop would bring him up, he'd get real hyper, and they'd get real nervous and they'd be quiet. And that would kind of mellow him down a little bit and then the other guy would start to talk to him to bring him down. And if they knew where they were going, then they would have known how to get him in the middle where he'd be rational. Because once you get him rational, you know he's not gonna cut his two little stepkids' heads off. When he's hyper, he might. And when he's down, he might. But not in the middle.

But they didn't know that. And we got there and one of the cops, I'll never forget, he's got this look on his face, and he was so scared. I was scared too.

We got this cop's partner away and then he and I traded places. Before this, I was writing him notes, things to say. Finally, I realized this isn't working. I wrote him a note: "Tell him you gotta take a leak or something." The cop says, "Listen, I gotta check on something. A friend of mine is here. Let him talk to you a minute."

So then I start talking to the guy in the basement. I'm standing by the doorjamb. The cop starts to go. I grab him. I couldn't tell him "You gotta stay with me," but I'm trying to let him know he shouldn't go anywhere because I don't know anything about this guy. There's gotta be things we don't know. First, I don't know if the father-in-law's dead or alive at this point. I don't know if the guy down *there* knows if the father-in-law's dead or alive. I don't know if they said to the guy, "Well, you killed him, but it's okay." It turned out he *didn't* know the father-in-law was dead.

I'm looking down at the two little kids the stepfather's holding. The little girl was real fidgety. The little boy was okay. You could tell with the boy, this guy was a definite father image for the boy. He didn't understand. He wasn't scared; he just didn't understand why his dad has this big knife and won't let him go.

The bond is there between the father and the little boy. You could tell. "It's okay. It's okay," he keeps telling the boy. But the bond isn't there with the girl. He's not saying anything to her. So right away, you're fearful for the little girl. Nobody else could sense that and nobody could see it because of my position. And unbeknownst to me, next door, there was a containment guy, a sniper, and the position I was standing in kept blocking their view of everything. But I just found the position I was comfortable in, and once in a while I'd move, but I kept coming back to that position. It was my comfort zone.

The other police are right next to me, but the guy in the basement can't see them. He only sees me. There are containment officers in the next building, looking down. The police inside don't communicate with me verbally; they write me notes. On occasion, I'd lean across and look at a note. One time, I put my cheek on the doorjamb like I was resting and they stuck an earphone in my ear.

The guy downstairs knows I'm a detective. "Where's your gun?" he says. I had already taken my gun from my ankle holster, put it in my back waistband, because if he's gonna ask me about my gun, I can show him, voilà!, an empty holster, right?

I said, "Listen, I don't have a gun anywhere." And I leaned to the left, up against the jamb, and fortunately the guy who was standing next to me had enough presence of mind to reach around, without being seen, and take the gun out of my waistband. So now I can do a pirouette, I can pull my shirt out, I open my pants and show him my underwear and I do everything possible to show him that I'm not armed, to take away what he thought was a threat.

The problem was, if he started cutting the kids, there's nothing I could do. My job is not to shoot. In that case, the only people that were in a position to do anything aggressive if necessary were the guys across the way and I didn't know they were there.

Anyway, we got to talking. I convinced him that his father-in-law wasn't dead. I convinced him that his father-in-law was the offender and he was the victim. I said the father-in-law was the offender—"He beat you with a baseball bat."

Fortunately, somebody picked up on what I was saying, and in about four minutes there was a case report brought to the scene that had him listed as the victim. "The Offender:" father-in-law's name. "Information Reveals That: Victim was trying to see his wife and was attacked." I mean, we had a police report that said that this man, who had just gotten done stabbing the shit out of his father-in-law, was a victim.

I could see that the little girl was scared. So I talked to her. "How do you feel?" "Oh, okay." "Are you sick to your stomach?" I kept returning to her. "How do you feel? Is your stomach bothering you? Your throat is real dry, isn't it?" I talked the kid into being sick. Pretty soon, she's got dry heaves. This poor little girl.

And now the stepfather starts to feel for her. I say, "Pat, she's gotta go to the bathroom." "Well, she can go in the sewer." Now, he had said to the little boy once to pee in the sewer. I said, "Pat, she's not gonna want to do that. Would you want to do that if you were a little girl, go to the bathroom in front of your father? Let her come upstairs."

And here's the thing that I'll be criticized for for the rest of my life. "If I let her come up, do you promise that she'll come back?" "I promise." Without hesitation, I said, "I promise." He's got a kid that he can cut his head off if I don't get the girl back. If you get one hostage out, you're never gonna get the second hostage back. *I* know we're not gonna get him back. But I'm gonna get one kid out. It's a decision I made and a decision they still don't like. Plus, I know the bond—nobody else could see the bond between the guy and the boy.

There were a lot of little things, but one thing convinced me the bond was really there with the little boy. At one point, the stepfather took the butcher knife and scratched the little girl's cheek with it. And he scratched the little boy's throat. He told *her,* "Stand still or I'll do it again," but he said to the little boy, "I'm sorry."

So we get the little girl up the stairs and they take her off and she goes to the bathroom, she threw up, she was sick. Now—*they're bringing her back.* And they've got her where I can see her. And I'm starting to think, "She's not going back down there. Wait a minute." And one of the bosses comes running to me, and he's standing there—see, after a while, you get to know the routine. You lean on the doorjamb whenever you want information. And the boss says, "That girl's not going back there." I kind of looked at him and then I said something to the guy in the basement so that I could respond, "What the fuck do you think I am? Stupid?" I said it to Pat but I meant it for the boss.

I could see that Pat was nervous. He's got the knife at the kid's throat. What if he says, "Bring her down right now or I kill him?" What do you do?

Now the case report's here. So I say, "We've got the case report. I'll show it to you." Now he says the magic words: "I believe you." Whoa. Okaaay.

Now he says, "What should I do, Tom?"

"We should take care of this."

"How do we do that?"

Now I've got him, but I don't know I've got him because he's still got this kid at knifepoint. For several hours, he's been holding the kids like that. He's had one or the other with a knife to their throat for hours.

So now we start to string him along like a violin. I say, "Well, let me tell you this, Pat. Let me see if we can get a complaint together. So you know and because you trust me, I want you to sign a complaint against your father-in-law. Battery."

I can hear people scrambling, so now they're looking for complaints and they're filling them out. In a few minutes, it's done. "Pat, here's the complaint. Here's what I want you to do. I'm gonna give you this complaint. I'll put it on the stairs." We'd already done that. I would put cigarettes on the stairs. I'd go down the stairs and come back up. And he'd come up one stair, holding the little boy by the collar. We went through this elaborate passing system on the twelve stairs.

"So I'll get the complaint down the stairs."

"No, you don't have to do that."

"No, I want you to see it."

"You don't have to do that."

"Well, okay. All right."

"Tom, I think I'm gonna give up."

"All right. Let me put the complaint on the stairway. Why don't you put the knife on the stairway, take the complaint, read it, and if everything is exactly what I told you, then you go back to the bottom of the stairs, and leave the knife right there."

"Okay."

I went down three stairs. And the next thing I see is this guy coming up the stairs with the knife. He's got his arm extended and the knife's pointed right at me. He left the little boy at the bottom of the stairs. And I'm thinking, "This isn't healthy. Where do we go from here?" If he had the little boy with him, I probably would have retreated. He didn't have the little boy and I'm thinking, "Do I run? Do I break up what we had going? Do I endanger the little boy? Do I want open heart surgery?" And all this is happening in just a second. And all of a sudden, he took the knife, turned it around, and turned the handle toward me.

I believe, and everyone agrees with me, that he was ready to give up long before he actually did. Probably when we first told him about the case report. I mean, we had brought him up and down and up and down so many times, this poor guy's mind, his mind was like rubber. But in that second . . . in the middle of that stairway . . . oh, shit.

All this stuff works great if you can get the guy inside to respond. But what happens if he won't respond—what if he won't even pick up the phone? That happens a lot.

The old thing was to use tear gas and smoke the bad guy out. But tear gas just doesn't work on everybody. Most of the time, it doesn't work on drunks and psychos. And that's what you're dealing with most of the time.

Plus the fact that a lot of the stronger tear gas is pyrotechnic. It can set the place on fire.

And if you have hostages in there, you can't use tear gas. A hostage might have a respiratory problem; it could be an older person you don't want to take chances with.

Also, the stronger stuff clouds the air. Tactically, you're going into a total darkness.

I went to a situation one time where a guy had killed his mother and he barricaded himself in his house. He never answered his phone. We were there twelve hours and the guy finally came out after they used tear gas—nuttier than a fruitcake. Who else would kill their mother in broad daylight and throw her body out on the front porch?

We rang the phone five, six hours. Just the thought of listening to the phone ring—I can't listen to the phone ring even five times in my own house, I go nutty. We did the bullhorn; that didn't work. They plugged his doorbell; that didn't work. Then they tried tear gas. That worked. He came out one minute later.

We had a real Norman Bates once. A sixty-five-year-old widower went barricade. The wife was dead and he was in there by himself. We got him on the phone; he'd wander off. What we heard was two voices. We figured out he was arguing with his dead wife—he'd talk in his own voice and he'd continue the argument in her voice. You could hear this.

It had gone on for about fifteen hours, with the guy talking to us and then going into his other voice. Finally, he hung up on us.

We called right back. The sergeant got on the phone, "Now listen, Mr. So-and-so, we've been talking for thirteen hours. You know we have policemen surrounding your home. There's not a lot you can do. We want you to come out and let's get this thing over with. That's it. Please let's get it over." The voice on the other end said, "What? What? What's going on? There are police around my house?" This was at two in the morning. The sergeant said, "Is this such-and-such at such-and-such address?" The fellow said, "No, I'm sorry. You dialed the wrong number."

The only time I've gone home feeling totally wrung out was when one of our guys got shot a couple summers ago.

There was a former police officer who went barricade on Stony Island. He'd been evicted from his apartment. When the sheriff and the deputy sheriff and five movers showed up, they were met with a shot.

It went on all day. It came to a point where people figured this is going to be another surrender; it's just a matter of time. All afternoon, we weren't able to get any response from this guy. We knocked on the door. We threw things through the window. Just to get a response from him. Then we could initiate negotiations.

He never responded. The only response he gave all afternoon was that one shot he took at one of the containment officers.

Our guy was in the alley and, after hours of the guy inside not responding to anything, our guy just peered around the corner of the garage—he just moved his head out at a little bit of a side angle rather than looking straight on.

He got shot in the forehead. The bullet went in and went around the skull, on the inside of his skull, rather than boring right through the meat in the center of the brain. He took a shot to the head. They say he'll be confined to a wheelchair for the rest of his life.

Your negotiations, and this sounds really great, a lot of times are yelling through a door or screaming across the rooftops. You find yourself yelling things through a door and you don't know if anybody's inside. They tell you just to keep on going. But how can you change the subject if nobody's answering you? You go on and on and on. You keep saying, "Come on, talk to me. I'd like to know what the problem is, why are you doing this, is there some way we can help you, da da da." How many times can you be vague? You feel really dumb.

We spend a lot of time talking to no one. We once negotiated with an empty building for twenty-five hours; the guy left before we even got set up.

You should see how many times we're watching a window. Somebody says, "Hey, I think I saw the window shade move." It's a breeze; there's nobody inside. Half the time we're not sure they're in there or not.

We were out one night three hours on the bullhorn. Finally, we go in the house. Empty. The guy had come out with a gun, made some threats, and left.

There was one incident—a shot fired. The neighbors thought the guy had gone barricade. He had gone to bed. We're out there for hours and hours, bullhorns, the whole bit. There's this whole world out there he knows nothing about. He's completely oblivious.

We talk to animals a lot. We talk to dead people a lot.

I talked down a hallway for six hours with a bullhorn with a man who shot a police officer and then killed himself in the same moment. And logistically, you couldn't go down the hallway. The decision was finally made to make the assault;

they brought out body armor, things like that. The assault team went in and found that the man was dead and he was in the initial stages of rigor mortis. He was dead the whole time.

A lot of these people got the idea that if they don't respond, maybe we'll just go away. Shit like that. So we start with a probe, maybe move on from there. It's to change the pace and to let them know that, hey, you're not playing the game—we're gonna start doing a little bit more.

Say we've been talking to the guy inside, yelling, calling him on the phone, but there's no answer to the phone, no answer to the bullhorn. Okay, now we'll start probing. You want to know, is he alive or dead? Maybe he slashed his throat and he *can't* talk to you; maybe he just doesn't *want* to talk to you. So you take a few steps to see if you can get him talking to you or whatever.

It might be taking a long pole and breaking a window. You'd be surprised how many times that gets a response out of these people. We're gonna bang on the doors. Throw a rock through the bedroom window. Throw a concrete block up against the door. Get these people to respond.

Sometimes you want to get the guy stirred up. You want to bring him up; maybe he's gotten down—they call it going to ground. He's just in there stagnating. So you go to a diversion. It's similar to a probe, but a little more. You make him think you're making an entry. You can break windows, fire tear gas in the front, make him move to the back, throw smoke bombs, turn the electricity on and off. A diversion is just something to get the person to think you're doing something you're not. It gets him up again.

If he thinks you're coming in, then he's gonna get real excited. "Wait a minute. Slow down. Relax," you say. "Why don't we just end this?" You work with noises, with lights, with anything. You keep the guy inside on the edge.

You bring him up and down. You want to wear him down so he recognizes the futility of staying barricaded in there. Turn on the power, turn off the power, the water, the electric, the gas. If it's wintertime and it's one of those twenty below zero days and you shut down his gas and his electric, he can't watch himself on TV and pretty soon he gets real cold in there. You break out a few windows and he gets a lot colder much quicker. After a while, he comes back into reason.

You might fool around with the lighting, with noises. We don't use sirens so much because sirens really irritate the shit out of *you*, too, if you're sitting out there. This guy can stand in there for ten hours and not give a shit. After about five minutes, the coppers are all going bats.

We might keep ringing his doorbell. If you're ringing the doorbell, he hears it; it's not affecting you. But say you're inside, and you've got some asshole from containment ringing the doorbell from the front porch and you're inside for a half hour listening to this asshole ring the front doorbell, pretty soon you're gonna shoot the guy on the front porch. Or you'll shoot yourself.

The whole idea is getting them real tired. Eventually, everybody has to go to sleep. And what you do is, you *bother* them. If you think he's going to sleep, you call him. If he hangs the phone up on you, you ring and ring and ring. Just bother them.

We want to totally control the environment of the hostage-taker: the electric, the gas, the air conditioning, the heating, no matter what it is, we want control of it. If you can pull these resources away, then they're negotiable items, and we can negotiate them back for the release of the hostages.

Anything you do can be tactical. If he's hungry, say, and you want to get something out of him, you might munch on a sandwich while you talk to him. If he's saying he's hungry and he wants some food, well, of course, you never let him have something for nothing. You might very well chew on a sandwich. Or pop a can near enough to the phone so he can hear it. Light a cigarette. Get him to give you what you want. It might be anything from a hostage to one bullet.

* * *

You negotiate everything. Basically, we take everything away and negotiate it all back.

One time, we had a trade involving a fellow down at the Criminal Courts Building. He had taken two lawyers hostage in a courtroom. And we traded him one lawyer for a can of 7-Up, which we thought was very humorous. And during the trade, we were able to get the other lawyer out.

Boredom is a horrible stressful factor in these things. It's much worse for containment officers than it is for the negotiators. You've got your position and you've got to watch that door, that window, whatever, the whole time. You can't relax or be diverted for one millionth of a second. Every time you light a cigarette, or take your eyes off that doorway or that window for even a second, that could mean someone's life.

It requires constant attention. We try to keep two guys at each post and one guy has to pay attention to that door. Nothing else. That means he can't be smoking, he can't be talking, these guys can't get into a bullshit seminar and start slapping each other on the back and joking and the whole routine, because pretty soon nobody's paying attention to where they should.

So, if the one guy's span of attention is one minute, the other guy will spell him after one minute. Hopefully, we've got people with enough training so they can stand there for fifteen, twenty minutes and watch.

Hostage-takers let their guard down after a while. The same thing happens with the police officers. It's how cops can get killed. The police officer starts off, say, in the garage—right behind the house where the bad guy is. He's very wary. He's got his gun out. He may have a mirror so he doesn't even have to put his head around the corner to peek at the guy.

What will happen is, if you leave an untrained officer there— you take a look at this guy at the beginning of the job, his gun is out, he's using his cover right. You leave him there four hours, he gets familiar with the environment—the smell of the place, the sound of the place. He keeps looking at the house; nothing's happened; the guy hasn't fired out of the house. All of a sudden, the gun's in the holster, he's having a cigarette, he's standing in the Kill Zone, talking to his buddy across the fence. So we constantly have to maintain our vigilance, because once you become complacent, that's when you're through.

You're always thinking what happens if the guy comes running out *now*. We had a naked woman thrown out at us one time. A guy threw his hostage out; she had multiple stab wounds all over her body. She was locked in the apartment with the guy; it was the fifth, sixth floor—and all of a sudden the door opens up, he throws her out, she's running down the hall, no clothes on her, she comes screaming at us, *Heyuhh!*, bare-ass naked, blood all over the place. He stayed in the apartment. He just threw her out. No warning. It could have been him.

You just never take anything for granted. Anybody comes out, we treat as a possible hostage-taker until we're able to secure that person and make sure that he's not the offender. Another thing you gotta look out for, somebody comes running out, it could be a hostage who's gone over to the side of the hostage-taker. So someone running out might be running out to help the hostage-taker—he runs out with the evidence, with the weapon, he could be running out as a diversionary practice. A guy comes running out the front shooting, you assume it's the hostage-taker, right?, but it's a cover for the hostage-taker.

We've had sightings where people have alleged the offender wore certain clothes—it turned out they were the victim's clothes. That's one of the reasons you just don't open fire. If the guy walks in front of the window wearing a blue shirt, and you have a description, the offender that stuck up the bank and took hostages was wearing a blue shirt and he had a handgun— subject wearing a blue shirt walks in front of the window, it could be the hostage-taker forcing the victim to do that with an empty gun just to see if we're gonna shoot. That's why you play it bare minimum. And you don't underestimate offenders, ever.

*   *   *

We had a robbery that went sour. A guy went into an old bookstore on the North Side and pulled out a handgun. Now, if he'd been thinking rationally, he'd know there's not that much money in a bookstore. Something happened that soured it, a patrol car pulled up or something, but anyway it turned into a hostage situation.

I myself had a position on the alley approximately three doors from where the guy was. On several different occasions, I could see him come to the back window and he'd take a mirror and stick it out so he could check our location and stuff without exposing himself. So I'd see the mirror come out with part of the hand.

When a guy does this, you know he's pulled some time in the joint. That's what they do in prison. They put the mirror outside their cell and they call out to the guy next door, they both look in their mirrors, and they talk to each other.

He talked about some guy he'd been in the joint with. An El Rukn street gang member. And the negotiators, they got this guy in there and he talked to the guy over the telephone. Then he went out in front of the place—across the street; he had a car for cover and talked to the guy over the bullhorn: "Come on out, Joe. Nothin's gonna happen to you" and all that kind of stuff. The guy finally came out.

What got us, though, was when this El Rukn first came out to talk to the guy inside, he let out with a yell—or a yelp; it was a sound an animal would make—to identify to the person inside that it was in fact him out there and nobody trying to trick him. It took us kind of off-guard. We weren't really ready for that kind of animal yell to come out.

As containment officers, we don't want to know what the negotiators are doing or saying. We don't listen to them, even if we're behind them or right next to them. Of course, if you're all in a hallway and the negotiator and the guy are hollering back and forth, you *have* to hear. The danger is, you might get to thinking, Gee, maybe the guy's right. It seems like he's had nothing but bad luck. But this can put you in a bad position. You might let your guard down while you're standing there. And then if you have to take the guy out, you might hesitate. You don't want to Stockholm. It's a great way to get hurt.

We had one a few winters ago—with the windchill, it was fifty-five below. This guy was a barricade, he had a gun; we had him contained in a first-floor apartment.

We broke all his windows out, turned off all the power, turned off the heat, tried to get him freezing too. As long as we were uncomfortable, we wanted to make him *really* uncomfortable.

But the guys on the rifle on the outer perimeter, they were outside containing; they couldn't last five minutes. They said they were spelling five on and ten off and working in three-man teams. With the cold, you couldn't remain alert and active longer than that.

When communications broke down, the negotiators had to go outside and use the bullhorn. In order to do this, they had to gather other clothes and stuff that we found inside and borrow from other police officers to go out there. They had to stand out below the front porch around the corner talking to this guy. We wound up, it was so cold out there, we had to get rugs to put on top of the ice so the cold wouldn't go up into their feet.

The war wagon got stuck. It has everything we need on it and we couldn't get it down the street. It's loaded to the max. We've got mirrors, poles, tape, wedges, crowbars, electrical connections, radios, tool bags, rifles, shotguns, gas guns, spotlights, sledgehammers. All that stuff is kept on the war wagon. And we couldn't move it on the ice.

It lasted about two, three hours. The guy gave it up.

Here was a case, where if you would have listened to his story, you would have agreed with the guy. The girlfriend wanted him locked up on battery or something. He owned the apartment; she was living with him. She calls the police. But before she called the police, she gets a moving truck and has it parked one block over. So he's gonna go to jail; she's gonna take the furniture.

So the tac team comes walking in. She says, "I want to have

him locked up." "Hey, man, what—what—? What did I do? I didn't do anything." She says, "He hit me in the head. I want him locked up." So they're gonna make the arrest on him, but he knew what she was gonna do. So he says, "You're not taking *my* furniture," and he went and got the gun and he fired a shot. And the tac team, naturally, backed out. They're not stupid. And he went barricade.

That happens all the time. The woman calls. The cops come. "Lock up my husband," she'll say. He goes off to jail and she moves out with all the furniture. She might have the new boy-friend come over to help.

No one in the whole current program ever had to shoot any-body. It's called getting the green light—they're supposed to say, "It's a green light"; "You've got a green light"—that means kill the guy. They haven't said it yet.

We've used gas; we've assaulted, but it's always been resolved without killing the guy. You don't *want* to start shooting; you might get hurt. The goal is always to come back home with the same amount of holes in your body that you came to work with. But you've got to be prepared to if you have to. That's why you don't want to listen to the negotiators. You don't want to put up mental blocks.

The last thing you ever want to do is assault. You want to negotiate *forever*. It's a difficult thing to do, waiting it out. Police are action-oriented. You know that somebody is holding a child, and that child's life is in danger, you want to go in. But that action will kill the child.

Usually, when the hostage *does* get killed, it's because there's too much push. There's an assault or something like that and the hostage-taker panics.

Police assault kills hostages. They did a study—the Rand Corporation analyzed over four hundred hostage situations and found that eighty-seven percent of the hostages who were killed were killed during police assault.

And assault kills police. Even if the guy just has a knife, one lucky lunge and you're through.

* * *

Chicago's very conservative about going in. Especially compared with the West Coast—they reach impasse a lot quicker than we do. Basically, the West Coast has started and characterized the SWAT team. We're much more low-key.

New York is even more low-key than we are. New York will sit there forever.

Assault comes when all other known avenues of approach are exhausted. You've done everything you can dream of. You've done everything known to man. Assault is all that's left.

We usually assault when somebody won't talk anymore. If the person's still talking, we'll sit out there forever.

What we try to do is get the advantage to us, initially, at the entry. So you introduce tear gas or use a diversion. They have this thing called a concussion grenade—it causes a loud noise, a big flash; it's almost enough to knock you out. It disorients the person.

You can use lots of different ways, though. If you get his attention diverted or get him disoriented for even a fraction of a second, that may be all you need to come in and overwhelm him or keep anybody else from getting shot. You draw the guy's attention away from where the shit is gonna hit the fan.

Usually, assault is very controlled, very limited. It's practiced ahead of time. But sometimes we have to move from containment to assault immediately. There's no time to set up.

We had a woman one time, up north, who said she had kidnapped a five-year-old child on his way home from school and had him in the house. She was pointing a rifle out the back window. Suddenly, we saw smoke coming out of the back porch. We had to run an assault and get the fire department in there right away—the place was on fire.

We make entry, get to the kitchen, the tile's on fire—the gas is off the tile; we couldn't breathe. She had the gas turned on on the stove with no fire and a fire set in a waste basket. The whole joint was about to go up.

We didn't know where she was; we had no idea. We couldn't find the kid who was supposed to be in there. We found two rifle bags and one rifle. We knew there was another rifle in there. She had it.

It turned out there *was* no child hostage. We found her underneath the stairs to the second floor, sitting amongst all the clothes, drinking a can of Old Style.

There was a guy once who held fifty coppers at bay with a pair of scissors. That's all he had that was lethal; we didn't know it, of course. Every time they'd say, throw out a weapon, he'd throw out something ludicrous: once he threw out a nail file; another time he threw out a screwdriver or something. Finally, they went in and took him out by throwing a ballistics blanket over him.

There was this two-hundred-and-fifty-pound body builder once who just *destroyed* his apartment. He started throwing furniture over his balcony. He thought the CIA was listening to him through the wall sockets. He cut holes in his walls with a machete. We had him cut a hole in the wall so we could talk to him.

So he kept handing things out to us through the hole in the wall. He wanted to show us things he had. He'd say, "Look at this gun"—It was a shoe. We'd say, "Gee, wow, look at that. How many bullets does it have? What else you got?"

And one time, he wanted to show us his machete. He handed the machete out. Then he wanted the machete back. We had him reach out and we looped a belt over his wrist and just pulled him out through the hole.

We were called out one Christmas morning because a woman wanted us to kill her brother. On Christmas. Her brother had beaten her, he had picked on her, he had pointed guns at her for so many years, she got pissed off and wanted us to kill him. She didn't say that, of course; she just thought that's what would happen when we showed up.

She said he was up there with a shotgun. She thought we'd just rush in there and kill him. That's exactly what she thought.

It took us about three hours. He never answered us. Finally, the containment guys stormed the door. He was asleep under a mattress. He had no guns at all. One of the containment officers dragged him out by the hairs of his head.

She wanted him done in. She would have done anything to get us to kill him. Then she would have sued the city and gotten money on top of it.

Sometimes, for no reason, they just give up. The negotiator gets upset. He's been talking to this guy for five hours. He's still vociferous. He's angry. The negotiator's like, "What do you mean, you give up?" We have to say to the negotiator, "Wait. This is good."

Other than the initial confrontation, when the police are running in, the most dangerous time in a hostage situation is the surrender.

Surrender is a psychological suicide. It's a loss of control. They've had all this control. Now, they have to give up this control. So, you know, he's gonna be very high-key, very emotional.

And the last thing, right before they give it up, they'll change their minds. Usually surrenders are on and off, on and off, on and off, back and forth. Usually there's a couple false surrenders.

It's a loss of control. He's been the center of attention. But now he's gonna become one of five thousand people at the county jail. They hate losing it. So all of a sudden they start thinking maybe the police are gonna hurt me and they want assurances.

Or you get someone who's crazy as a loon, with all this paranoia. You may get somebody who's seriously paranoid, where his whole life has been dominated by it, his dreams—and all of a sudden he's surrounded by the police. "My God! Look out the window!" It looks like what they've been dreaming about for years. You make this guy walk out in the middle of all these police, it's very difficult.

So we have to be very careful with them, because they change their mind a lot. If they change their mind, and we expose ourselves, things can happen.

* * *

Surrender is especially dangerous for police because when we think that we've won, the police will let their guard down. They'll step back into that Kill Zone. They'll relax. The bad guy could still have a gun. And he's going through probably more psychologically traumatic times than ever. And *that's* the time police start to let their guard down and move into the Kill Zone.

The last thing you want to do is do something or not do something that's the cause of him going off. Say he comes out and everything's all screwed up; now he runs back into the building. Now you're stuck with another four hours of this shit.

You have to have a very regimented surrender procedure. You just can't have fifteen guys standing there saying, "Put your hands up." The poor guy comes out and there's three different guys telling him, "Put your hands up." "Put your hands down." "Stand up." "Kneel down." "Lie down." "Turn around." You gotta have *one* guy giving him directions. It's gotta be regimented. And it's all planned ahead of time. It's practiced.

It's not a thirty-second thing. We'll prepare everybody for it. We won't take a surrender sometimes until everybody knows what they're supposed to do, everybody's in place, everybody's been briefed, including the asshole.

You bring him to you; you don't go up to meet him. You can step into a world of trouble that way. You have him come out past the point of no return. You make it harder for him to go back than for you to go back.

We don't go with hands on the head, hands on the neck. We like their arms outstretched. The further his fingers are from his body, the harder it is for him to get to a weapon.

The guy always comes out looking like a wet rag. He's under a tremendous amount of stress. He's embarrassed. He's trying to save face.

We had one guy blow his brains out because he couldn't stand the humiliation of surrendering. I talked to him for sixteen hours.

We did everything right, everything by the book, everything was working great—the phone system, the intelligence, and the only guy not cooperating was the Italian guy on the other end of the phone. He kills himself.

He had a hostage in with him, his sister-in-law; he had a gun to her head the whole time. When he was twenty-one years old, he went to Italy and brought back a fourteen-year-old girl and married her. Over the years, they found out she couldn't have children. What set this thing off was, he wanted his pregnant girlfriend to move in with them and they'd take the baby. The wife said, "Fuck you," and left.

His demand—"I want to talk to my wife." We knew that if he even got on the phone with her, he'd kill himself, or he'd kill the sister-in-law. I knew I couldn't say anything about his barren wife or kids, or that would trigger him off.

We had him convinced we could not find his wife. The phone company cooperated—they popped the line to the girlfriend's house in case he called her on the second phone line and she said, "Oh no, she's there. I saw her on TV." We got the media to squash that. He'd call the girlfriend's; the phone would ring and ring and ring; no answer.

We got talking about baseball. We're friends. He got to like me, he's b.s.-ing with me.

Finally, after sixteen hours, he kills himself. He knew that the plan was shot because they couldn't find his wife. He couldn't walk out in disgrace. He went in the bedroom, put on a three-piece suit and his gold chains and he blew his heart out.

I went in to see him. He was just a skinny little pukey guy, not what I had pictured at all. I thought he'd be some big iron worker, a macho guy, a big soccer player. He was just this little guy. Some people were worried about me, going in to look at this guy. I did it out of curiosity. I had talked to this guy for sixteen hours. I wanted to see him.

Hostage/Barricade Incidents:
Contributing Police Officers

YOUTH OFFICER KIM ANDERSON, Area Five. Anderson has worked as a hostage negotiator (she was one of the CPD's first seven woman negotiators) since the inception of HBT in 1979. Anderson's seventeen-year career with the police has included work in the Youth Division from 1974 to 1980; assignments within the Organized Crime Division's Gangs, Narcotics, Prostitution, and Gambling units and the Intelligence Section from 1980 to 1983. Anderson was detailed to the Chicago Terrorist Task Force from 1983 to 1985. Anderson has been working as a youth officer in Area Five since 1985.

SERGEANT JAMES BIEBEL, Area Six Property Crimes; hostage negotiator. Biebel, who joined the CPD in 1967, worked patrol and tac in the Twentieth District till 1971, when he was promoted to detective and assigned to Area Five Burglary. In 1973, Biebel was assigned to Area Six Burglary, where he served as a detective for seven years before joining the CIU, a unit that tracked down career criminals. In 1982, Biebel was promoted to sergeant. Biebel worked in Area One Property Crimes from 1982 to 1984. In 1984, he joined Area Six Property Crimes. Biebel has been with HBT from its inception in 1979.

LIEUTENANT E. FRED BOSSE, watch commander, Gang Crimes West; in charge of Chicago's HBT containment. Bosse joined the CPD in 1970. He worked patrol in the Thirteenth District and tac in the Special Operations Group until his promotion to detective in 1972. As a detective, Bosse worked Area One General Assignment for a year and was then assigned to Area Four Robbery in 1973. In 1975, Bosse was promoted to sergeant and served as a tac sergeant in the Twentieth District for three years. Upon Bosse's promotion to lieutenant in 1978, he served as tac lieutenant in Eighteen for a year, and then as tac lieutenant in Nineteen and Thirteen. In 1981, Bosse became the commanding officer of Gang Crimes West. That same year, Bosse helped establish the Bureau of Field Tactical Services. From 1982 to 1987, Bosse ran the Summer Mobile Force and was watch commander in Gang Crimes West. Bosse has been with the HBT program since 1982 and has worked on more than a hundred HBT incidents.

SERGEANT JAMES DOLAN, Outlying Range Program, Training Academy; former containment officer. Dolan's thirty-two-year career in the CPD has included patrol in Morgan Park, serving in the Area Two Task Force (1961), and work in the old TUF Squad (the Tactical Undercover Function Squad, in which police acted as robbery decoys) from 1961 to 1963. After the TUF Squad was disbanded, Dolan returned to the Area Two Task Force, serving as a supervising sergeant till 1965. From 1965 to 1968, Dolan worked in the Narcotics Unit. Dolan was assigned to the Area One Task Force from 1968 to 1970, served six years in the Marine Unit, then served as supervising sergeant and watch commander, Special Operations, Area One, from 1976 to 1988. In 1982, this unit became the Gang Crimes Unit, and Dolan worked Gang Crimes South from 1982 to 1988, when he was assigned to Prostitution. Dolan was a containment officer for twenty-five years, first with Special Operations and then with HBT.

DETECTIVE JOHN C. ESHOO, Intelligence Section, Organized Crime Division; hostage negotiator. Eshoo joined the force in 1968, worked patrol in the Thirteenth District for three months, and then was assigned to a tac team in the Eighteenth District, where he worked for four years. Eshoo was promoted to detective in 1972, was a robbery detective in Area Six from 1972 to 1976 and a homicide detective in Area Five from 1976 to 1980. In 1981, Eshoo was assigned to the Intelligence Section of Organized Crime. He's been detailed to the Chicago Terrorist Task Force, which works jointly with the FBI and the Illinois State Police, since 1982. Eshoo has been a hostage negotiator since the program's inception in 1979.

DETECTIVE PATRICIA HARRISON, Crime Analysis Unit, Detective Division Headquarters; hostage negotiator. Harrison joined the force in 1974 as a policewoman and was assigned to Area Two, Youth Division, where she served as a youth officer for the next seven years. Harrison was promoted to detective in 1981, assigned to the Area Two Homicide Unit. From 1985 to 1991, Harrison worked Area One Violent Crimes. Harrison has been a hostage negotiator for eight years.

LIEUTENANT JOHN P. KENNEDY, lieutenant-in-charge, aide to the Chief, Special Functions Division; Hostage/Barricaded/Terrorist Incident Coordinator. Kennedy was chosen to design Chicago's HBT Program in 1979. Kennedy selects and trains personnel, develops the procedures to be used by the CPD at hostage/barricade scenes, and oversees the actions of the negotiators and containment officers at the scenes themselves. Kennedy also advises the U.S. State Department's office of Diplomatic Security on counterterrorist programs.

SERGEANT JOHN LOUGHNANE, Gang Crimes North. Loughnane is one of the containment operation's supervisors. Loughnane joined the force in 1968, became a sergeant in 1978 in the prestigious Special Operations Group, which investigated patterned crimes in burglaries, rapes, robberies and, after SOG merged with Gang Crimes in 1981, continued as a street gangs specialist in Gang Crimes North.

OFFICER WALTER MUSZYNSKI, Gang Crimes South; containment. Muszynski worked patrol for nine years, spent three years as a tactical officer, and has worked in Gang Crimes South for eight years.

DETECTIVE RICHARD SCHAK, Area Five Violent Crimes; hostage negotiator. Schak joined the force in 1968 as a cadet and worked from 1970 to 1973 in the Eighteenth District as a patrol officer, a tactical officer, and on the Michigan Avenue pickpocket detail. Schak has been a homicide detective since 1973.

THE STREET

Sometime in the fifties, TV ran out of cowboy scripts. Suddenly, TV discovered cops.

And a whole generation got suckered into police work. A lot of women, too, who would ordinarily have gone into careers like teaching or nursing, decided, with men, that it would be great to be a cop.

And then they found out about the grueling boredom and the horror of it all. . . .

Sergeant Ted O'Connor
Twenty-third District

Seeing things other people don't, that's this whole job. I saw my first gunshot victim when I'd been three months on the job. I was fascinated by it. It didn't bother me at all.

I tell all the recruits, "If you look at it like you're seeing a Steven Spielberg horror movie, it won't bother you."

Youth Officer Linda Reiter
Area Five

Pure Cop ends where *What Cops Know* began: on the street. "The street" is the generic term given to the world of predators and victims outside the police station or specialized unit headquarters (in cop terms, "outside the building"). Anyone working a case, from street gang specialists to vice cops to hostage negotiators to evidence technicians to bomb and arson and major accident investigators, works the street to solve it. "On the street" has a gutsy ring to it. One time, I called my sister, a supervising sergeant, and the desk sergeant responded in tones worthy of the old intro to "Superman": "She can't talk to you right now. She's out on the street fighting crime . . . and *evil.*"

While all cops work the street to solve cases, some cops, especially beat cops and undercover cops, inhabit the street. And the street inhabits them. What they see on the street, their knowledge that the landscape the rest of us see is actually a backdrop for ludicrous and hideous dramas, changes them.

I remember sitting in a pancake house with a police officer. There was a pause while the waitress dispensed pancakes to us. The officer took a long look around the restaurant. I thought he was going to say something like "Nice joint." Instead, he said, "If somebody pointed a gun in here, sure these people would be nervous, but do they know what a gun could do? Only veterans of combat and cops know what high-velocity gunfire does to a body. You'll see heads completely exploded, limbs torn off.

"The people sitting here . . . ," indicating the tables jammed with oblivious pancake eaters, "If somebody pulled out a large hunting knife and went to attack someone else, nobody here knows what would happen. They haven't seen somebody's eye carved out of the head. Do these people in here know how much blood there is with a stabbing—that the heart keeps pumping and there'd be a geyser shooting to the ceiling with every pump? When you've seen this and somebody draws a knife on you, you know you've got just one chance.

"But once you've seen this stuff, it takes away a lot of the gentleness. It brings the survival instincts up."

Part of the survival instinct is to protect the family. How do you raise kids when you know the world out there is filled with danger—and *evil*? According to one ex-cop, "You get goofy with your kids after all you see. I really wrestled with that—Should I teach them the right way or to be street-smart? If I teach them just to be good, when they get out in the world, will some sharpie take advantage of them?

"I took teaching them the right way. I figure the sharpies are in the minimum; they'll be mostly with good people." A female officer told me, "My kids are teenagers now. All their lives they've thought I was nuts. I was always the mom who wouldn't let them take the bus by themselves, walk home from school by themselves, go downtown. When you know what's out there, you *are* nuts with your kids. When they were little, and I'd be working the midnights, I'd rush home and run into their bedrooms to make sure they weren't murdered in their sleep."

The street changes cops, and it separates them from us. Father John Nangle, chaplain for the CPD, sums up street cops' work as "wrestling with evil spirits": "When you check out your radio, put your squad car keys in the ignition and head out on the street, you're dealing with the evil spirits of crime, suffering, degradation, and that's almost all you deal with. It has to take a toll. It has to be abrasive and corrosive on the human spirit. I think what it sometimes takes away from some of the police officers is the ability to love and to let themselves be loved, to trust. Sometimes it takes away a sense of God, a sense of beauty in life. That's a hell of a price to pay for $30,000 a year.

"But the other thing is we always tend to stereotype and lump cops together. I can't say this strongly enough. What amazes me is that the vast majority of them are as healthy and stable and adaptive as they are."

The street is a book best interpreted by cops. Like any good book, it cannot be read attentively without working a profound change on the reader. . . .

This happened when I was in the Academy. We were all in the Crime Lab auditorium for a class. And they brought in the hat of a guy who had just been killed. A piece of the skull was bouncing around inside it. He'd been killed . . . he was writing a case report. He had taken the information from the family on a missing young girl, and he went and parked his car. He's sitting there, writing his case report, and two guys walked over with a shotgun and shot him right in the head.

They took his guns. As luck would have it, they committed a traffic violation about eight or ten blocks away. The guys that stopped them found the guns and brought them into the district where he was assigned. When they ran the gun registration, the revolver comes back registered to the policeman. And they think, "Well, damn! He's out on the street working." So now they start calling for him. He wouldn't respond to the radio, and by this time a citizen had seen the car and called in. So within minutes of this happening, the people were apprehended.

My class was at the Crime Lab for some kind of demonstration. They just had to bring the hat in—"This guy was just killed this morning, people. This could happen to you." Everybody's thinking, "Gee, thanks for telling us. Great."

The majority of people meet police officers just one way. Traffic stops. Here comes the guy with the hat, the mirrored glasses. Here's somebody like their parents—"You did somebody bad. You will be punished. You're in a heap of trouble now." That's all most people see of us. That's their entire conception of the police.

People get visibly shaken when a car stops them. They can't talk right, they fumble for their driver's license, they do all kinds of weird things. They're *scared* of the police. You talk to all kinds of people, they say, "Police make me nervous."

Sometimes you have to say to these people, they get so agitated, "Let me tell you something, pal. This is not the end of the world. It's only a ticket."

They have excuses. "Why were you speeding?" "I wasn't. The car was." I asked another guy, "Didn't you realize you were going too fast?" "I forgot to wear my glasses. I couldn't see the speedometer." "How can you drive?" "I can see far away."

People do things like—they park their car right in front of a NO PARKING sign. You come up. "Officer, is it okay if we park here for five minutes?" "Hmmm. Let's see. Does it say 'No Parking—except for maybe just five minutes'?"

I once stopped Mr. Yuppie Lawyer who blew a stop sign. I go up to him. "Can I help you, officer?" he says. He's in his act. "You went through the stop sign." "But officer, I paused." He paused! I gave him a pass. Anyone that creative deserves to go.

My partner and I are driving one night in an unmarked car. A guy gives us the finger and cuts us off. We go up to him.

"Hey, I didn't realize you were the police." "Wait a minute, pal. What if we were just two wackos with a shotgun?"

People write their own tickets. They really do. Your conduct to me will predict how I'll act to you. The ultimate outcome of that traffic stop is always in your hands. Your attitude writes your ticket.

I've talked to a lot of old-timers, and they say they miss the good old days. They tell me they used to make more money on traffic stops than the city was paying them, okay? They miss those good old days. They do. They miss them. And I told them at one point, "Shit, maybe *I* should have worked in those good old days."

Even in today's world, there are still a few out there who are taking . . . they're *crazy*. You've got IAD [Internal Affairs Division], you've got all kinds of goofy . . . running around, setting the traps for you.

But it's still going on. It's not as prevalent today as it was fifteen, twenty years ago. When I say it's still going on, I mean, I refuse to believe that there are no police officers taking money. I refuse to believe that. Can't nobody tell me—if someone was to tell me that there are no police officers taking money, I'd tell them to their face they're a damn liar. Because there are guys out there taking money. But they're *fools*. Sooner or later, you know that old saying, "Whatever you do in the dark comes out in the light"? It's true. Sooner or later, you fall into the trap all these internal agencies set. A guy may have twenty, twenty-five years on the job, a couple kids in college, and he loses his job? It's not worth it.

This job, right now. I've got almost eight years, it pays about $36,000 a year. If I lose this job, where am I gonna go and make this same type of money and have the same fun? I'm not. I'll be reduced to flipping hamburgers in McDonald's someplace. I love my job too much to go out there and take a nickel.

I locked up one guy, it was a traffic stop and he attempted . . . I asked him for his driver's license, he gave me the license with a fifty-dollar bill on a paperclip. Unfortunately for the individual, the day before, I had just read a training bulletin on what to do if someone offers you a bribe, the procedure. So, *he was fucked*.

There's a lot of danger in traffic stops. People forget burglars have cars. People forget rapists have cars. There could be the time that the beat car sees a mover. What if that person *just* committed a crime and you're thinking, "Look at that jerk who went right through the light," and they're thinking, "They know what I just did."

So you approach the car with the idea—maybe he just stuck someone up or he's a serial killer with a body in the back seat. You have to be aware. Yes, it's a traffic stop. And it also could be something else.

We were writing tickets on the expressway. And there's a hazardous spot, marked by two big signs on the ramp: ENTRY TO EXPRESS LANES PROHIBITED. But you always get people who come flying down a ramp, jump over the white line, and go into the express lanes.

So we stop a guy for doing this; he had Indiana plates. And he's going through this long story about how his driver's license got all washed in the washing machine and he hasn't had a chance to go to Evansville, where there's the only state driving office in Indiana.

So while my partner's talking to him, I'm looking at this woman in the back seat of his car. And she's just like a chipmunk; she's like a bead of water on a hot skillet; she's jumping all over the back seat of this car. I walk up. She doesn't even pay any attention to me. And as I look in the back seat of this car, she's pulling one syringe from her arm where she's injected something and she's about to inject herself again. At that point, I reached in, grabbed the hand with the syringe, and drug her out of the car.

I look and I say, "What the hell is going on *here?*" And she came up with a farfetched story that her aunt, who lives on the

West Side of Chicago and is a diabetic, had no insulin. She just happened to have insulin at her house in Indiana, so she was bringing her a syringe—full of *brown* insulin.

Listening to this fairy tale, I also noticed that she was pencil thin. And she had these enormous breasts. There was something a little odd about those, too, because one was higher than the other. Looking closely, you could see coming through where the blouse she had on was buttoned; there was a corner of a Baggie sticking out.

So my partner and I elected to search her to find out what this was. And what we found was two kilos of heroin stuffed into her brassiere. Her brassiere must have been a mini-A cup, way too small for the heroin, so one had shifted up and one had shifted down, and the one that shifted up had the corner coming out.

After the preliminary hearing on probable cause, we never saw her again. She never showed up at her first court appearance.

We later found out that she was a runner for a black crime syndicate in Gary called "The Family," which is a notorious drug/violence little group. We figured she lost them two kilos of heroin. She may be part of the expressway now.

Auto thieves. It's hard to prove auto theft; to actually charge a guy with auto theft, you gotta have eyeball, you gotta have somebody *see* him: "I seen that guy break that window. I seen that guy get in the car and drive off."

You stop the car, you know it's a hot car, you catch him, he's in it, he's the guy—you can only charge him with possession of a stolen motor vehicle.

And they say—"My friend gave me the car." "I found the car." Or—"The car was running and I just took off on it." They got all kinds of goofy stories.

I had one guy—"I was walking down the street. Here this car was, moving real slow. There was no driver. So I went to jump in to stop it from running into the fire hydrant. And I was just gonna keep it till I found out who it belongs to."

* * *

Most guys out on the corner selling dope, you stop them, you ask them what they do for a living, the number one response is: "I work for my uncle." "Well, what does your uncle do?" "He's a carpenter." "Where's your business card?" They never have business cards.

I mean, most established businessmen—"You have a card?"—they whip out that business card. Your dope dealers—"You have a business card? Because I want you to do some work for me." "Oh. Wait. I don't have no cards on me today." They *never* have a card.

I bought dope undercover. *One time.* I'll never buy dope again. If they ever ask me if I want to do it, "No." It's the scariest thing. . . . Some people can do it and not blink. It's scary.

First of all, I was looking at an eyeball when I bought it. I was looking at an eyeball through a keyhole. I knocked on the door, there was a gate on the door, and where they used to be a lock, there were paper towels stuffed in the peephole. When I knocked on the door, the paper was taken out. Now you're looking at this eyeball that's checking you, looking you up and down. "What do you want?" "Give me a dime bag." "Just a minute." Stuffed the paper back in there. In about two, three minutes later, the eyeball comes back. Looks at you again. "Pass the money through." You stick the money through the little keyhole, they take the money, give you the dope, stuff the paper back in, you're on your way.

But—the reports before we even went to the location told us—there's generally two people inside the location and they're *heavily armed.* Okay. So, if you look at me right now, I'm a clean-cut. . . . I don't fit your usual dope user. . . . So it surprised me that they sold.

It was an unnerving situation. It was the eyeball checking me out. Because it was like—"Who are you? You don't fit the mold for the person who usually buys dope in this quantity, or uses dope." And I was upstairs by myself. It was summertime; I didn't have my vest on, because if I had my vest, it would probably be very easily detected. I always kept in the back of my mind this female police officer who worked tac; she was blown away, she got killed inside a place trying to buy dope maybe four, five years ago. She got locked *inside* the dope house. I'm gonna tell you, dope is risky, risky business.

I'd be lying between my teeth if I said I never get scared. I wouldn't want to work with a police officer who said he's never scared. That macho act—can't nothing hurt me; can't nothing touch me—that's all it is, an act.

People say, "You have such a dangerous job." I say, "Not really; I just have a slightly higher chance of getting hurt by a nut who knows I'm the police and wants to kill a police officer."

When you're a woman cop, everybody says to you, "Aren't you afraid?" You know, it's just as easy to walk out of the kitchen to the living room and hit your head on the coffee table and die. You can't think about it. You can't think about it.

A lot of cops are too scared to work the street. Why do you think there are so many inside jobs?

Do cops get paranoid? I never saw anybody who was afraid of every shadow. If you were that way, you would be in an institution or drunk all the time.

But you have to be alert. Constantly alert. You pick up a sixth or seventh sense. You know if somebody's doing something or they've done something or they're *about* to do something.

You go into depressed areas, you're the police, the citizens look at you like you're a piece of dog meat. This is true whether you're white or black. They look at black officers as working for the white establishment, so we're lumped in with the rest of them. You might get the little old ladies who will say, "Hi, Officer," or an older man . . . and the gamblers will speak to you. Police don't really bother the gamblers. I mean, we raid them, but they never really seem to mind. I've never hit a gambling joint where the people are hostile. They're always like, "Yeah, well, you got us." The gamblers are cool. The dope dealers, they don't like you at all.

So when you get a call in a depressed area, they give a general description—you might have, say, five male blacks in front of a place where something is going on. And unless there's something unique in the description—say it's "male black wearing a dark jacket" and they've all got on dark jackets—four of these guys with the dark jackets on are all hardworking, upright citizens, and it's just one of them that's the bad guy. So everybody suffers for the acts of one.

The upright citizens, the police come up, there's hostility. But the person who comes up—"Oh, hi Officer, how are you?"— something ain't right about it. So if one of these five guys on the corner is the first to speak, he's gonna be the first one I search.

Or you're sitting in the car and a guy comes walking along, he goes out of his way to say something to you—there's something wrong. In my experience, ninety percent of the time were hits where I found something, and I say later, "Well, why did you come up and speak to me?"—"Well, I figured if I spoke, you wouldn't bother me."

A call came—what it turned out to be was a federal security guard for the Veterans Administration who called. She was trying to have her live-in boyfriend killed—by us.

She called in a 10-1, which is "a police officer needs help"— the cars arrive, she's standing in front of this apartment building, her clothes are torn, she's scratched in the face, hysterical. "He's up there! He's got my baby! He's got a gun!" "Well, where did he get the gun?" And she explained to us about her occupation.

Most of the policemen were in front of the apartment building and in front of the stairwell. I came around the back and was able to go in the back door. Crept through the house. And the guy was standing, holding a child, and holding a gun. I came up behind him and snatched the gun from him. All he said was,

"Please don't shoot me, don't shoot me, don't shoot me."

He had—prior to all this happening—called 911, and told them he was not going to hurt anyone, that he and his wife were arguing, she pulled the gun on him, he took it from her, he put her out of the house, and all he wanted was the police to come. As I was creeping through the house, I could hear the guy talking on the phone to the dispatcher, and the dispatcher was constantly talking to us over the radio, saying, "I got the guy on the phone. He's not going to hurt anybody."

But that's not the way the woman brought it out to us when we arrived. And had everyone overreacted and not restrained themselves, he and this baby could have been killed. Or more to what she seemed to want, *he* would have been killed.

One of these late mornings, about eleven-twenty-five, nothing really going on. And we could have stormed in and killed the guy. She was trying to set this guy up to be killed and she was going to use us as the executioners.

No charges were brought against the woman. You can't charge somebody with what you think; you have to have an act.

People lie to us eight hours a day. Everybody lies to us: offenders, victims, witnesses. They all lie to the police. It gets so bad, you go to a party, somebody comes up to talk to you. You're thinking, "Why is this guy saying this to me? What's his game?" You can't turn it off.

People think of us as the enemy. The only time they contact us is when they're in trouble. Then all of a sudden it's in a different light.

One night, we go right from a domestic in the projects to a domestic in a Gold Coast apartment. Going in, we're thinking, "Hey, it's nice in here. They got elevators that work." We talked to the man and the wife. The only difference between this couple and the one in the projects is this couple is white and they have more money. Were they more obnoxious? *Both* were obnoxious.

*   *   *

The big difference in arresting a gang member from the projects and a LaSalle Street lawyer is this: White people are a pain in the ass. They can both be criminals. But you won't get the aggravation from the gang-banger that you would from the attorney. They're the real assholes.

My daughter told me she wants to study to be a lawyer. I told her I'd kill her first.

I tell people—When I came on this job, I was prejudiced. Now I'm prejudiced against everybody: I don't care if you're white, black, Hispanic, whatever—I want to know what kind of game you're trying to run on me.

You know what I hate? I *hate* when people condescend to me. They explain things; they talk down to me because I'm a cop. They just assume you've got a block of wood between your ears.

If you want respect, don't become a cop. The recruits come up to me: "We don't get any respect." I tell them, "You want respect? Be a whore. Whores get respect—and money."

People from other walks of life don't really go for police. It's tough to make a relationship with a person with a normal job because when they think of police they think of getting parking tickets or speeding tickets. It's tough for them to get close to us. It's hard to identify with us.

And that's why cops hang with cops. The only time people think of talking to us is if they need us.

We get a call of a domestic, which turns out to be a rape. We get there, and this woman is being comforted by relatives. It was her husband's birthday; everyone had been over to the house having a drink. The brother-in-law was upstairs sleeping. She went upstairs, took a shower, and was ironing a dress in the same room where he was asleep. And all she had on was a brassiere and panties and a robe. And all of a sudden the brother-in-law gets up from where he was sleeping and starts making advances toward her, which resulted in him forcibly raping her. And then he went back to sleep.

She calls the police. Now here we are talking to her. "Well, is he still here?" "Yeah, he's still upstairs asleep." "Fine."

At this, the husband bursts into the house. "What happened?" She tells him. He makes a beeline up the stairs. He goes in; he's trying to kill his brother.

Now my partner and I are trying to arrest the brother and get the husband off of his brother. We began to wrestle with these two guys—no one's fighting us; it's just us trying to get these two guys apart.

Well, the storm window was knocked out as the four of us wrestled into the window; we bounce off of this into this enormous saltwater fish tank—I mean clown fish and all kinds of . . . gorgeous thing—well, it went into the stereo system, a console stereo with TV, it went into that, the tank's destroyed, the console stereo TV set is destroyed, numerous lamps and other odds and ends, tables and so forth. . . . We finally get the husband subdued and the brother handcuffed. Other units had arrived and that's how we finally got these two apart.

A couple weeks later in court, the family wants to know if they could have a copy of our report for their insurance company and did we put anything in our report about what was damaged in their apartment. "Well, no, we didn't." Well, they had figured about $2700 worth of damage that had been done—while these two were wrestling and we're trying to get them apart. We're just thinking, well, "Sorry! Chalk it up to experience, or *something*."

It used to be if you were a copper, you'd have at least two physical fights a day. Nobody would obey us when we did anything, so we went hand to hand a lot. There was a place called the Bucket of Blood in the fifties, we fought there every night. One night, I had most of my teeth knocked out in a fight. I had the rest of my teeth pulled and had false teeth put in in the morning and kept working that day. My wife said I was nuts.

In the fifties, you could punch out anybody you wanted. In the sixties, you had to go in an alley or a basement. From the seventies on, you can't do anything; some citizen will bring a complaint against you.

In the sixties, if you said to a citizen, "Get off that corner," and they said, "I know my rights," you could say, "I don't know anything about that, but I do know I have this nightstick."

Remember the Democratic Convention of '68? Remember the cameras rolling and all the cops with their clubs swinging over their heads? Well, for six months before the convention they taught us the right way to use the clubs—you're supposed to hold them out straight in front of you. We were drilled in this. But, I was there, and when push comes to shove, you're gonna do what they did a thousand years ago; men used to put the clubs over their heads and hit on people. It's something that's inbred in you.

When I came on the force in the late sixties, being a Chicago cop was something else. We were the rompin', stompin', ass-kicking Chicago police. All you had to do was pull up, not even get out of the squad, just see some kids on the corner and give them the look. Man, they'd scatter.

When you think you're bigger than God, then you're in trouble. I came on this job, 5'5", maybe 145 pounds. And right now, I'm still 5'5", maybe 150 pounds. But I put my gun on, my star, and you know, all the equipment, I'm still 5'5", but now I might be 160, maybe 170. I'm *still* 5'5". It doesn't make me John Wayne. I'm still the same person.

And I realize that there are people out there: Police? Fuck the police. They don't give a shit about you. Hey, fine. I'm goin' home the same way I came here. Eight fingers, two thumbs . . . I'm going home *intact*. I'm not gonna let nobody get the best of me. I'm gonna do whatever I have to do.

But in doing so, I'm not gonna abuse or misuse anybody. Because there was a time of the day when I wasn't a police officer. I was just John Q. Citizen like everybody else. Didn't like the police. When I got stopped, I'd say, "Don't fuck *over* me."

If you're a burglar or a stickup guy, and you've gotten away with some money, your objective is not to get arrested. Our objective is to arrest you. So if we get you, we're not gonna say, "Oh. We realize you don't want to be locked up, so go on your merry way."

We get a lot of brutality beefs from offenders. I'm 5'8" and weigh 180 pounds. If you're 6'3" and 250, I'm gonna have to do some things to subdue you. It's common to have an offender report us to OPS (Office of Professional Standards)—this officer beat me. They don't mention the biting and scratching and kicking they did to you during the arrest.

Brutality is when we hit back.

People are always saying: "Oh, the police. Police brutality." Like we pick somebody out of a crowd—"You. Come here"— and beat them.

Oddly enough, it's far more gentle on a guy to have three or four coppers subduing him than one or two. With one or two, they'll have to use far more force to gain control over the guy. With three or four, it's not so rough on the guy to bring him down.

It's cops with fewer than five years on the job that tend to be involved in brutality incidents. There's so much power that goes with that piece of steel you put on. They want to be part of the police, they've seen all the Dirty Harry movies, they think the way to impress the bosses is to appear reckless. The more you're on the job, the more you know power is much better served with a pen than with a club.

* * *

You know what the best brutality is? Stop him, search him, cuff him, read him his rights, pull out your pen, and smile. You got him. You won.

A lot of this job is knowing how to talk to people. You could fight with people every day of the week if you wanted to, three, four times a day. If you start at the bottom, you can always gear yourself up. If you start at the top, you have nowhere to go. Then you have to back down. You don't want to back down. If you come out like a bull in a china closet, be prepared.

I try to deal with people on a human level, on the human side. Even the lowliest asshole that I'll confront on a day-to-day basis, I'll give him his due. "Good morning, sir" or "May I be of service to you?"—something to that effect. I let them go off on me.

Because once you go off on me, or you call me out on my name, or you're disrespectful to me, now it's my rules. Now we're gonna play this by my rules.

But if you give the people a "Good morning, ma'am," a "Good morning, sir," "May I be of service to you?"—for a lot of people, it kind of throws them off, because they're used to dealing with this "Hey, asshole" or . . . and for some people, they don't understand that "Good morning, sir"; you *have* to "Hey, asshole." They understand that. Or—"Get your ass out of here. Move your fucking ass." They understand that better than that "Good morning, ma'am." So we use that terminology. . . .

You've gotta be on the street constantly. You've gotta know who the bad guys are; you eliminate the bad guys from the hangers-on. You've got to know how to talk to people.

We go from gang to gang—"What's up, guys? Anybody shooting at you? What did they look like? What kind of car?" The whole cornerstone is being able to approach somebody— "What do you know about this or that?" You take that approach. You cultivate anybody and everybody in the neighborhood, the old women and men, the young, everybody. You treat them right.

You know how to judge policemen? How you know the ones who are really good? By no other factor than the number of call slips on their spindle back in the station. You can't have too many people calling you on the phone.

Police are called upon to do everything. A woman was out gardening and she kills a snake. So she calls the police. I get the call: "See the woman about the animal."

I get to this house and here's this lady and she's a perfect picture out of *House and Garden*. She's got on a little cap, little gloves, shorts, and a little kneeling pad. Trowel in hand. I ask, "Can I help you?" "Yes. I was gardening and I killed a snake. I want you to identify it for me." I said, "Do I look like Marlin Perkins to you?" I said, "I believe it's the common, everyday-variety garter snake. It's green. It's got the little orange and red stripes." "Are you sure?"

I had another lady. I got a call and the dispatcher, I mean he was in tears talking to me: "Check this out. A felony alert. Suspicious bird on lawn." So I go out. Here's a male ring-necked pheasant. He's sunning himself. This little old lady is terrified. "What is that? Is that a hawk? Is it an eagle?" "No, lady. That's a pheasant. You know, the pheasant-under-glass type? Pheasant. A pheasant." "Oh, no, that's not a pheasant. A pheasant is . . ." "Lady, that is a pheasant. Trust me." "Well, what should I do?" "Nothing. It'll go away. Maybe it'll stay. It'll be a conversation piece."

Police become police because they want to help people. They really do. It takes you a while before you find out no one wants to be helped.

As a rookie, I was sent to the ghetto. I had my brand new uniform. I was all spit and polish, 6'1", slender.

I was out on a minor call. A little eight-year-old boy says hi. I said hello back. He started walking with me. It was just like every Norman Rockwell picture I had ever seen. I put an arm around him and said, "What do you want to be when you grow up?" Of course I thought he'd say he wanted to be a policeman. The kid said, "A pimp."

A battle had already been waged and been lost for this kid. That kid was sharp. That's where the money was and where the respect was.

When you first become a police officer, you think you're gonna change a lot of things and do a lot of good. You really can't. And you don't. And here's another thing—you don't really give a fuck about the people out there. There are times when, naturally, if you can help save a baby's life or help save someone from a burning building, or a robbery in progress, you do what you can. But on a day-to-day, you don't give a fuck. You don't have time to solve everybody's little problem in the street. When it counts, then you do care. But everything else, fuck it.

You've got a prostitute coming up to you and telling you that her pimp is beating her up or just threw her out of a moving car. When you first come on, you care. Later it's, "So what? You're lucky to be alive. You're not going to town; you're going to jail."

I don't care what they say about police becoming callous. I have never found police to be callous and I've been doing this for thirty-three years. I've found the good ones to be the biggest softies in the world. They're empathetic.

I don't want any cynical police working for me. I want police who can empathize with the situation at hand.

Some cops do get much harder; it's kind of a defense mechanism. Just to protect your own sanity, you become hardened. But I find it's much easier to become more tolerant and a little softer approaching people.

Hey, but mark it well, police officers are not without fault. There are dog asses who are scared shitless of their own shadow, who don't do a fucking day's work—all they're worried about is their two checks a month and when they're gonna get their retirement. There are police officers who have never made a felony arrest in ten years, sometimes for their whole careers. They wouldn't know what to do with one if they got it.

You go through three very definite stages as a policeman. Stage one that you go through is where you get an education off the street. And it's one that nobody can teach you. That you're gonna have to learn all by yourself; you have to learn the street. Then you go in Stage two, which is probably the nicest stage of all of them, because you sort of taper off learning—I mean you would never stop learning in a hundred years on this job, but your learning process tends to taper off—and now you start seeing humor in a lot of this stuff. Now it starts getting funny. And this is a good period of time. Then you go into Stage three, where you start to realize that things you're finding humor in are either sick or it's somebody's ignorance that you're sitting there laughing about. But you have to see the humor in this stuff to live with it.

Clout is alive and well in the Chicago Police Department. Even though there's the union and some seniority, a lot of it is still who you know. All the Machiavellian intrigues—the KGB pales by comparison.

I'll give you two examples. One—I remember when I was going through the Academy, this guy was just doing some horseplay, he cocked someone else's gun in their holster, a shot went off. Now, if this was anybody else, he'd be *gone*. When you're on probationary patrol, they can get rid of you real easy. But this guy was heavy. He stayed.

Here's another example. I have a friend, twenty years on the job. After twenty years, you want to slow down, you don't want to go out and bust heads all day long. He's out on the street and his sergeant said, "There's a spot open. Go in the office and apply." He went off the street, went in to apply, and the desk guy said, "You were on for about an hour. But two rookies came in, and one of them has it." The rookie who got the job was politically connected.

Things are not as bad as they once were in the CPD. Time was, whenever there was a political change, you stood to lose your job. At every election, if there was a change in City Hall, you'd look around for another job.

A true policeman doesn't care about politics, about who's in, who's out, as long as he can stay with his friends and do his job.

Ball-busting is a big part of police work. It's a great stress reducer, like humor. For example: The Case of the Kidnapped Cup.

There was a guy in the office who had a cup, it had something like WORLD'S GREATEST DAD on it. People were always using his cup; he got real upset with this. He threatened that the next time somebody took his cup, he'd make out an official police report that his cup was stolen, treat it like a theft case.

You talk about running a red flag in front of a bull. The cup went missing. This guy fumed around. Then he got the first ransom note, and he saw the humor in it and went along. The note went something like, "Please, Dad, get me out of here. They're doing terrible things to me."

There was a series of ransom notes, all saying that dire things would happen to the cup unless he performed some strange ritual to get the cup back. Accompanying the notes were photos of that day's newspaper next to it, so he'd know the cup was alive. One of the photos showed a gun pointed at the cup, held up against it.

Sometime down the road, he got a note with the ear of a cup inside. Ultimately, he did get the cup back, but it was sort of anticlimactic.

Camaraderie in the police. You're real close to your partner. If you get a new partner, they say you got a divorce from your old one. It's like a marriage.

If you work with a team or in a specialized unit, you work with them day in and day out. After a while, after you stick with them

for a number of years, they're like part of you. They're the first
ones to make fun of you and the first to help. When you're going
through a door, any one of us could get killed, and you all know
that. There's always a chance we won't be together anymore. We
count on each other.

We were at the station. It was pretty late, almost two in the
morning, almost time to go home. And we were called down by
the desk sergeant.

A guy had come in. He was in his late twenties. He complained
that he was being held prisoner in an apartment down the block,
not far from the station, and he had tricked his way out of this
other guy's custody.

He told us that he was being held by this guy and being tortured. I said, "What do you mean, being tortured?" He said, "He
was trying to make me drink ammonia. And when I wouldn't
drink it, he held a gun on me and he tied me up to the chair. And
then he pulled my pants down." And the guy told us the other guy
took an electric iron and he took the iron part off the wire and
held the electrical wires against this guy's testicles.

But I didn't believe this guy. See, the thing is, being what we
were—tac officers—you want to believe the fact that the guy had
a gun, but it's hard to believe the torture thing.

What he said happened was, he met the guy on the street. He
knew him way back when, and this guy had just gotten out of
prison. We found out later he was in for armed robbery. They
bought some booze and they went up to this guy's apartment and
started drinking and he said this guy started talking crazy-like
and said he wanted to kill the attorney that represented him, so
he needed money to go to New York and he needed a sawed-off
shotgun.

So the guy says, "You're crazy." "Don't call me crazy"—they
start having a big argument. The other guy says, "Drink this"—
but instead of handing him a glass of booze, it's a glass of ammonia. "Go ahead. Drink it." The guy goes, "No," you know, "I'll
die. It's poison."

And then at that time, he said the guy pulled a gun. He tied
him up. He pulled his pants down and stripped the ends off the

wire, plugged it in, and said, "I'm gonna electrocute you." The other guy says, "Come on. Whatever you want to do, I'll do it. Just, you know, give me a break here." "Can you get me a gun?" "Well, you got a gun." "A sawed-off shotgun." "Yeah, I can get you a sawed-off shotgun." The other guy goes, "Don't bullshit me." "No, I can get it for you." What else are you gonna say? The guy goes, "How long will it take you?" "About a half hour." "Okay, but if you don't come back with a shotgun, you're dead meat," and all this other stuff.

He tells us this story and we say, "Okay, we'll go over and check it out." We don't believe this guy a hundred percent, but he appears to be pretty shaken, and he's willing to come up to the door with us.

There were four of us; one of us went out to the fire escape, to cover the back door.

We had the alleged victim call the guy out. "Henry, I'm here." He knocks on the door. "Who is that?" "It's me, Freddy." "What do you want?" "I got the shotgun." "You're full of shit." "No, I got the shotgun." "You're with the fucking police, man." "No, I'm not—" We know there's something going on, whatever it is, so we have our guy, the victim, step aside. We knock on the door—"Police. Open the door."

The guy shoots through the door. The bullet goes between me and my partner. Hits the wall behind us.

Our reaction was, we kicked the door in. We're yelling "Police!"—the guy fires a couple more rounds, but we don't know where they're going. So now we more or less lay down on the floor on either side of the doorway, the door's open—and there's a throw rug all bunched up in front of the door from when we kicked it open. A couple shots are fired. We return fire. And the guy's yelling at us the whole time, "You motherfuckers, you fucking police!" and all this shit. All right.

Next thing I know, there's a big thump. Here's a pipe, hit the door, landed on that bunched-up throw rug.

Now I'm incensed. I pick up the pipe and I yell, "You dirty motherfucker!" and I throw it back at him. My partner goes, "That's a goddamn pipe bomb!" Technically, that was the last of the pipe bomb. It didn't go off.

He ended up shooting fifteen times at us. He was in a one-room apartment and he was hiding behind a dresser slightly to the right of the furthest wall where the bed was.

We ran out of bullets. I ran to the back of the building and I got the guy who was covering the fire escape—I get to him and I say, "Give me some bullets." He ends up giving me his gun.

So I take his gun and I go back into the hallway. We had put in a 10-1, you know, "Officer needs assistance," at the first or second shot. So now we're getting assistance, they're coming up the front, but we won't let them in the hallway because we're afraid they'll be in the line of fire. The problem was, we didn't have time to reload. So they're handing us guns so we could return fire. We shot through the doorway at the direction the fire was coming from. All we could see was some object—it turned out to be a bedroom dresser—part of this guy's leg, and the flashes from his gun.

The man inside knew what he was doing. He would fire like one or two rounds and stop and then reload a different magazine on a small semiautomatic weapon, it was a .25 automatic.

We were shooting, we were shooting for the legs. We'd hear him yell, but then he'd shoot right back. The man was hit thirteen times, the torso, the arms, the legs.

There were forty rounds fired by us and fifteen by him—the Mobile Crime Lab counted the expended shells. We had shouted to him at least a dozen times to drop his gun and give up. He ignored the order. We figured we had the upper hand, because we had as many guns as we needed; there were at least ten assisting units behind us on the stairs and going out the apartment. We later found he had over fifty rounds of ammunition plus the damn pipe bomb and all the chemicals.

Finally, the hallway was all full of gunsmoke. My partner's gone to get a gun and I had just gotten a gun from somebody else. Now the guy starts coming out. He's saying, "Okay, okay." I'm telling him, "Come out with your hands up." He's coming out into the hallway of the apartment and he's more or less silhouetted in the doorway of the apartment. He doesn't have his hands up; he's just standing there; his gun's in his hand.

I'm telling him, "Drop the gun." You can tell he's hurt, his head's down, more or less. "Drop the gun. Drop the gun." "Okay, okay. Don't shoot. Don't shoot."

I got my gun pointed at him. Instead of dropping the gun, he fires the gun at me. This time, the bullet just misses my head and goes into the wall. So I now emptied the gun I had at him. I hit him in the upper torso. He goes down. Now my gun's clicking.

I turn around the little corner there and I'm yelling to my partner. I go, "Tim, he's out. He's down. He's out. He's down." Tim looks out and he says, "Yeah, he's down." That's what I wanted to hear. So I go inside with Tim— and this guy's moving his arms. He's moving his arms to his belt, and on his belt he's got a hunting knife. He grabs the hilt of the knife and he's pulling it out and we step on his arms. I've got one arm, my partner's got the other arm. We kneel on his arms. That's when he expires. You know, we saw this white stuff come out of his mouth. He's dead.

They took him away. The whole thing took about fifteen minutes. They called Bomb and Arson to the scene and they dismantled the pipe bomb. They told me that if this had gone off, it probably would have taken off the whole apartment, the ceiling, the roof. It was a six-inch pipe bomb, two inches in diameter. Inside were all kinds of screws and nails and washers and things like that. Surrounded by phosphorus. And inside *that* was a glass cigar tube filled with sulphur. So what's supposed to happen is that when you throw this thing, the glass tube filled with sulphur breaks and mixes with the phosphorus, causing the combustion, and because the pipe is serrated, it breaks, and all the stuff inside becomes shrapnel.

They said it didn't go off because of luck. It hit the carpet, the carpet was all bunched up. And then when I threw it back, it landed on the mattress. But I wasn't thinking in technical terms when I threw it. I was just hot.

Being a policeman, you can go to work, and you can have the same type of call: a burglary-in-progress, a robbery-in-progress—eighty-five percent of the in-progress felony calls are not bona fide. You see somebody going into a house, the police are called, we get there, and it's, "Well, I'm the brother-in-law and they're visiting so-and-so and I've got the keys and I've got to feed the cat."

But the calls that you get that are going to be a pain in the rear are your domestic disturbances, and rarely do you get called to a domestic disturbance and it's not bona fide—somebody's fighting somebody about something. With the calls you get, you begin to treat things routinely, and . . .

That's how cops get hurt sometimes. They begin to treat things routinely. You answer another domestic. You feel it's all pretty much the same. You knock on the door of John and Mary Doe and stand there. John Doe has a gun. He snatches the door open and pulls the trigger. He thinks you're the boyfriend standing there. He just killed Officer Friendly.

But never is anything the same. The call might have the same label: burglary-in-progress, domestic disturbance; but when you get there, the circumstances are always unique and ofttimes totally hilarious.

Call of a burglary-in-progress, shots fired. I was working the wagon, we were right around the corner. We pulled up. From the apartment building, you could hear what sounded like shots.

As you came up the stairs, here are carpet installers, with compressed air-powered nail guns, shooting staples into the carpeting. They're laying carpet.

The lady on the second floor, who had been the victim of a burglary, or a robbery, and was also extremely drunk, heard these nail guns going off, went to her door—"Who is it? Who is it?" No one answered, so she just shot through the door a couple of times. And then goes in and calls the police.

Now the guys laying the carpet never knew that the woman had fired shots. They were right on the stairs outside her apartment door. But their nail guns drowned out the gunshots. And when we told them what had gone on, they had to shape up— "Oh, my God, what . . ." "We gotta get outta here. You can get *killed* here."

* * *

We went in this real dark apartment once; we were looking for a guy wanted for homicide. We sneak up the back steps and go into the third-floor apartment. We tap on the door. They wouldn't answer the door. We kind of like burst in, we've got our guns out, we're saying, "Where's José? Where's José?" They're going, "No, no, no. No José here. No José."

So we're walking through the apartment and there's no lights on in the place. And it's like there are . . . pretzels all over the floor; we're crunching every step. We've got our guns out; the sarge is walking right behind us. All of a sudden, I hear the sarge go, *"Ooo-whooo-ooo"*—I whip around with the gun; he says, "A *rat* just ran by." Aw, jeez, you know. I nearly killed him.

Finally, the sarge says, "You got any lights here?" They turn them on—millions of cockroaches just scatter. Their clothes and belongings were hanging from bags. So now we're really spooked. We're talking to the Mexicans; we find out it's nothing; we want to get the fuck out of there.

So the sarge is right next to me and just looking at all the roaches all over everything, he goes, *"Blagh!"* and I nearly blast him again. And all the Mexicans start laughing at us—*"Cucarachas! Cucarachas!"*

I had a nickname—you know one of those black exploitation movies that came out in the seventies, *Shaft*? I have the dubious distinction of having landed with that name because of an incident where I jumped through a plate glass window. Robbery-in-progress, a head shop, a guy was standing holding a gun and no one knew what to do. So I said to hell with it. And I just jumped through the window and luckily, nothing happened to me or to anybody else. I just came through it, landed, gun in hand, and the guy looked and said, "Oh, shit." He dropped his gun and that was the end of it. My sergeant said, "Why would you do something that stupid?" "It seemed like a good thing to do at the time." Nobody else was doing anything.

There's entertainment out there. All it is is a game. Make it a game. Make it an enjoyable game.

* * *

Over in Eighteen, there was a guy who dressed up as Superman and secreted himself behind a steel door in the subway. He got the frame loosened before he went behind it. He was with a robbery decoy; this guy lay down on the platform and let this street person pick his pocket. With that, the steel door comes crashing down. Out comes Superman; the guy was arrested by Superman. When it gets to court, the judge says to the officer, "Were you the arresting officer?" "Yes, Your Honor, I was." The street person goes, "That ain't the arresting officer. That was Superman that arrested me."

One night, working the midnights, investigating some call, man with a gun maybe, and we're knocking on doors. Remember that old Landshark sketch from "Saturday Night Live"? My partner and me would knock on a door, this is around five in the morning. "Who's there?" "Candygram." *"Who?"* "Landshark. Candygram." It helps pass the time.

You really would have had to see this guy to believe this. This was when I was in Traffic. We get a call from the state police about an accident on the Dan Ryan Expressway. We get there— there's no state truck. The only thing that's there, hanging on the guardrail, is a car. And the only thing that's stopping it from rolling down this hill are the front tires hanging over the guardrail. We wait. The state truck pulls back up, says the accident was already handled, will we call for a tow? We say all right, and a couple minutes later here comes the tow truck with the car owner who's as drunk as whiskey, and this tow truck that looks like a Tonka Toy, it's so little. So this guy is telling us how he was forced off the road. And now his car is hanging here.

So while we're talking the guy is hooking up his tow truck. He's trying to lift the car off the guardrail and then pull it across. The tow truck is too small. All that's happening is the hook is lifting the front of the tow truck up. So the guy says, "There's nothing I can do. I've got to go."

So the guy says, "Will you get me another tow truck?" "Sure, we'll be glad to. We'll call. That's what we're doing." Idiot. So while we're sitting there waiting, this guy says, "Well, I gotta go try something." "Hey, it's your car. You do whatever you want to." This guy goes—he had to climb up into the car—gets behind the wheel, starts the car, revs the engine, turns *on* the headlights, puts the car in gear, and tries to drive—up.

When he turned on the headlights, my partner and I just about died. Where in the hell is he going? Then he puts the car in reverse, and tries to go backwards. Now, had he been able to get enough traction to pull the front wheels off this guardrail—it was on about a forty-five degree angle—the car probably would have gone down and flipped and killed him.

It was like—you watch somebody get in their car, turn on the lights, and now . . . I'm going to drive away. And we're looking—"Now . . . where . . . do you think . . . *you're* going?"

When I was in the Sixth District, I was a Field Training Officer, and one of my recruits, a female, was a nurse in a hospital psychiatric ward before coming on this job and she was telling me the horror stories . . . the things that she had to tolerate as a nurse.

Well, one afternoon, we were working days; we were to get off at three-thirty. At about a quarter to three, we get a call of a disturbance at McDonald's. So when we get there, there's one of our plainclothes cars already on the scene, with this disturbance, which was a man, I'd say in his fifties, who obviously had some type of psychological breakdown or something, as he was . . . kind of *nuts*. There was spit flying, mucus flying out of his nose, and he was just kind of bent over, and looked real weird.

So, the tac team had got this guy out of McDonald's. "Well, what are we gonna do with him?" I said, "If you let him go, he's just gonna go back to McDonald's. So we might as well try to find out where he lives and get him to his house." Asking *him* was like talking to a typewriter—he just *"Annnnhhhhh."* So we searched him and found some type of identification; he lived over near Ninety-fifth and Jeffery which was out of our district and a good ways away from Eighty-seventh and the Dan Ryan. So we got permission from the sergeant to take this guy home.

We get him in the back seat of the squad. The recruit I was training had just purchased this beautiful leather attaché case, and she grabbed it out of the back, clutched it like a child, and put it in the front with her.

This guy is in the back seat. And the recruit and I get to talking. The whole day I had been telling her war stories. See, all the recruits I trained, the watch commander would tell them, "Oh yeah, he's been shot up. He's wild and he's crazy. You've gotta watch him. He does all kinds of crazy things. So you'll learn a lot from him." So all the recruits, they come out all bright-eyed, bushy-tailed, they want to hear all these tales of horror and gore and people that are shot and stabbed and cut. And you begin to tell them and then after a while, they start looking at you like, "Man, you have weird dreams at night. You're making this stuff up." And then they find out it's reality.

I said to this recruit, "Now, some of the things that I told you sound like utter fabrication. But the longer you're on the street, every day something will happen, and you will go back and you are going to tell somebody. And it's going to be totally hilarious and people are going to think *you're* fabricating."

So as we're driving along, discussing, you know, the war stories that have happened and that *will* happen, I begin to hear what sounds like water running. And what I mean by water running—the splash as it hits a solid object. I looked in the back seat, and this guy that we had was urinating straight up into the rear of the squad car and it was splashing down on the rubber mat on the floor.

The recruit looked at me and said, "That's not what I think it is, is it?" I said. "Yep!" With this, she leapt from the seat and up *on to* the dashboard. She was *in* the dashboard of the squad car. How she did it, I don't know. She's an average-size woman, but she was up into the dashboard.

She came down finally, and with that, I looked at her and I said, "See? Now *you* got a story to tell. And the longer you're out here, the more stories you're gonna have. Six to eight months from now, you'll be telling a story, and people will be looking at you a little cross-eyed. They won't believe you. And it's all true."

The Street:
Contributing Police Officers

SERGEANT ED ADORJAN, Area Six Violent Crimes. Adorjan joined the CPD in 1959, worked Vice and Gambling in Eighteen, was assigned to the CPD's first tactical unit in 1963, and became a homicide detective in 1967. Adorjan worked Homicide for twenty-four years, first as a homicide detective in the old Homicide Unit, and then for eleven years as a supervising sergeant in Area Six until his retirement in 1991.

YOUTH OFFICER KIM ANDERSON, Area Five. Anderson joined the CPD as a policewoman in 1974 and worked in the Youth Division for six years. In 1980, Anderson was assigned to the Organized Crime Division. Over the next three years, Anderson served in every unit in Organized Crime: Gangs, Narcotics, Prostitution, Gambling, and Intelligence. From 1983 to 1985, Anderson was detailed to the Chicago Terrorist Task Force. Anderson has worked as an Area Five Youth Officer since 1985. Anderson has served as a hostage negotiator from the inception of the CPD's Hostage/Barricaded/Terrorist Program in 1979.

OFFICER ELMER ATKINSON, Third District. Atkinson joined the CPD as a cadet in 1967, where he worked with the Sixth District tac team in making narcotics buys and infiltrating a street gang. In 1970, Atkinson became a patrol officer, and was reassigned to Sixth District Patrol till 1972, when he was assigned to the Traffic Division. Atkinson attended the Northwestern University Traffic Institute in 1972. Atkinson stayed with Traffic, working the expressways, till 1976, when he was assigned to the Englewood District, where he worked patrol and tac till April 1981. Atkinson returned to the Sixth

District, tac, and served as a field training officer from 1982 to 1987. Atkinson served as the administrative aide to the commander of personnel from 1988 through 1990.

YOUTH OFFICER AL AUGUSTINE, Area Five.

Augustine is a twenty-one-year veteran of the CPD. Augustine worked the wagon in the Fourteenth District for two years, then was assigned to the Area Six Task Force, Special Operations, till 1980. Augustine then worked patrol and tac in Sixteen, Eleven, and Twenty-three. Augustine became a youth officer in 1989.

OFFICER ANTHONY BERTUCA, Twenty-third District tactical unit.

Bertuca, a former linebacker with the Baltimore Colts and the Miami Dolphins, joined the force in 1976. Bertuca has served in Twenty-three for the past sixteen years: two years on patrol and fourteen years on the tac team.

SERGEANT JIM BIEBEL, Area Six Property Crimes.

Biebel, who joined the CPD in 1967, worked patrol and tac in the Twentieth District till 1971, when he was promoted to detective and assigned to Area Five Burglary. In 1973, Biebel was assigned to Area Six Burglary, where he served as a detective for seven years before joining the prestigious CIU, a unit that tracked down professional thieves. In 1982, Biebel was promoted to sergeant and served in Area One Property Crimes from 1982 to 1984. In 1984, Biebel joined Area Six Property Crimes. Biebel also serves as a hostage negotiator; he's been with the CPD Hostage/Barricaded/Terrorist Unit from its inception in 1979.

OFFICER STEVE BOCCONCELLI, Twenty-third District tactical unit.

Bocconcelli joined the CPD in 1973 and was assigned to patrol in the old Nineteenth (now Town Hall). In April 1974, Bocconcelli was named Police Officer of the Month. In 1975, Bocconcelli was assigned to tac in Twenty-three. In 1984, he was detailed to the Narcotics Unit, Special Enforcement. Later in 1984, Bocconcelli returned to Twenty-three tac.

SERGEANT SAM CHRISTIAN, watch commander, Special Investigations Unit. Christian came on the force in 1973 and was assigned to the Twenty-third District, where he worked tac for five years. He then served as a patrol specialist, training recruits on the street. In 1980, Christian went to Area Five, Youth Division, where he was assigned to the crime car. He was assigned to SIU in 1981 and, in 1985, was promoted to sergeant and assigned to Area Five. Christian returned to SIU in 1989.

CAPTAIN TOM CRONIN, Fifteenth District. Cronin was selected by the CPD in 1985 to be trained in investigative profiling by the FBI's National Center for the Analysis of Violent Crime. Cronin joined the force in 1969, working patrol in the Thirteenth District until 1971, when he became a crime analyst. In 1973, Cronin was promoted to detective and worked Robbery in Area Two for two years and Robbery in Area Five for two years. Cronin made sergeant in 1977, lieutenant in 1985, and captain in 1990. Cronin, who holds a master's degree in social justice, is one of twenty-seven FBI-trained investigative profilers in the world.

OFFICER SIDNEY DAVIS, Eleventh District. Davis joined the force in 1983, and was assigned to the Seventh District. Davis and his partner, Clarence Williams, were patrol officers until 1986, when they were promoted to patrol specialists. Davis served on the tac team in the Seventh District for two years, and was assigned to the Eleventh District in 1990, where he works patrol and serves as a district evidence technician.

OFFICER JIM DILLON, Eighteenth District, Rush Street Detail. Dillon spent eleven and a half of his eighteen years on the force working in the Vice Control Section, Prostitution Unit. Dillon worked patrol for six months after joining the force in 1973, and then worked on the Sixteenth District tac team for four years before being assigned to Vice. Dillon has served on the Rush Street Detail since 1989.

SERGEANT ELLEN EGAN, Nineteenth District. Egan, who joined the force in 1980, worked the beat car for a year and a half and worked with the tac team full-time for six years in Eighteen. Egan worked crime patterns, the projects, and Operation Angel (decoy prostitution assignments) in Eighteen. In 1988, Egan was promoted to sergeant.

LIEUTENANT TED HEAD, field lieutenant, Seventeenth District. Head is a thirty-one-year veteran of the CPD. Head worked one year as a patrol officer before being assigned to the old Task Force, a mobile, citywide crime unit that sent police as troubleshooters into areas and situations deemed out of control. Head's five-year assignment with the Task Force included a stint in the TUF (Tactical Undercover Function) Squad. Head became a vice cop on Rush Street in 1966. In 1967, Head was promoted to detective, and worked in General Assignment in Area Four and Area Six. After his promotion to sergeant, Head worked on the street in the Nineteenth and Twentieth districts. In 1970, Head represented Chicago police as president of the original Chicago police union, the Confederation of Police (COP). Head was promoted to lieutenant in 1984 and has been field lieutenant in Seventeen since 1986.

LIEUTENANT HUGH HOLTON, commander, Third Division. Holton joined the force in 1964 as a cadet, served in Vietnam from 1967 to 1970, and became a patrolman in 1970, assigned to the Nineteenth District. In 1971, Holton went to the Second District tac team. Holton was promoted to youth officer in 1972, assigned to Area Four. Holton made sergeant in 1975, working the First District (the Loop) patrol till 1978. He then studied at the Northwestern University Traffic Institute. In 1979, Holton became administrative assistant to then-deputy chief Fred Rice, who, while Holton was still administrative assistant, became chief and then superintendent of the Patrol Division. In 1984, Holton became administrative assistant to Robert A. Williams, deputy superintendent, Bureau of Investigative Services. Holton was promoted to lieutenant in 1984, and appointed in 1985 as director of the Beat Rep Program Division.

In 1986, Holton became the commander of the Sixth District. Holton served as commander of personnel from January 1988 through 1990, when he was appointed commander of the Third District. Holton writes a monthly column on police procedure for *Mystery Scene Magazine*.

DETECTIVE BRIAN KILLACKY, Area Six Violent Crimes.

Killacky worked in a suburban police force for two years before joining the CPD in 1976. Killacky worked Vice and tac assignments for five years. In 1981, Killacky was promoted to youth officer and assigned to Area Four. In 1982, Killacky, along with Sam Christian and Michael Dolan, was selected to implement the Special Investigations Unit, designed to target child pornography, child molestation, and juvenile prostitution and pimping. In 1990, Killacky was promoted to detective, assigned to Area Six Violent Crimes, where he specializes in sex crimes.

SERGEANT JIM LANE, head of tac team, Twenty-third District.

Lane joined the force in 1970 and was assigned to the Monroe Street District, where he worked tac for three years. In 1973, Lane was assigned to Special Operations, working hostage/barricade calls until 1980. Lane was promoted to sergeant in 1980, assigned to the Twenty-third District to head a tac team. Lane was also detailed to SNIP: Street Narcotics Impact Program, for a couple years during the mid-eighties, and then returned to heading the tac team in Twenty-three.

DETECTIVE JOE LASKERO, Area Four Property Crimes.

Laskero worked on the tactical unit in the Town Hall District for twelve years. He came on the force in 1970, served on the West Side, Fillmore District, on patrol for three and a half years, and then was transferred to Town Hall, where, before joining the tac team, he worked the prostitution car for a year and a half. Laskero was promoted to detective in 1987.

SERGEANT ROBERT LOPEZ, Twentieth District tactical unit.

Lopez joined the force in 1978 and was assigned to

the Twenty-third District, where he worked tac for ten years.
Upon his promotion to sergeant in 1988, Lopez studied at
the Northwestern University Traffic Institute and was then
assigned, in 1989, as tac sergeant for the Twentieth District.

SERGEANT ED MINGEY, Area Five Violent Crimes.

Mingey has been with the CPD for twenty-five years, working
four years on patrol, three years as a youth officer, and sixteen
years in Gang Crimes North, both as a gang crimes specialist,
from 1973 to 1977, and as a gang crimes supervising sergeant,
from 1977 to 1989, when he was assigned to Violent Crimes.

SERGEANT TED O'CONNOR, Twenty-third District.

O'Connor was promoted to detective and assigned to Homicide
three years after joining the force in 1967. O'Connor worked in
Homicide till 1978, when he went undercover in an operation
targeting Outfit-controlled businesses. O'Connor then served in
the DEA's Narcotics Task Force for five years. O'Connor next
worked as sex crimes analyst for the CPD and as administrative
aide to the deputy chief of detectives. From 1988 until his
promotion to sergeant in 1990, O'Connor worked in the Joint
FBI/CPD Task Force, investigating unsolved Outfit murders.

DETECTIVE BILL PEDERSEN, Organized Crime Divi-

sion. Pedersen, who joined the CPD in 1968, has worked in Auto
Theft, the Special Investigations Unit, and for ten years (from
1973 to 1983) as a narcotics detective. Pedersen then worked for
six years as an Area Two violent crimes detective before joining
the Organized Crime Division, Asset Forfeiture Unit, in 1989.

LIEUTENANT CINDY PONTORIERO, field lieuten-

ant, Twenty-first District. Pontoriero joined the force as a
policewoman in 1967 and became the first woman detective
in the CPD, assigned to Area Five Homicide in 1972, to Sex
Crimes North in 1980, and to Area Five Violent Crimes in 1981.
Pontoriero has twenty-five years on the force and seventeen
years as a violent crimes detective. After being promoted to
sergeant, Pontoriero served as Area Six sex crimes coordinator

from 1985 through 1988. In January 1989, she was assigned to Detective Division Headquarters. Pontoriero was promoted to lieutenant in 1990.

OFFICER EDMUND PYRCIOCH, investigator, Inspector General's Office. Pyrcioch has worked tac for a total of fifteen years out of his twenty-five with the CPD, a career that's included work with Gang Crimes North for four years and work as a homicide investigator for a year and a half in Area Four, called "the Murder Factory" by Chicago cops for its usual number-one ranking in homicide statistics. Pyrcioch worked tac in Eighteen for eleven years before being detailed to the Inspector General's Office in 1989.

YOUTH OFFICER LINDA REITER, Area Five. Reiter came on the force in 1982, worked patrol in the Eighteenth District for seven years, including work in Operation Angel (decoy prostitution) and female search in Cabrini-Green, until her promotion to youth officer in 1989. In 1991, Reiter was assigned to the crime car, which responds to notifications from the Child Abuse Hot Line pertaining to the physical/sexual abuse of children.

GANG CRIMES SPECIALIST JOE RODRIGUEZ, Gang Crimes North. Rodriguez joined the force in 1972, spent a year and a half in the Town Hall District on patrol, and has been with Gang Crimes North since 1974.

YOUTH OFFICER ROBERT J. SIMANDL, Area Four. Simandl is a national expert on street gangs, founder and chairman of the Midwest Gang Investigators Association, and a member of the California Gang Investigation Association. Simandl is also a nationally recognized expert on ritualistic crime. Before becoming a youth officer in 1989, Simandl served fifteen of his twenty-four years on the force as a gang crimes specialist.

DETECTIVE VINCE STRANGIS, retired. Strangis's career in the CPD included fifteen years in the high-crime

Englewood District, one year on patrol and fourteen as a detective working Burglary, Robbery, and Homicide, and sixteen years assigned to the Organized Crime Division, one in Vice Control, Prostitution Unit, and fifteen in the Intelligence Section.

OFFICER EDWARD TANSEY, SR., wagonman,
retired. Tansey, a policeman from 1951 until his retirement in 1986, worked patrol for twenty-one years and then the wagon, always in Area Six.

OFFICER EDWARD TANSEY, JR., Inspector General's Office.
The elder Tansey's son worked patrol for eleven years after joining the CPD in 1966, was promoted to detective in 1977, and served in Area Six Property Crimes from 1977 to 1990.

OFFICER T. WARD, Eighteenth District.
Ward joined the CPD in 1973 and spent the next seven years working patrol and tac in Fourteen and Nineteen. In 1980, Ward requested transfer to Cabrini-Green. Ward and his partner work Special Investigations in Narcotics and Gang Activity, centering on Cabrini-Green.

SERGEANT JEFFREY WILSON, Twentieth District.
Wilson joined the force in 1980 and was assigned to patrol in Twenty-four. In 1981, Wilson went to Twenty-three, where he worked tac for six years. In 1988, following his promotion to sergeant, he was assigned to the Eleventh District. Wilson came to Twenty in 1990. Wilson holds a law degree.

OFFICER JUDY ZYDOWSKY, Vice Control Section, Prostitution Unit.
Zydowsky joined the CPD in 1983; she worked in the Twentieth District for four years as a tac officer, including work as a prostitution decoy in Operation Angel. Zydowsky had been in Vice Control since 1987.

About the Author

CONNIE FLETCHER developed an interest in crime during a typical Chicago girlhood, when her father, James T. Fletcher, took her every holiday to visit the site of the St. Valentine's Day Massacre and to finger the bullet holes left in the stones of Holy Name Cathedral, where Little Hymie Weiss was gunned down. Like her father, Fletcher was educated at Loyola University Chicago, where she is now an associate professor in the Department of Communication. Fletcher teaches journalism. She has a doctorate in English literature from Northwestern University. Fletcher lives with her husband, Trygve, her daughter, Bridget, and her son, Nick.

He joined the Fort Lauderdale police force to protect and serve. But what he found was a war as devastating as the one he'd fought in Vietnam. A skyrocketing crime rate fueled by drugs had turned a vacation paradise into a sun-drenched battlefield with beaches—and he was on the front line.

Now the ten-year veteran officer exhibits the same tough, uncompromising courage that made him a legend. You may hail him as a hero or damn him as the product of a brutal system, but Cherokee Paul McDonald is one cop you'll never forget.

BLUE TRUTH

CHEROKEE PAUL McDONALD

"A scorching, devastating book...McDonald as a writer is unsparing, unapologetic, and dead honest. BLUE TRUTH is not a pretty story...but by God, you won't stop reading it."
—Lawrence Block

BLUE TRUTH
Cherokee Paul McDonald
_____ 92773-8 $4.99 U.S./$5.99 Can.